Dislocating Cultures

Dislocating Cultures /

Identities, Traditions, and Third-World Feminism

Uma Narayan

Routledge
New York and London

Published in 1997 by
Routledge
29 West 35th Street
New York, NY 10001

Published in Great Britain by
Routledge
11 New Fetter Lane
London EC4P 4EE

Copyright © 1997 by Routledge

Printed in the United States of America on acid-free paper.

Library of Congress Cataloging-in-Publication Data

Narayan, Uma.
Dislocating cultures : identities, traditions, and Third-World
feminism / Uma Narayan.
    p.   cm.
Includes bibliographical references and index.
ISBN 0-415-91418-3 (hb). — ISBN 0-415-91419-1 (pb).
1. Feminism—Developing countries. 2. Women—Developing
countries—Identity. I. Title.
HQ1870.9.N37   1997
305.42'09172'4—dc21   97-12405
                                                 CIP

For Usha

Contents /

Preface /

The essays in this volume represent my attempts to begin thinking through a number of feminist concerns and questions that are connected to the category of "culture." This volume consists of five essays that are thematically connected, but that can also be read by themselves as independent essays. They explore, in a variety of ways, a number of questions regarding Westernization, tradition, and national and political identity in the context of Third-World feminist politics. Taken together, these essays constitute attempts to contest, criticize, and complicate some prevalent understandings of notions such as "culture," "tradition," and "national identity," by pointing to the problematic assumptions they embody, and by emphasizing the importance that such contestations have to Third-World feminist perspectives.

The first chapter, "Contesting Cultures: 'Westernization,' Respect for Cultures, and Third-World Feminists," criticizes attempts to dismiss Third-World feminist politics as symptoms of "Westernization." While such dismissals predominantly emerge today from a variety of Third-World fundamentalist movements, the charge that Third-World feminist politics is tainted by "Westernization" is not exclusive to such perspectives. I respond to these charges in two basic ways. First, I point to the ways in which Third-World feminist contestations are responses to problems women confront *within* a variety of Third-World national contexts, and an integral part of the political debates and disputes within these nations. Second, I argue that the charge of "Westernization" is intimately connected to the contrasting views of "Western culture" and specific Third-World "cultures" that were constructed in colonial times, drawing attention to the ideological and problematic nature of these characterizations of "culture." Using concrete examples, I draw attention to the selective, self-serving, and shifting ways in which certain social changes in Third-World contexts (notably, but not exclusively, those involving gender roles) are castigated as symptoms of "Westernization," while other changes are regarded as innocuous and consonant with "preserving our culture." My intention is to caution against taking terms like "Westernization" and "cultural preservation" as innocuous descriptive terms, and to urge critical attention to the agendas that are served by the deployment of these terms.

The second chapter, "Restoring History and Politics to 'Third-World Traditions': Contrasting the Colonialist Stance and Contemporary Contestations of *Sati*," begins by analyzing how Mary Daly's discussion of *sati* replicates important aspects of "colonialist representations" of "Third-World traditions." In so doing, I attempt to clarify the notion of "colonialist representation" and to draw attention to the ways in which colonialist representation participates in problematic pictures of "Third-World cultures." I go on to discuss the odd and interesting maneuvers that led to *sati* acquiring the status of "an Indian tradition" in colonial times, and its role in the construction of the "contrasts" between "Indian" and "Western" cultures. Pointing out the similarities that link problematic representations of *sati* by nineteenth-century British colonialists and Indian nationalists, representations of *sati* by Western feminists such as Daly, and the picture of *sati* endorsed by contemporary Hindu fundamentalists, I analyze the ways in which contemporary Indian feminist contestations of *sati* challenge all these "colonialist" representations of *sati*. I end by arguing that commitments to a transnational and global feminism require that Western feminists refrain from buying into historically inaccurate and politically dangerous pictures of "Third-World traditions" such as those that are presupposed by Daly's critique of *sati*.

The third chapter, "Cross-Cultural Connections, Border-Crossings, and 'Death by Culture': Thinking About Dowry-Murders in India and Domestic-Violence Murders in the United States," explores the features of national contexts that might help explain why the Indian feminist movement has tended to focus on a fatal form of domestic violence, namely dowry murder, while domestic violence *fatalities* have a noticeably low profile in U.S. domestic violence activism. I go on to point to the ways in which national agendas around domestic violence shape the *data* that are available for making "cross-cultural connections" on these sorts of issues of violence against women. I discuss the ways in which the nature of the data available, as well as the decontextualization and reframing that occur when Third-World feminist issues cross over into Western national contexts, complicate such feminist attempts at cross-cultural comparisons. I end by exploring the ways in which forms of violence against Third-World women, such as dowry murders, get represented as instances of "death by culture" while analogous forms of violence in Western contexts, such as domestic violence murders, often do not. As a whole, this chapter strikes a series of cautionary notes about "cultural explanation" and about the project of cross-cultural understanding of problems that affect women in a variety of national contexts.

In the fourth chapter, "Through the Looking-Glass Darkly: Emissaries, Mirrors, and Authentic Insiders as Preoccupations," I describe and critically examine the roles of Emissary, Mirror, and Authentic Insider, roles that are often assigned to individuals from Third-World backgrounds in academic contexts interested in promoting multicultural education. I connect these three roles to strategies that appear designed to comport with the imperatives of what I call an "anthropological perspective" towards Other cultures—whose commitments are that Westerners should take an interest in Other cultures but refrain from moral criticisms of these cultures. I examine the problematic approaches to "Other cultures" that result from the "anthropological perspective," and analyze the ways in which the roles of Emissary, Mirror, and Authentic Insider are particularly burdensome for Third-World feminists. Finally, I suggest some strategies for dealing with these roles and for developing a richer vision of multicultural education.

The final chapter, "Eating Cultures: Incorporation, Identity, and Indian Food," uses food, curry in particular, to think about the constructions of colonial and postcolonial identities. The first section explores the connections between colonial British attitudes to Indian food and their attitudes to India, describing different versions of the colonial project, as well as Indian nationalist responses to colonialism. It also examines the connections between religious and caste-based food norms and contemporary political animosities in India. The second section uses curry as an example of "ethnic food" in Western contexts to examine Indian diasporic identity in contemporary England, and to address the problematic roles assigned Indian women in attempts to "preserve Indian cultural identity" in immigrant Indian communities. The third section examines the ideas of "food colonialism" and "culinary imperialism," and thinks about the role food plays in the construction of ethnic identities in contemporary Western contexts. I argue for the need to pay attention to the selective processes that mark certain commodities as "exotic" or "ethnic" or "Western" in different national contexts, and to the political implications of these characterizations in contemporary contexts marked by multidirectional transnational flow of commodities.

Overall, these essays suggest that a historically attentive and politically astute understanding of nineteenth-century colonial constructions of "Western" and "Third-World" cultures can help us avoid totalizing, reified, and problematic pictures of "Western culture" and of specific "Third-World cultures." They point to the problems certain understandings of "culture," "tradition," and "cultural identity" pose for versions of multiculturalism as well as for transnational feminist political collaboration.

The form of this volume, a series of thematically linked essays, has benefits as well as burdens. Writing discrete essays was instrumental in giving me the freedom to change gears and to focus on a range of topics that each allowed me to explore a different set of issues connected to the notion of "culture." The essay format also permits readers to engage with these essays singly, and in no particular order, without the necessity of getting their bearings from previous chapters. However, I am aware that the format leaves my readers with the task of articulating the ways in which these essays manage to "connect" with each other. I am aware, too, that distance from these essays, as well as the questions and criticism they elicit, will be instrumental in facilitating my own ability to grasp their connections and to acquire a better sense of the many issues they leave unaddressed.

Writing these essays left me struggling with a number of difficult issues and choices pertaining to writing about the sorts of issues I address. At a number of points in these essays, I have tried to combine personal narrative with more analytic modes of writing, a process that has had its excitements as well as uncertainties. It is a process that has often left me unsure about how well particular narratives helped to illuminate the general point I was trying to make, and about how to handle transitions between these two modes of writing. At different points, the process of writing these essays raised difficult and painful questions with regard to whether and how to tell stories that involve people one knows and cares about, and about how to discuss to conversations and experiences that involved other people. There were seldom easy answers, and I continue to think about these questions.

While I have relished the opportunity these essays provided to engage with and learn from work done in many disciplines other than my own, I remain aware of the perils of wandering into intellectual territory where I lack grounding. Working on these essays has forcefully brought home to me the importance of attending to work outside one's own discipline, even as it has made me see how one's disciplinary background structures and limits these engagements and shapes the uses one can make of work in other areas. Furthermore, these essays all bear traces of my struggle to move between the particular and the general. While using specific personal experiences, particular texts as support or as objects of criticism, and examples that pertain to concrete moments of a particular point in colonial history, have helped me to make my points concretely, I am aware that there are real risks in using such concrete examples to make the more general points I often wished to make. While I have tried to draw attention to the possible limits and limitations of my use of particular examples, and have attempted caveats and cautions about overgeneralizing from them, I remain aware of irreducible tensions that remain between the particular and the general.

This book is, like many things in life, a result of a fortunate conjunction of events. Shortly before I was to begin my first sabbatical, Linda Nicholson asked me if I had any ideas for a book. Linda's unstinting encouragement and the year's leave provided by Vassar College were both crucial to enabling me to work on the essays that constitute this volume. With the exception of the fifth chapter, a previous version of which was published in *Social Identities*, and a preliminary version of the first chapter that was written earlier, the bulk of the book was written during my year of sabbatical leave. While I am pleased to have pulled this volume together in that time, I am also aware that there are liabilities to not having more time to reflect on and rework these essays. I have benefited tremendously from the comments and suggestions of friends and colleagues who have generously given time and thought to these essays.

I owe a great deal to the many people who have read versions of the various chapters in this book and have given me helpful comments and criticisms. My colleagues, Michael McCarthy, Jesse Kalin, Michael Murray, Mitchell Miller, Jennifer Church and Douglas Winblad, Giovanna Borradori, Bryan van Norden, Ellen Feder, and Herman Capellan have read some of these essays at our departmental colloquia, and I have gained a great deal from all their comments, questions, and criticisms. Special thanks to Ellen Feder who took time, at a very busy moment, to read some chapters. I owe special thanks, too, to Jennifer Church, who has been extraordinarily generous with her time and energy in responding to my work ever since I joined the department.

I have received helpful comments on these chapters from people outside my department. I thank Luke Harris and Kathe Sandler for reading various chapters, and for their ongoing encouragement of my work. Susan Zlotnick, whose work on theorizing curry prompted my own, read many of these chapters, and I have profited greatly from her sharp eye for split infinitives and mixed metaphors. Radhika Balakrishnan's comments helped me improve these chapters at many points, and her assistance and reassurance have meant a great deal to me. In addition to reading these chapters, Beth Kelly has also dealt with my many moments of panic with her unique blend of asperity, wacky humor, intellectual acuity, and levelheadedness. Those I would like to thank for reading and commenting on various drafts of some chapters include Andrew von Hirsch, Marque Miringoff, David Theo Goldberg, and Sandra Harding.

There are many people I would like to thank for their encouragement, friendship, and support over the years. I am indebted to Molly Shanley, Leslie Dunn, Peter Antelles, Donna Heiland, Pinar Batur-Vanderlippe, John Vanderlippe, Robert Prasch, Tina Sheth, Karen Robertson, Jim Brain, and Margaret Fusco for their friendship and support during my time at Vassar. I would like to thank Alison Jaggar, Joan Callahan, Howard McGary, Mary Gibson, Jeffrie Murphy, and Hugh LaFollette for their interest in and encouragement of my work. I am grateful to Sarah Boone, Anjana Mebane-Cruz, Anna Vittola, Joyce Tigner, and Josie Rodriguez-Hewitt for friendships that sustained me through graduate school and that continue to sustain me today. John Stouter's wonderful silliness and Guy Colvin's acid wit have contributed to my life since my earliest weeks in this country. I heartily thank Rosette Uniacke and Kathy Magurno for the innumerable forms of assistance they have provided as secretaries of the philosophy department, and for the comfort of their departmental mothering. I also appreciate the many students whose comments, questions, and concerns have inspired to me think about some of the issues in these essays.

Linda Nicholson has read each of these chapters with care, and her comments have been invaluable. This volume would not exist without her encouragement, assistance, and support. I would also like to thank Maureen McGrogan, Laska Jimsen, Ronda Angel, and Lai Moy of Routledge for the assistance they provided at various stages of this project.

My partner, Jim Hill, has dealt with the periods of panic and the periods of elation that have punctuated the writing of these essays with his admirable calmness and good humor. He has coped with messy piles of books and papers, helped me with the vagaries of computers, and plied me with coffee, aspirin, or dinner, as the moment required. I am grateful both for his ability to take me seriously, and his ability to prevent me from taking myself too seriously.

One / Contesting Cultures

"Westernization,"
Respect for Cultures,
and Third-World Feminists[1]

Language becomes "one's own" only when the speaker populates it with her own intention, her own accent, when she appropriates the world, adapting it to her own semantic and expressive intention. Prior to this moment of appropriation, the word does not exist in a neutral and impersonal language . . . but rather it exists in other people's mouths, in other people's contexts, serving other people's intentions. . . . Expropriating, forcing it to submit to one's own intentions and accents, is a difficult and complicated process.

—Mikhail M. Bakhtin[2]

For who among us, after all—white or nonwhite, Western or not—is not always caught precisely in the space between "inherited traditions" and "modernization projects"? And where else, how else, do "cultural interpretations" come from—"theirs" or "ours," local or global, resistant or complicit, as the case may be—other than from the spaces between the two, and with the ensemble of materials they provide (or, indeed, from the lack of space, the sometimes desperate need for new conceptual and material resources).

—Fred Pfeil[3]

Introduction /

To try to define oneself intellectually and politically as a Third-World feminist is not an easy task. It is an unsettled and unsettling identity (as identities in general often are), but it is also an identity that often feels forced to give an account of itself. There is nothing inherently wrong about the project of giving an account of oneself—of one's specific location as speaker and thinker; of the complex experiences and perceptions and sense of life that fuel one's concerns; of the reasons, feelings, and anxieties that texture one's position on an issue; of the values that inform one's considered judgment of things.

Giving such an account of oneself has much to recommend it, for all of us. It enables one to see, with humility, and gratitude, and pain, how much one has been shaped by one's contexts, to sense both the extent and the boundaries of one's vision, to see how circumstances can circumscribe as well as inspire, and to become self-aware to some extent of one's perspectives on things. What is strange, I believe, for many Third-World feminists, is the sense that, in our case, such an account is especially called for, *demanded* even, by the sense that others have that we occupy a suspect location, and that our perspectives are suspiciously tainted and problematic products of our "Westernization." Many Third-World feminists confront the attitude that our criticisms of our cultures are merely one more incarnation of a colonized consciousness, the views of "privileged native women in whiteface," seeking to attack their "non-Western culture" on the basis of "Western" values. This essay attempts to reveal some of the problems and paradoxes that are embedded in these charges of "Westernization" as well as to understand what provokes them.

I should admit at the outset the peculiarities of my own location. I have grown up and lived in a variety of places. I was born in India and lived in Bombay until I was eight, when I moved with my family to Uganda. I returned to India when I was fourteen and lived there until I was twenty-five. As is the case with many middle-class Indian children, my formal education was in the English language. For the last dozen years I have lived in the United States, which makes my currently calling myself a Third-World feminist problematic, in contrast, say, to feminists who live and function as feminists *entirely* within Third-World *national* contexts. Calling myself a "Third-World feminist" is problematic only if the term is understood narrowly, to refer exclusively to feminists living and functioning within Third-World countries, as it sometimes is. But, like many terms, "Third-World feminist" has a number of current usages. Some feminists from communities of color in Western contexts have also applied the term "Third World" to themselves, their communities, and their politics, to call political attention to similarities in the locations of, and problems faced by, their communities and communities in Third World countries. As a feminist of color living in the United States, I continue to be a "Third World feminist" in this broader sense of the term.

In writing this essay, I was caught in a struggle between my political desire to endorse this broader use of the term, and aspects of my project that seemed to indicate the narrower usage. For the most part, I have decided to use the term "Third-World feminist" more narrowly in this essay, to refer to feminists who acquired feminist views and engaged in feminist politics in Third-World countries, and those who continue to do so, since it is my project to argue that feminist perspectives are not "foreign" to these Third-World *national* contexts. Another reason for this choice is that the charge of being "Westernized" or having a "Westernized politics" that concerns me in this essay, is more commonly leveled at feminists within Third-World national contexts. While feminists from *some* communities of color in Western contexts, such as feminists from Indian diasporic communities, are sometimes charged with "Westernization," the charges of "inauthenticity" leveled at many Black or Chicana feminists often take the form of asserting that they are embracing a "White" rather than a "Westernized" politics.[4] When confronted with such difficulties about terminology, perhaps the best one can do is to clarify one's use of the terms and give an account of the reasons for one's choices.

I wish to speak as a Third-World feminist in this essay for three important reasons. First, having lived the first quarter-century of my life in Third-World countries, and having come of age politically in such contexts, a significant part of my sensibilities and political horizons are indelibly shaped by Third World national realities. Second, this essay is an attempt to explicate the ways in which the concerns and analyses of Third-World feminists are rooted in and responsive to the problems women face within their national contexts, and to argue that they are not simpleminded emulations of Western feminist political concerns. I need to speak "as an insider" to make my point, even as I attempt to complicate the sense of what it is to inhabit a culture. Finally, though calling myself a Third-World feminist is subject to qualification and mediation, it is no more so than many labels one might attach to oneself—no more so than calling myself an Indian, a feminist, or a woman, for that matter, since all these identities are not simple givens but open to complex ways of being inhabited, and do not guarantee many specific experiences or concerns, even as they shape one's life in powerful ways.

I do not "locate myself" or specify who I am because I "*assume . . . who I am determines* what and how I know"[5] (italics mine), but rather to point to the complications of saying who I am, and of my assuming specific identities as a speaker. I do, however, wish to suggest some *linkages* between the complexities of who I am and what I claim to know. By "linkages," I wish to suggest *weaker* forms of influence or connection than is suggested by the term "determined." I do not simply *assume* such linkages, but attempt to give an account of them, a gesture that both "authorizes" my speech and opens the nature of this "authority" to evaluation and interrogation. To surrender the possibility of any connections between who I am and what I know is, for the purposes of this paper, to surrender my standing to speak as an "insider" to Third-World contexts, a standing that many Third-World feminists are often denied simply by virtue of their feminism.[6] This is a denial whose legitimacy is precisely what I wish to question.

The first section of this essay attempts to contest charges of "Westernization" used to insinuate that Third-World feminist politics are "inauthentic" and "irrelevant." The second section attempts to explain why "Westernized" is the epithet of choice leveled against Third-World feminists. It turns to colonial history, arguing that the contrasting self-definitions of "Western culture" and the "indigenous national culture" of specific colonies that were constructed in the political conflicts between colonialism and nationalist movements, and the place assigned to different groups of women in these conflicts, help illuminate contemporary charges of "Westernization" leveled against Third-World feminist politics. The third section explores the "selective" ways in which social changes in Third-World contexts are labeled as "Westernization" and argues that trying to carve Third-World feminist voices, and the changing economic, social, and cultural realities of Third-World contexts into "Western" and "non-Western" components, is a much more complex task than it is often perceived to be. I do not intend to provide an analysis of the term "Westernization" but rather concretely to point to tensions and paradoxes in the use of the term "Westernization," and to discuss what strike me as selective and problematic about its applications. In the concluding section, I examine the implications of problematic pictures of "national culture" and "national identity" for feminist politics in Western as well as Third-World national contexts. Although many of the concrete examples I use to make my points in this essay are from an Indian context, I believe parallel examples can be found in other Third-World contexts.

Speech and Silence in
the Mother Tongue /

I have been working to change the
way I speak and write, to incorporate in the manner of telling
a sense of place, of not just who I am in the present but where
I am coming from, the multiple voices within me. . . . When
I say then that these worlds emerge from suffering, I refer to
the personal struggle to name the location from which I come
to voice—that space of theorizing.

—bell hooks[7]

Many feminists from Third-World contexts confront voices that are eager to convert any feminist criticism they make of their culture into a mere symptom of their "lack of respect for their culture," rooted in the "Westernization" that they seem to have caught like a disease. These voices emanate from disparate sources, from family members, and, ironically enough, from other intellectuals whose own political perspectives are indebted to political theories such as Marxism and liberalism that have "Western" origins. This tendency to cast feminism as an aping of "Westernized" political agendas seems commonplace in a number of Third-World contexts.[8] For instance, Mary Fainsod Katzenstein points out that while Indian feminist activism has "been of critical importance in eliciting media attention and in shaping a new consciousness around gender violence," it has also provoked criticism that "portrays feminist activism as originating out of a Western, bourgeois, modernist perspective."[9] I shall try to reveal the problematic assumptions that underlie these rhetorical dismissals of Third-World feminist voices as rooted in elitist and "Westernized" views, and argue that, for many Third World feminists, our feminist consciousness is not a hot-house bloom grown in the alien atmosphere of "foreign" ideas, but has its roots much closer to home.

My sense of entitlement to contest "my culture" is threaded through with both confidence and doubt. I grew up in a fairly traditional, middle-class, South Indian family, in the urban milieu of Bombay. Besides my parents, both my paternal grandparents also lived in the household, making us what in India is called a "joint family." As the eldest grandchild, and for several years the only child, I was raised with considerable indulgence. And I also remember the boundaries and limits to this indulgence. I remember my mother saying, "What sort of a girl are you to talk back like that to your father?" and my thinking, "But his reprimand was not deserved, and he will not listen to me, and she will not even let me speak."

I remember minding particularly that the injunction to be silent came from my mother, who told me so early, because she had no one else to tell, about her sufferings in her conjugal home. I remember my mother's anger and grief at my father's resort to a silencing "neutrality" that refused to "interfere" in the domestic tyrannies that his mother inflicted on my mother. The same mother who complained about her silencing enjoined me to silence, doing what she had to do, since my failures to conform would translate as her failures to rear me well.

I also remember my mother years later saying, "When I came to Bombay right after I was married, I was so innocent I did not know how to even begin to argue or protest when my mother-in-law harassed me," with a pride and satisfaction that were difficult for me to understand. That "innocence," that silence, indicated she was a good wife, a good daughter-in-law, well-brought up, a "good Indian woman," a matter of pride, even to her whose "innocence" had not prevented her from recognizing that what she was being subjected to was wrong, but which had prevented her from explicitly contesting it. And for once choosing to hold my tongue, I did not say, "But mother, you were not entirely silent. You laid it all on me. My earliest memory (you were the one who dated it after I described it to you, and were amazed that I remembered it) is of seeing you cry. I heard all your stories of your misery. The shape your 'silence' took is in part what has incited me to speech."

I am arguing that my eventual feminist contestations of my culture have something to do with the cultural dynamics of the family life that surrounded me as a child, something to do with my early sense of the "politics of home." My grandmother, whom I loved and who was indulgent to me in her own way, tormented my mother, whom I also loved, in several petty and some not so petty ways, using her inventiveness to add color and detail to the stock repertoire of domestic tyrannies available to Indian mothers-in-law. My father, clever and able and knowledgeable in so many other ways, would not "interfere." After all, "our" cultural traditions did not deem it appropriate for a son to reprimand his parents, providing a convenient cultural excuse for my father, despite his having had a "Westernized education" not very different from that which would later be blamed for the intransigence of his daughter! How could my loyalty and respect for "my culture" fail to be tainted by the fact that there was little justice or happiness for my mother in our house?[10]

So it is strange, and perhaps not strange at all, that my mother adds her voice to so many others that blame my being "Westernized" for my feminist contestations of my culture. And I want to remind her, though I cannot bring myself to it, of her pain that surrounded me when I was young, a pain that was earlier than school and "Westernization," a call to rebellion that has a different and more primary root, that was not conceptual or English, but in the mother-tongue. One thing I want to say to all who would dismiss my feminist criticisms of my culture, using my "Westernization" as a lash, is that my mother's pain too has rustled among the pages of all those books I have read that partly constitute my "Western-ization," and has crept into all the suitcases I have ever packed for my several exiles.

I would argue that, for many of us, women in different parts of the world, our relationships to our mothers resemble our relationships to the motherlands of the cultures in which we were raised. Both our mothers and our mother-cultures give us all sorts of contradictory messages, encouraging their daughters to be confident, impudent, and self-assertive even as they attempt to instill conformity, decorum, and silence, seemingly oblivious to these contradictions. Thus, both my mother and many others in the specific caste and middle-class Indian context in which I was raised saw education as a good thing for daughters, encouraged us to do well at our studies, saw it as prudent that daughters have the qualifications necessary to support themselves economically, saw it as a good thing that we learned to master tasks in areas of life that had been closed to women of my mother's generation. At the same time, they were critical of the effects of the very things they encouraged. They were nervous about our intoxication with ideas and our insistence on using ideas acquired from books to question social rules and norms of life. They were alarmed at our inclination to see careers as not something merely instrumentally valuable in the event that our marriages failed but as essential elements of fulfilling lives. They were anxious about the fact that our independence and self-assertiveness seemed to be making us into women who lacked the compliance, deference, and submissiveness deemed essential in good "Indian" wives.

It is not just that mothers and mother-cultures often raise their daughters with contradictory messages, but also that they often seem unaware of these contradictions. They give voice to the hardships and difficulties of being a woman that have marked their lives, teaching us the limitations and miseries of the routine fates that await us as women, while also resisting our attempts to deviate from these cultural scripts. And so they tend to regard their feminist daughters as symptoms of their failure to raise us with respect for "our" traditions, as daughters who have rejected the lessons they were taught by their mothers and mother-cultures. In seeing us in this mode, they fail to see how much what we are is precisely a response to the very things they have taught us, how much we have become the daughters they have shaped us into becoming.[11]

Thus, my mother insists on seeing my rejection of an arranged marriage, and my general lack of enthusiasm for the institution of marriage as a whole, as a "Westernized" rejection of Indian cultural values. But, in doing so, she forgets how regularly since my childhood she and many other women have complained about the oppressiveness of their marriages in my presence; she forgets how widespread and commonplace the cultural recognition is in India that marriage subjects daughters to difficult life-situations, forgets that my childish misbehaviors were often met with the reprimand, "Wait till you get to your mother-in-law's house. Then you will learn how to behave."

I would thus argue that my sense that marriage is an oppressive institution for many women is something that predates my explicit acquisition of a feminist politics, and is something I initially learned not from books but from Indian women in general, and my female relatives in particular. After all, many women like my mother, whose "cultural authenticity" and "Indianness" are not at issue, commonly acknowledge the mistreatments women are subjected to within their marriages. Such mistreatments are also staple ingredients of the "family dramas" depicted in Indian movies, and thus openly acknowledged elements of popular cultural awareness.[12] I would argue that seeing the perspectives of feminist daughters simply as symptoms of our "Westernization" and as "rejections of our cultures," fails to perceive how capacious and suffused with contestation cultural contexts are. It fails to see how often the inhabitants of a culture criticize the very institutions they endorse. It fails to acknowledge that Third-World feminist critiques are often just one prevailing form of *intra-cultural* criticism of social institutions.

Many Third-World women who do not consider themselves feminists know and acknowledge that women face mistreatment within their social contexts and cultural institutions. Feminist daughters are not the only ones who see that motherlands are spaces where fathers still have most of the privileges and power, and that mothers and mother-cultures relate differently to their daughters than they do to their sons, imposing different demands and expecting different forms of conformity. What may set feminist daughters apart is the ways in which they insist that these differences require us to rethink notions of what it is to "be at home" in a "culture," and to redefine notions of "cultural loyalty, betrayal, and respect" in ways that do not privilege the experiences of men.

Just as daughters seldom recount their mothers' stories in the same terms as their mothers tell them, feminist daughters often have accounts of their mother-cultures that differ in significant ways from the culture's own dominant accounts of itself. Telling the story of a person whose life is intertwined with one's own, in terms different from her own, is often a morally delicate project, requiring accommodation and tact and an ability to leave room for her account even as one claims room for one's own. Re-telling the story of a mother-culture in feminist terms, on the other hand, is a *political* enterprise. It is an attempt to, publicly and in concert with others, challenge and revise an account that is neither the account of an individual nor an account "of the culture as a whole," but an account of *some* who have power within the culture. It is a political challenge to other political accounts that distort, misrepresent, and often intentionally fail to account for the problems and contributions of many inhabitants of the context. It is a political attempt to tell a counter-story that contests dominant narratives that would claim the entire edifice of "our Culture" and "our Nation" for themselves, converting them into a peculiar form of property, and excluding the voices, concerns, and contributions of many who are members of the national and political community.

Both mothers and mother-cultures often inspire the same sorts of complicated emotional responses from their feminist daughters—love and fear, the desire to repudiate and the desire to understand and be understood, a sense of deep connection and a desperate desire for distance. Acquiring one's own "take" or perspective on one's mother-culture seems no less vital and inevitable than developing one's own sense of one's mother, perspectives where love and loyalty often coexist, uneasily and painfully, with criticism. And no matter how far from them we move, we carry with us the shapes of their influence in much of what we do, even in our contestations and reworkings of the very lessons they taught us. Those who perceive our feminism as merely a symptom of our "Westernization," or accuse us of lack of "respect" for "our cultures," fail to see how complicated are an individual's relationships to powerful influences that shape both their conformities and their conflicts, fail to see the closeness between us and the contexts in which we have become both daughters and feminists.

I do not wish to suggest that there is any *necessary* connection between one's early experiences of oppressive gender roles within the family and one's subsequent feminist politics and perspectives. Some individuals might well acquire feminist political perspectives in ways less connected to familial experience; others might well experience oppressive gender roles without developing feminist perspectives on them. However, I also want to insist that, for many of us who do subsequently develop feminist perspectives, our early experiences of gender within the family do play a powerful part in our coming to see feminist perspectives as illuminating.

The lessons about gender that I learned were not confined to my immediate family. As I grew older, I learned a great deal more about the fates of several women who are my kin, for "grown women's matters" that are often concealed from small children are less hidden from an older child. I was seven when my father's cousin and his wife came to visit. I remember how his wife cried and cried in the kitchen to my mother (desperately but quietly, so that her husband who was chatting with my father in the living room would not hear) about the miseries inflicted on her by her in-laws and her husband. My grandmother was away, her absence making the kitchen a place where these revelations were possible, one young wife to another, although my mother was a virtual stranger to this woman. I remember this young woman talking about beatings and humiliations, about how her in-laws and husband were trying to alienate her from her two young sons, and about how she could not go back home to her parents because she had two sisters as yet unmarried. I was told a few years later that she had "gone mad," and will never forget her passionate weeping or my terror in that kitchen, helping my mother in a bustle of noisy activity that was surely, in part, designed to conceal the sounds of that young woman's sobbing.

An aunt whose husband beat her did not talk about it for a decade, even to her sister who lived in the same city, silenced by what my mother names "innocence," and by the cultural shame of articulating such "private" matters. Some twenty years later, those same norms and material structures that enabled those mistreatments, those "innocent" silences, that "madness," have not ceased to flourish. My second cousin was married not that long ago to a "wonderful catch" settled in the United States, who turned out to have been involved all along with a white woman. He locked his wife in his house and burned her with cigarettes, perhaps venting against her body his rage against those cultural traditions that insisted he marry an Indian woman chosen by his parents, and that his "respect for his parents" did not permit him to challenge. Although this cousin was twenty years younger and "better educated" than those older women, she let no one know for over two years. Her "innocence" conspired with international distances, lack of income, dependent immigration status, and isolation in a foreign land to produce a silence that was broken only when a relative happened to visit and helped her to escape.[13]

These stories I have told are both undoubtedly part of my "education" though they had little to do with school, and are incontrovertibly "Indian." While I wish to make connections between women's experiences in their families and their feminist politics, I do not wish to make these connections simplistic. An awareness of the gender dynamics within one's family and one's "culture," even a critical awareness, does not suffice to make women feminists. Women may be aware of such dynamics but may consider them to be *personal* problems to be dealt with personally, without seeing them as a *systematic* part of the ways in which their family, their "culture," and changing material and social conditions script gender roles and women's lives, or without feeling that they must contest them in more formal, public, and political ways. It takes *political connections* to other women and their experiences, political analyses of women's problems, and attempts to construct political solutions for them, to make women into feminists in any full-blooded sense, as the history of women's movements in various parts of the world shows us.

Many Third-World feminist criticisms—say, of the position and treatment of women within their families or of institutions such as dowry—are both influenced by, and bear some resemblance to, criticisms voiced by many nonfeminist women within the culture reflecting upon their life-experiences as affected by these institutions. In this respect, many Third-World feminist issues are hardly "foreign imports" or "Westernized agendas" imposed by feminists onto contexts where "culturally authentic" nonfeminist women would entirely fail to see what the feminist fuss was about. However, the fact that feminist critical analyses are *political* analyses also works to make them different in important ways from criticisms of the same institutions voiced by women like my mother. Feminist criticisms of problems such as dowry deaths and dowry-related harassment seek to make these issues matters of *general concern and public debate*, while the criticisms voiced by my mother are articulated in more private contexts. Feminist criticisms also differ in their *terms of analysis*.[14]

One thing that divides me from my mother is that we have quite different *explanatory accounts* of the sufferings that mark the lives of the women we know. My mother's account explains these sufferings by references to the cruel dispositions of particular in-laws, the brutal natures of particular men, seeing them as "unfortunate accidents" rooted primarily in human propensities for greed, cruelty, and evil. While I acknowledge human propensities for evil, my account insists that that is not the whole story, and that these mistreatments are significantly rooted in particular practices and institutional arrangements, embedded in a material reality that includes our culture and traditions as well as a variety of ongoing changes, and the powerlessness they inflict on many women. The difference perhaps is that while my mother acknowledges that these dice can result in unfortunate outcomes, I insist these dice are loaded. Feminist critical analyses of institutions and practices tend, like political analyses in general, to point to the *systemic and systematic* nature of the problems they focus on. I would argue that what differentiates my accounts from those of my mother has less to do with her "cultural purity" or with my "Westernization" than with certain contingent features of our respective histories that mark the space between our generations. Women like my mother grew up with an awareness that problems such as dowry-related harassment and mistreatment of daughters-in-law were fairly common-place,[15] but my mother did not come of age in a context where dowry-murders were a growing problem, or where feminist groups were engaged in generating political analyses and public protests about these problems, as I did.

Feminist movements in various parts of the world develop when historical and political circumstances encourage public recognition that many of the norms, institutions, and traditions that structure women's personal and social lives, as well as the impact of new developments and social change, are detrimental to women's well-being, and enable political contestations in which the status quo is criticized and alternatives envisioned. Those in Third-World contexts who dismiss the politics of feminists in their midst as a symptom of "Westernization" not only fail to consider how these feminists' experiences within their Third-World contexts have shaped and informed their politics, but also fail to acknowledge that their feminist analyses are results of political organizing and political mobilization, initiated and sustained by women *within* these Third-World contexts.

Issues that feminist groups in India have politically engaged with include problems of dowry-murders and dowry-related harassment of women; police rape of women in custody; issues relating to women's poverty, work, health and reproduction; and issues of ecology and communalism that affect women's lives.[16] Indian feminist political activities have ranged from public protests, to publicizing and writing about these issues, to pressing for legal and public policy changes. Such activities clearly make feminists and feminism part of the *national political landscape* of many Third-World countries.[17] I am arguing that Third-World feminism is not a mindless mimicking of "Western agendas" in one clear and simple sense—that, for instance, Indian feminism is clearly a response to issues specifically confronting many *Indian* women.

I would argue that if there seems to be considerable resemblance, at least at a certain level of abstraction, between the issues addressed by Third-World feminists and those addressed by Western feminists, it is a result not of faddish mimicry but of the fact that women's inequality and mistreatment are, unfortunately, ubiquitous features of many "Western" and "non-Western" cultural contexts, even as their manifestations in specific contexts display important differences of detail. Thus, while women in Western contexts might be unfamiliar with the violence against women connected to the contemporary functioning of the institutions of dowry and arranged marriages, they are no strangers to battery and violence prevalent within their own various forms of marriage and family arrangements. They are no strangers either to the sense of shame that accompanies admitting victimization, or to a multiplicity of material, social, and cultural structures that pose serious impediments to women seeking assistance or to their leaving abusive relationships. There is considerable irony in the fact that our "Westernization" is blamed for our feminist cultural contestations, while the similarities I have mentioned suggest that "Western culture" has hardly displayed an easy willingness to take the fate of women seriously!

The Burdens of History:
Colonialism, Nationalism,
Feminism, and "Westernization" /

> If "woman" has been
> a part of the colonial and nationalist discourse of modernity, it
> is difficult but necessary to dismantle this construct without
> recuperating the also problematic discourse of "role" within
> the patriarchal family (of wife, mother, sister) and consequently
> of "tradition." . . . Thus, even while it is important to critique an
> ahistorical category of "woman," it is just as problematic to
> seek authentic versions of women's locations within societies.
>
> —Inderpal Grewal[18]

In this section, I would like to provide an historical account of why the charge of "Westernization" is so frequently leveled against Third-World feminists. Terms such as "Westernized" or "Westernization" function as negative epithets in several Third-World contexts, used to castigate not only individuals or political movements but also various forms of social change. I believe that one cannot account for why these terms function as pejoratives without reference to the history of colonization of Third-World countries by Western powers. The "colonial encounter" resulted in problematic pictures both of "Western culture" and the "indigenous culture" of particular colonies, pictures that relied on a sharp sense of contrast between the "two cultures." Views of gender, and of norms and practices affecting women, were seen as central to this contrast. I wish to argue that understanding the broad historical contours of these "cultural contrasts," and of the places assigned to different groups of women within these contrasts, helps make sense of why "Westernized" is the negative epithet of choice where dismissals of Third-World feminists are concerned. A critical understanding of the "cultural distinctions" constructed in colonial struggles is salient to contemporary Third-World feminist agendas.

Anticolonial struggles for national independence in many Third-World countries not only rejected the legitimacy of Western colonial rule but also often constructed a nationalist political identity by contrasting the indigenous "culture" and "its values" to those of the West, calling for a rejection of the latter.[19] This valorization of the values and practices of "the indigenous culture" of the colony was often a response to colonial attempts to eradicate or regulate customs and practices in the colonies that Western colonial governments found unacceptable or inexpedient. Ironically, the contrast between the values of "Western" culture and the values of colonized cultures was initially something insisted on by the colonizing powers. In their rhetoric, the "superiority of Western civilization" functioned as a rationale and justification for the colonial project, casting colonialism as, in part, an attempt to bestow the benefits of "Western civilization" on colonized peoples. In a manner of speaking, one could say that important strands of these anticolonial nationalist movements concurred with the colonizing powers concerning the differences in their values and cultures, but disagreed about the respective value of these values, inverting the colonialist contempt for "indigenous cultures" into a contempt for the "culture" of their colonizers. Each side in this colonial encounter had different political reasons for this shared insistence on the "Otherness" of the other culture.

The picture of "cultural differences" between "Western culture" and the cultures of various Third-World colonies that was constructed in colonial times, and that persists in contemporary postcolonial incarnations, was never a simple *descriptive* project of describing "cultural differences." It was inevitably implicated in the *political and discursive struggles* that marked the colonial encounter, and was an important part of attempts to justify, and interrelated attempts to challenge, the legitimacy of colonial rule. The pictures of both "Western" culture and particular "Third-World" cultures that resulted from these struggles were often marked by some interesting peculiarities.

For one thing, these pictures of different "cultures" and "cultural values" were "*idealized*" constructions, which were far from being faithful descriptions of the values that *actually pervaded* their institutional practices and social life. Thus, "Western culture" could see itself as staunchly committed to values like liberty and equality, a commitment that was often upheld as its distinguishing feature, a mark of its "superiority." This self-perception was untroubled by the fact that Western powers were engaged in slavery and colonization, or that they had resisted granting political and civil rights even to large numbers of Western subjects, including women. Similarly, some Indian nationalists could insist that Indian culture saw women as "goddesses"[20] without attending to the fact that poor and lower-caste women were far from being considered "goddesses," and without attending to the problematic implications of "goddess" status even for women of their own middle-class families.

Furthermore, both pictures of "Western" culture and "non-Western cultures" were "*totalizations*"—pictures that cast values and practices that pertained to *specific* privileged groups within the community as values of the "culture" *as a whole*. In the case of anticolonial Indian nationalism, "Indian culture" was often problematically equated with aspects of upper-caste Hindu culture, ignoring the actual cultural and religious diversity of the Indian population. Sucheta Mazumdar points out with respect to the Indian National Congress that, "since the vast majority of the leadership came from upper-caste Hindu backgrounds, Hindu religious culture was effortlessly equated with Indian culture."[21] This picture of "Indian culture" was not merely a distortion, but one that had detrimental practical consequences with respect to the manner in which many of the political struggles of Indian nationalism were constructed. Mazumdar notes, "Religious festivals were promoted by Hindu landlords and converted into sites for mass political rallies; religion, nationalism and anti-Muslim activism became one and the same."[22]

In the colonial context of nationalist struggles, both "Western culture" and the "non-Western culture" of a particular colony were often presented as *preexisting* schemas that were being compared and contrasted in relation to their respective merits. Often obscured was the fact that representations of what these "cultures" amounted to were *products of these very comparisons and contrasts*, where each side's sense of its cultural distinctiveness resulted from *discursive maneuvers* dedicated to constituting and refining their distinction. For instance, several interesting historical studies reveal not only the extent to which "Indian tradition" was produced and defined by colonial and nationalist discourses but also how "all the oldest English traditions were invented in the last quarter of the nineteenth century."[23, 24]

From the viewpoint of colonizing Western powers, an important "difference" between "Western culture" and various colonized cultures was the alleged singular openness of "Western culture" to historical change—cast, not surprisingly, as "progress." Colonized cultures were conversely often represented as victims of a static past of unchanging custom and tradition, virtually immune to history. Thus, even history-intoxicated philosophers like Hegel and Marx could complacently place entire colonized regions of the world "outside" of history, at least until the advent of colonialism. Hegel proclaims that Africa "is no historical part of the World. . . . What we properly understand by Africa, is the Unhistorical Undeveloped Spirit, still involved in the conditions of mere nature."[25] Marx confers the same distinction on India when he pronounces that "Indian society has no history at all, at least no known history," making it an "unresisting and unchanging society."[26]

To the degree that colonized societies were seen by Western colonialists as open to and affected by change, as in some Orientalist views of certain colonies, the changes were regarded as symptoms of cultural "decline" and "degeneration."[27] In either case, "Western culture" was regarded as suffused by the ingredients of world-historical progress, while colonized cultures were contrastingly regarded as entities paralyzed by Tradition, cast either as static and inert, or in a process of "decline." As Andre Beteille puts it, "The contrast is between western civilization which is dynamic and ever-changing and other civilizations in which change is so slow that it need not be taken into account."[28]

Many Third-World nationalist struggles against colonialism bought into aspects of these totalizing pictures of "their Traditions and Culture," even as they attempted to reinterpret them and reform them in directions more conducive to nationalist pride and resistance to colonial rule. Independence from colonial rule was imagined in a number of Third-World contexts as (at least partially) a future return to the values and culture of a hoary Past. In the perspectives of many Third-World nationalists fighting against Western colonial rule, the longstandingness of their "Culture and Traditions" had positive rather than negative connotations, since it was used to portray colonialism as merely a brief interruption in the autonomous and "authentic" life-story of the Nation. In these contexts, the "Traditions and Culture" of specific Third-World contexts became focal points of what was threatened by colonial rule and "Westernization," and vital strands of "the national fabric" of the envisioned independent Nation that would emerge after the demise of colonialism.

Many of these "cultural" conflicts between Western colonizing cultures and colonized indigenous cultures involved issues pertaining to women's roles and female sexuality, rendering the figure of the "Colonized Woman" an important site of the political struggles between "Western Culture" and the "Culture" of the colony. Veiling, polygamy, child-marriage, and *sati* were all significant points of conflict and negotiation between colonizing "Western" culture and different colonized Third-World cultures. In these conflicts, Western colonial powers often depicted indigenous practices as symptoms of the "backwardness and barbarity" of Third-World cultures in contrast to the "progressiveness of Western culture." The figure of the colonized woman became a representation of the oppressiveness of the entire "cultural tradition" of the colony.

Male-dominated Third-World elites often responded by constructing these very practices as sacred and longstanding traditions that were constitutive of their values and world views, and as practices that were tied to the spiritual place of, and respect for, women in their cultures. There were both "modernist" and "traditionalist" sides in a number of anticolonial nationalist discourses. "Modernist" segments of these anticolonial nationalist narratives accepted to a greater degree that some aspects of their "Traditions and Culture," including practices affecting women, were in need of a certain degree of reform and change. However, they often combined endorsement of such change with an insistence that "their Culture" had distinctive, special, and valuable views about women and their "cultural place," views preferable to those of "Western culture." The "traditionalists" tended to be more resistant to some of the changes in their "Traditions" that the "modernists" endorsed, seeing them as deeply corrosive of their way of life and a capitulation to the cultural domination of a colonizing Western culture.[29]

Given a background where colonial agendas faced-off against anti-colonial nationalist agendas, it often became impossible to extricate discussions of indigenous practices that adversely affected women from this conflict-laden political and discursive background. There could be little serious discussion of the impact of these practices on women's well-being and agency that could escape becoming embroiled in the struggles between colonialism and nationalism. This situation left women and women's issues vulnerable to co-optation by both colonialist and nationalist agendas. Discussions of problematic practices affecting women often became hostages to a discursive background of cultural muscle-flexing about the relative moral superiority of "Western" culture and the "culture" of particular colonies. Partha Chatterjee points out that the "woman question" in nineteenth-century India "was not so much about the specific condition of women within a determinate set of social relations as it was about the encounter between a colonial state and the supposed 'tradition' of a conquered people."[30] The sound and fury of these "my culture is better than your culture" conflicts between male-dominated colonial governments and male-dominated Third-World nationalist movements often served to obscure the fact that women were clearly second-class citizens in *all* these cultural contexts.

Some colonial women (including feminists) as well as some colonized women participated in this complex process, often playing their part in these games of cultural one-upmanship, pledging allegiance to their respective "national cultures," and insisting on their difference from, and cultural superiority to, each other. Antoinette Burton shows how British feminists used the colonial context to "undermine the Victorian construction of woman as Other by identifying her with the Self of nation and empire."[31] She describes how Victorian feminists often grounded their claims for political agency and rights in a reform ideology of women's special moral responsibility for the downtrodden, both at home and in the colonies. Burton concludes that in domestic politics, Victorian feminists transformed "the poor into the symbolic nation that British women were responsible for saving"[32] while, in the colonial context, "Indian women appeared to them to be the natural and logical 'white woman's burden.'"[33]

It was often not only the women of the colonizing nation but also nationalist men engaged in anticolonial struggles who built their claims for self-representation by appealing to their role in improving the lot of colonized women. For instance, Indian nationalist men saw their political role as crucially connected to "improving the status of Indian women."[34] Thus, both Victorian feminists and Indian nationalist men constructed "the Indian woman" as a site upon which to ground their own demands for political liberation and agency, giving them both an

Other to "speak for" in a context where "speaking for" was "one of the prerequisites of political subjectivity."[35] The position of "the Indian woman" as someone to be "spoken for," in both British feminist and Indian nationalist discourse, provides a clear example of how challenges to the political status quo often repeat and replicate *aspects* of its "political logic."

The fact that one is confronted with a choice between problematic pictures of one's social and political role does not necessarily mean one has no reason to prefer one over the others. Thus, there were often aspects of nationalist discourse that made it more appealing to many colonized women than the discourses of colonialism, including that of "imperial feminism." These nationalist perspectives, despite their problems, often accorded colonized women both a more "reverential" status and also a more significant political role and agency compared to any of the visions of their colonizers.[36]

Thus, in the Indian context, many nationalist women as well as men subscribed to a posited "dichotomy between the 'material West' and the 'spiritual East,'" within the terms of which nationalist women often embraced their roles as "repositories of a national spiritual essence" who must remain untainted by "Westernization" and its implied pollution.[37] Indian women often also subscribed to nationalist views that "their culture" treated women with more veneration, regard, and honor than did "Western" culture, and to views of Western women as women who "were fond of useless luxury and cared little for the well-being of the home."[38] On the other hand, these women also challenged to some degree the views of appropriate gender roles held by nationalist men. Thus, some nationalist women used nationalism to better their own positions, demanding full rights to higher education for women, in ways that went beyond what nationalist men wanted for them, even as they were "careful to link this achievement with better motherhood and a better home."[39]

Gender thus played its part in the ideological service of both colonial Empires and of Third-World nationalist movements, helping to position "Western" and "non-Western" women against each other as competing cultural embodiments of appropriate femininity and virtue. Simultaneously, colonialism and nationalism played their own ideological parts in the construction of gender roles, in both Western contexts and in the colonies, sometimes with surprisingly similar results. The "Indian woman" of Indian nationalist discourse bears a striking resemblance to "Victorian womanhood" not only in her imputed "respectability" and "refinement" but also in the explicit contrast between her and her "coarse and vulgar" lower-class sisters![40]

These contours of colonialist and nationalist "cultural self-definition" help clarify why "Westernization" is a popular expression of cultural disapproval in many Third-World contexts. The construction of national identity in opposition to "Westernization" and "Western culture" has continued into postcolonial times in a number of Third-World contexts, assisted by the fact that many Third-World countries have remained vulnerable to economic exploitation and political manipulation by Western powers even in the aftermath of colonialism. The rapid transformation of economic and social structures in many Third-World contexts in recent decades, a process often influenced by Western economic agendas and visions of "development," has only re-evoked and intensified the feeling that the "traditional culture" is under threat from "Westernization."

Among the more noticeable changes in recent decades in many Third-World countries is the entry of increasing numbers of women from the ranks of local elites, predominantly middle-class urban women, into professional and public life, spheres of activity that used to be exclusively male. The sense of cultural anxiety created by rapid social change often results in responses that focus on changes in gender roles as the paradigmatic symptom of cultural threat and loss. This in turn results in calls for a return to and restoration of "our traditional way of life," a return that is to be accomplished by returning women to their "traditional place."

The nationalist cultural pride that was predicated upon a return to "traditional values" and the rejection of "Westernization" that began under colonial rule thus re-emerges today in a variety of postcolonial "fundamentalist" movements, where returning women to their "traditional roles" continues to be defined as central to preserving national identity and cultural pride. In such contexts, the fact that a number of Third-World feminists are middle-class urban women who have entered formerly male professional and political spheres, combined with the fact that they often demand greater equality and participation for women in various arenas of national life rather than a return to "traditional roles," facilitates casting them and their political visions as embodiments of the demon "Westernization." Third-World women engaged in struggles over women-centered issues in Third-World contexts—women who are not urban or middle-class—are ignored and marginalized by an insistence on seeing only urban middle-class women as "feminists." As a result, Third-World feminist criticisms of practices and ways of life that are harmful and oppressive to women are depicted as mere symptoms of an antinationalist cultural disloyalty and as forms of "cultural inauthenticity" rooted in an adoption of "Western" ways and values.

The political location of many Third-World feminists makes it particularly clear that the scope of feminist struggles needs to include not only contestations of *particular practices and institutions* detrimental to women, but additionally to include challenges to the larger pictures of Nation, National History, and Cultural Traditions that serve to sustain and justify these practices and institutions. These are often "pictures of History" that *conceal their own historicity and their own status as representations*—suggesting that the Nation and its Culture are "natural givens" rather than the *historical inventions and constructions* that they are.

These pictures of "Culture and History" also serve to conceal the degree to which calls for a "return to past traditions," in Third-World contexts as elsewhere, are motivated by *present* economic and political agendas. Such narratives of "National Traditions" and "National Culture" often present themselves as talking about *factual and descriptive* features of a national and cultural past, but are always in fact *political* notions—used to prescribe which groups among the body of citizens are important, which ways of life deserve honor and respect, and how a particular nation should imagine its political future. They require feminists to combine critical contestations of particular practices and institutions with attempts to reimagine their Nation, Culture, and History in ways that more adequately accommodate women's contributions as well as attention to their problems. While I have focused on how the dynamics of colonial history complicate the present political locations of many Third-World feminist struggles, feminists in all nations confront problematic nationalisms and different versions of these "burdens of history." I will argue later that feminist political struggles in any national context crucially involve new ways of perceiving and retelling that nation's history.

Selective Labeling and the Myth of "Continuity" /

> The starting-point of critical elaboration is the consciousness of what one really is, and is "knowing thyself" as a product of the historical process to date which has deposited in you an infinity of traces, without leaving an inventory.
> —Antonio Gramsci[41]

In this section, I would like to shift to exploring some ways in which the sense of "cultural distinctiveness" from "Western culture" that developed in colonial contexts affects the ways in which the term "Westernization" is deployed in contemporary Third-World national contexts. I will argue that "Westernization" is often used to define "national culture" in ways that imagine more "cultural continuity" than is in fact the case. National cultures in many parts of the world seem susceptible to seeing themselves as *unchanging continuities* stretching back into a distant past. This picture tends to reinforce powerfully what I think of as the "Idea of Venerability," making people susceptible to the suggestion that practices and institutions are valuable *merely* by virtue of the fact that they are of long-standing. It is a picture of Nation and Culture that stresses continuities of tradition, (often imagined continuities) over assimilation, adaptation, and change.

In some Third-World contexts, the past history of colonization seems to exacerbate this problem. For instance, many versions of Indian anti-colonial nationalism relied greatly on appeals to a totalizing vision of "our ancient civilization," casting independence from colonialism as a recovery of this "ancient civilization" while simultaneously casting "Western civilization" as an uppity and adolescent newcomer to the stage of world history and civilization. Such discursive backgrounds often obscure the extent to which actual cultural practices, the significance of particular practices, as well as the material and social contexts of these practices, have undergone, and continue to undergo, substantial change. A frequent and noticeable peculiarity in these portrayals of unchanging "national culture, traditions, and values" in Third-World contexts is the degree to which there is an *extremely selective* rejection of "Westernization." What interests me is that while *some* incorporations of "Western" artifacts and practices are perceived and castigated as "Westernization," not all are, making some of these borrowings and changes contested and problematic in ways that other changes are not.

I believe that the term "Westernization" functions in colonial and post-colonial Third-World contexts primarily as a sort of rhetorical term, and that the term is often deployed in inconsistent as well as problematic ways.[42] Certain artifacts and not others are "picked out" and labeled "Western," and certain changes and perspectives are arbitrarily attributed to "Westernization" while others are not. This "selective labeling" of certain changes and not others as symptoms of "Westernization" reflects underlying political agendas. For instance, such "selective labeling" enables Hindu fundamentalists to characterize Indian feminist issues as symptoms of "Westernization" even while they skillfully use contemporary media such as television to propagate their ideological messages. Their commitment to "Indian traditions" seems unconcerned about whether the entry of television into Indian homes affects our "traditional way of life"! Feminist commitment to autonomy or equality for women can be portrayed as "Western values" by the same fundamentalists who discern no paradox, for instance, in appropriating the language of rights when it suits their interests.[43]

Dismissing feminist criticisms as "Westernized" is, unfortunately, not unique to right-wing fundamentalists, but is a practice that can be found at various places in the political spectrum. Many Third-World intellectuals who are not fundamentalists also collaborate in depicting feminism as "Western" and a "foreign import" into Third-World contexts. Feminist political agendas are presumably deemed "tainted" by their alleged "origin" in the West. Many of these allegedly "Authentic Upholders of their Culture" seem to have few personal qualms, however, about using "Western" technology or buying "Western" consumer goods. Nor do they have political qualms about their Third-World nations spending their scarce monetary resources on the purchase of Western armaments.

This "selective labeling" of certain changes and not others as symptoms of "Westernization" enables the portrayal of unwelcome changes as unforgivable betrayals of deep-rooted and constitutive traditions, while welcome changes are seen as merely pragmatic adaptations that are utterly consonant with the "preservation of our culture and values." It has often struck me that many in Third-World contexts who condemn feminist criticisms and contestations as "Westernization" would like to believe that there was a pristine and unchanging continuity in their "traditions and way of life," until we feminist daughters provided the first rude interruption.

Both my grandmothers were married at the age of thirteen. This was quite typical for the women of this particular community in that generation. I try not to think about what this meant to them,[44] and above all what it could have meant to me if that particular "tradition" had continued. Like many other women of her generation and class and caste background, my mother was not married until she was twenty-one. How would my grandmothers have explained so significant a change in the space of one generation, a change that, however else it is to be explained, cannot be explained in terms of their daughters' rebellion against the practice of marriage following on the heels of the first indications of puberty?

It is not clear to me how illuminating or intelligible it is to attribute such a change to "Westernization," given *the complex interaction of local and colonial structures* that operated to produce this change. For instance, there were many more colleges for women by the time my mother was in her teens ("Westernization"?) than existed in my grandmothers' youths. A community that valued education as part of its particular caste-ethos (both my grandmothers had some schooling despite their early marriage, and were literate) was thus encouraged to educate its daughters longer, postponing the age of marriage. Indian nationalists (many of them men with "Westernized educations") whose attempts to "reform Hinduism" were linked to an attempt to create nationalist pride, and who criticized the practice of child-marriage, undoubtedly had some impact on this change.[45]

It is not my intention to suggest that these startling changes with respect to women's education and the age of marriage happened without cultural notice or negotiation. Education for middle-class Indian women was clearly a contentious issue early in the nineteenth century, in part because it was initially predominantly organized by white Christian missionaries.[46] This raised the specters of both religious proselytization and the exposure of Indian women to the "harmful influences of Western culture." However, by the 1850s Indians opened their own schools for girls,[47] and before the end of the century, formal education "became not only acceptable, but, in fact, a requirement for the new *bhadramahila* [respectable women]."[48] This process interestingly led to a few Indian women receiving university degrees "before most British Universities agreed to accept women on their examination rolls."[49]

There are difficulties in attempting to characterize changes such as education for Indian women as "Westernization." For one thing, education for *Western* women, especially college and professional education, was a deeply contested issue in the nineteenth century, and bitter struggles around higher education continued to be a part of Western feminist suffrage struggles of the early twentiethth century.[50] Thus education for women could hardly be seen as an uncontroversial and longstanding aspect of "Western culture." For another, while Westerners, especially missionaries, were initially crucial causal components in setting up educational institutions for women, the success of these projects also depended on their being embraced and endorsed by segments of the Indian elites. Such endorsements were often couched in nationalist terms that specifically *resisted* seeing educating Indian women as "Westernization," seeing it variously as "making Indian women better wives and mothers," as helping to fulfill the urgent need for women doctors, and even as restoring to women the freedom, equality, and access to education they were believed to have enjoyed in the remote "golden age" of Hinduism. In many colonial and postcolonial contexts, it is difficult to clearly distinguish between the facts of change over time and "changes due to Western influence," since many of these changes involve complex "complicities and resistances" between aspects of "Western culture" and Third-World institutions, agents, and political agendas.

I wish to call attention to the fact that these undeniably significant changes in women's access to education and in the age of marriage were not, by my mother's lifetime, seen by my mother's family as a "surrender of our traditions" or as a problematic symptom of "Westernization." The traces of cultural conflict and negotiation that gave rise to them had vanished from view. For large segments of this particular Indian community, college education for its daughters and the correspondingly older age of marriage had, within a generation, become matter-of-fact elements of its "way of life."

It is far from my intention to suggest that the changes that led to my mother not being married at thirteen have affected the lives of *all* Indian women. Class, caste, religious, and ethnic differences pose problems for generalizations about women in Third-World contexts, in much the same way as differences among women pose problems for generalizations about women in Western contexts. Thirteen year olds continue to be married off in many poor and rural Indian communities. The forces of "modernization" that prevented my mother from being married at thirteen are, paradoxically, also responsible for the marriages of some contemporary thirteen year olds. Take the publicized recent case of Ameena, found sobbing in an Air India plane by an alert flight-attendant, in the company of a sixty-three-year-old Saudi man, who was taking her out of the country as his "wife."[51] Today, there are businesses, paradigms of efficiency, organization, and modern entrepreneurial spirit, where skillful middle-men mediate, for a price, between poor Indian families anxious to marry off their barely teenage daughters and those with the foreign currency to purchase them as "wives": a complex interplay of "tradition" and "modernity," poverty and perversity, that has hundreds of Ameenas sobbing on their way to foreign fates that make my grandmothers' fates seem enviable.

I have been struck by the fact that it is not only religious fundamentalists who believe they are continuing "longstanding traditions" while ignoring the changes in which they have collaborated, but also women like my mother. My mother's vision manages to ignore the huge difference between her marriage at twenty-one and her mother's marriage at thirteen and sees both her life and her mother's as "upholding Indian traditions," while my life-choices are perceived to constitute a break with and rejection of tradition. My calling attention to the changes that mark the historical space between my mother's life and that of my grandmothers is an attempt to drive home the fact that it is not merely Third-World "intellectuals" or "Westernized feminists" who have been affected by profound changes in traditions, ways of life, and gender roles.

Third-World feminists, whose political agendas are constantly confronted with charges that they constitute betrayals of "our traditional ways of life," need to be particularly alert to how much relatively *uncontested change* in "ways of life" has taken place. We need to redescribe and challenge this picture of "unchanging traditions" that supposedly are only now in danger of "betrayal" as a result of feminist instigation. Some of these changes, while historically pretty recent, have become so "taken for granted" in our lifetimes that I am often amazed to confront the details and the extent of these changes.

I remember the surprise I felt in listening to one of my mother's stories about her girlhood, when her mother was a young wife and mother, married to my grandfather, who was a lawyer. My mother recounted how my grandfather's clients would come to the house hoping to meet with him, only to find that he was away in court. It was then not deemed "proper" for my grandmother to meet directly or converse with these male clients, posing a "communication problem" that was rather ingeniously resolved. My grandmother would stand behind the front door and send her child, my mother, onto the front steps, whereupon the client would address the child, requesting that she ask her mother about her father's whereabouts. My grandmother behind the door would then tell her daughter to inform the client that her father was in court and would return at a particular time.

My mother's telling of this story was centrally motivated by her amused recollection of standing on the front steps, saying nothing, while the entire conversation proceeded by means of the two adults addressing her. What I registered in listening to this story were other facts: how the grandmother I knew two decades later no longer hid from her husband's clients; how my mother had, in sharp contrast to her mother, accompanied my father to mixed-gender gatherings where she socially interacted with his male colleagues and coworkers; how many of the women of my generation had male colleagues and clients of our own and took our public lives and interactions with men for granted. Looking at these rapid generational changes, I find it impossible to describe "our traditional way of life" without seeing *change* as a constitutive element, affecting transformations that become "invisible" in their taken-for-grantedness.[52]

Not surprisingly, the gender of the actors seems to be one factor that determines whether a particular change is regarded as an example of "Westernization that is disrespectful of our traditions." My paternal grandfather and my father, for example, wore trousers and shirts to work, not "Indian" clothes.[53] I have no idea how this particular transition was initially conceptualized or categorized. Even if it was considered "Westernization" at the start, I do not think that the millions of Indian men who wear shirts and trousers today think of themselves as putting on "Western clothes" as they get dressed. However, the women in my family of my grandmothers' and mother's generations have worn traditional "Indian" dress all their lives, and I am sure that any attempt at a similar "transition" on their part would have been a matter of cultural consternation. My female cousins who grew up mainly in the cities wore an eclectic mixture of "Indian" and "Western" clothes into their teens; but most wear only "Indian dress" after marriage.[54] In this context, it is interesting to note that the particular version of the sari, which functions as the cultural paradigm of "traditional Indian dress" today, and has become standard for middle-class women, emerged via a series of *nineteenth-century* experimentations.[55]

I am aware that in some contexts within the Third World, some Southeast Asian countries for instance, many men and women have both adopted "Western" modes of dress without it appearing to be much of an issue.[56] In yet other Third-World contexts, groups of both men and women may retain local forms of dress as an ethnic or regional marker, as an articulated resistance to "Westernization," or as an assertion of nationalist identity and pride. My point is not that the adoption of "Western" dress functions in similar ways in *all* Third-World contexts. Rather, I merely want to use the dress-related examples I give to underscore the fact that, in many instances, men seem to be permitted a greater degree of cultural latitude in making changes than are women, and are less frequently accused of "Westernization." (And, in many other instances that seem less linked to gender, artifacts, ideas, and practices originating in the West, from cars to computers to constitutions, have been adopted into and adapted for local use, without engendering a discourse that constructs them as emblems of "Westernization," while other such borrowings are seen as "problematically Western.")

I have only fairly recently begun to see that a common thread linking what was forbidden to me at various times under the rubric of "Westernization" involved cultural norms relating to female sexuality. When I was twelve, my family came to India on a holiday from Uganda and went South to visit relatives who lived in much more "traditional" contexts than Bombay. My mother made it clear that, marked as I now was by puberty, I could not wear my "Western" skirts and dresses there, though they had seemed "Indian" enough to both me and her when I wore them in Bombay. The primary principle that seemed to determine what I could wear when I was South visiting my relatives was that it fully covered my legs.[57] I have since wondered in what sense this "culture" that was bothered by my spindly twelve-year-old legs was the "same" culture that produced the polymorphously perverse erotic sculptures on the temples of Khajuraho, festooned with dozens of sexually acrobatic "divine" bodies, in a variety of positions, some of which are undoubtedly only possible for the gods!

My story reveals that what counted as "inappropriately Western dress" differed from one specific Indian context to another, even within the same class and caste community. This suggests to me that the more details one attends to, the less neat and tidy is likely to be one's picture of what constitutes "Indian culture" or "Indian values," or even one's picture of somewhat narrower categories such as "Indian attitudes to sexuality" or "Indian attitudes to female bodies." Any attempt to create a neat and totalizing picture of "Indian culture's" attitudes to sexuality and women's bodies is going to run up against the undeniable tensions between my relatives' anxieties about my adolescent legs and the equally "Indian" celebration of the erotic embodied in the carvings at Khajuraho.

Other stories, other confusions, other contradictions: I was about five when I went over to play with the little girl next door, and we discovered a bottle of her mother's nail polish. We had a wonderful time painting each other's nails a garish pink. I returned home pleased with my shiny nails, to face a torrent of my grandmother's wrath. She made it clear to me, though I did not quite understand why, that I had done something shameful, that only "loose" women and Westerners wore that sort of thing, that "our" women did not. I remember crying as she scraped the polish off, not primarily because I was disappointed at losing my pretty pink nails, but because it was clear I had done something horrible and I did not really understand what the nature of its shamefulness was. And the irony of course is that the same grandmother did not bat an eye when I came back at the end of every summer from visits to my maternal grand-parents' home with my hands and feet patterned with the lovely dark red of henna that would not fade for months.

And the same grandmother often took buses across town to watch movies with her cronies, sometimes taking me along, and would not have ever dreamed of considering the bus or the movies "Western." By travel-ing in public conveyances and venturing out for public entertainment such as movies, without the benefit of a male escort, my grandmother was not only engaging in conduct that would have seemed unseemly to her mother, but in conduct that would have seemed problematic and "West-ernized" to many women of her own generation living outside large urban cities. It was also conduct that my grandmother would not permit her daughter-in-law, my mother, to engage in, on the grounds that it was unseemly for younger women! What counts as "Westernization" seems to vary considerably with time and place and community, and the very things that were forbidden in its name to women of one generation, such as employment outside the home, often seemed to become commonplace in the next, remarkable only in their unremarkability.

Partha Chatterjee helps make sense of many of the examples I have given when he argues that the project of nineteenth-century Indian nationalism was not a total rejection of the West but rather comprised an "ideological justification for the selective appropriation of Western modernity."[58] This project, he argues, disproportionately conferred on women the task of preserving the "spiritual distinctiveness" of Indian cul-ture, a distinctiveness that was located within the home. Changes that affected women and the domestic realm were thereby rendered more contentious than changes with respect to men in the "outside world." I suspect that the allocation to women of a "special role" in preserving national culture and traditions was fairly commonplace in a number of other Third-World nationalist movements, making changes that affect women and family life matters of greater consternation.

I agree with Chatterjee that such selective appropriations of modernity *continue* to be pervasive in many postcolonial Third-World contexts, and that women continue to be disproportionately assigned the tasks of "preserving national culture and traditions." I also wish to point out that appropriate "public" roles for women also continue to be reinterpreted, to make some changes, but not others, consonant with "preservation of tradition" at particular times. As my stories reveal, ideas of what constitute appropriate appropriation seem to change with remarkable rapidity. These stories also show that there is often considerable disagreement on what constitutes "inappropriate Westernization" within various regions and social groups within a Third-World national context at any given time.

This process of designating certain changes and not others as "problematically Westernized" is often carried out as if the label was picking out something descriptively obvious. Pointing to the fluid, fractured, selective, and changing deployment of this "labeling" is one important strategy for Third-World feminists who face delegitimization via accusations of "Westernization." I believe Third-World feminists need to elicit greater public debate about what the label of "Westernization" means. We need to point out that it often is a rhetorical device, predicated on double-standards and bad faith, used to smear selectively only those changes, those breaks with tradition, that those with the authority to define "tradition" deplore. We need to ask forcefully what sets off our transgressions, our changes, the breaks we would make with "our culture" from all these breaks, changes, and adaptations that have been going on all along.

I believe there *is* something about the political contestations articulated in Third-World feminist voices that single us, and the changes we would make, out for rhetorical attack. We are often young women, vocal and articulate, who clearly assert our entitlement to contest "our cultures" with a confidence that many "cultures" find unnerving in their women. We provoke anxiety and resistance because we publicly hold up to our fellow-citizens the shame of what "our" traditions and cultural practices, and the changing economic and social contexts in which they function, have so often done to the women: the deaths, the brutalities, and the more mundane and quotidian sufferings of women within "our" culture, with which "our" culture has been complicitous. And we have the temerity to justify our refusal to be "innocent" and silent. We provoke nervousness and condemnation because we insist that the choices and happiness of women should matter considerably more than the preservation of "Tradition" even as we call attention to the selective and problematic ways in which these "traditions" are understood.

Despite these accusations of "Westernization," our voices will not quietly vanish, shamed into silence. We are the sisters, the wives, the daughters, of those who would dismiss us, and our points of view are no more able to be "outside" our national and cultural contexts than the perspectives of those who dismiss us as "Westernized." We are very often no more products of a "Western" education than our critics who position themselves as unproblematic preservers of "our traditions." And while we know only too well that our criticisms and contestations are not uniquely "representative" of our "culture," we have the power and the ability to question whether the voices of our critics are any more uniquely "representative" of our complex and changing cultural realities. I firmly believe Third-World feminists are entitled, in our own ways, to respond to our critics in the same way I once responded to my mother when she accused me of being "decultured" (an English neologism that she seemed to invent in the heat of an argument-laden moment). I told her that what she refused to see was that I was not just a feminist, but an Indian woman with particular views about what "her" culture was and what it had to offer women.

I do not wish to deny that "cultures" in general are always being contested, and not only by feminists; nor to imply that Third-World feminists always have *"the* right take" on their cultures. Feminist critiques in any context, like other intellectual endeavors, might be mistaken in their assumptions, insensitive to context, inadequately attentive to the interests of those who are marginalized and powerless, and so forth. Such flaws, when present, should elicit serious critical dialogue instead of attempts to *dismiss* the views put forward by questioning the "authenticity" of the speaker or by characterizing feminism as a purely "Western" political agenda.

These strategies of dismissal, where political positions are characterized as "alien," as "foreign," as "representing the views of Others," and whereby individuals who endorse these positions are categorized as "betrayers" of their nation or "traitors to their communities," seem fairly ubiquitous and are not only directed at feminists.[59] These strategies of dismissal have also been used against feminists of color in Western contexts, where their perspectives are often dismissed as an espousal of a political agenda that is "white." As Cherrie Moraga points out:

> Over and over again, Chicanas trivialize the women's movement as being merely a white middle-class thing, having little to offer women of color. . . . Interestingly, it is perfectly acceptable among Chicano males to use white theoreticians, e.g. Marx and Engels, to develop a theory of Chicana oppression. It is unacceptable, however, for the Chicana to use white sources by women to develop a theory of Chicana oppression.[60]

I would argue that attempts to dismiss Third-World feminist views and politics as "Westernization" should be combatted, in part by calling attention to the selective and self-serving deployments of the term, and in part by insisting that our contestations are no less rooted in our experiences within "our cultures," no less "representative" of our complex and changing realities, than the views of our compatriots who do not share our perspectives. Third-World feminists urgently need to call attention to the facts of change within their contexts, so that our agendas are not delegitimized by appeals to "unchanging traditions." We need to point to how demands that we be deferential to "our" Culture, Traditions, and Nation have often amounted to demands that we continually defer the articulation of issues affecting women. As an Algerian feminist puts it:

> (It is never, has never been the right moment to protest . . . in the name of women's interests and rights: not during the liberation struggle against colonialism, because all forces should be mobilized against the principal enemy: French colonialism; not after Independence, because all forces should be mobilized to build up the devastated country; not now that racist imperialistic Western governments are attacking Islam and the Third World, etc.) Defending women's rights "now" (this "now" being ANY historical moment) is always a betrayal—of the people, of the nation, of the revolution, of Islam, of national identity, of cultural roots, of the Third World.[61]

I am not suggesting that all the changes that have taken place within Third-World contexts are for the better. I am not advocating that Third-World feminists simplistically invert traditionalist, nationalist, or fundamentalist attempts to convey the message "Change is Bad, Traditions are Good" by insisting that "Traditions are Bad, Change is Good." While some of the changes that have taken place in Third-World contexts have arguably improved the lives of women, others have clearly made things worse. In Third-World contexts, as elsewhere, changes that improve the lives of *some* women may do little for others, or might affect them adversely. Feminists need to be alert and attentive to all these various possibilities and to encourage widespread and critical dialogue on various aspects of social change.

All national contexts need to promote the abilities of their various members to think critically about the elements that should be preserved and those that need to be challenged, to distinguish cultural changes that should be valued from those that should be resisted, opening up these questions to widespread political debate. The charge that Third-World feminists lack the "cultural legitimacy" to name what is wrong about the ways in which women are affected by the persistence or change of economic, social, and cultural structures in their national contexts is often an attempt to curtail and cut short this political dialogue about particular practices, institutions, and changes, and to preserve a misguided sense of "cultural pride" that equates respect for a "culture" with blindness to its problems.

Conclusion /

No discussion of the feminist international perspective is complete unless it rests on a lucid analysis of one's own national roots, of one's own inscription in the network of power and signification that make up one's culture. . . . Feminists cannot avoid confrontation with our own national ties, our location within a specific national framework. Unless this kind of feminist analysis gets elaborated, women run the risk of waving the international flag as an empty rhetorical gesture, slipping into a fantasy world, . . . a no (wo)man's land. Proposing an international perspective without critical scrutiny of our roles in our cultural, national contexts would be only a form of supranationalism, that is, ultimately, a form of planetary exile.

—Rosi Braidotti[62]

My intention has been to point to a number of assumptions that impede Third-World feminist criticisms of their cultures, and to challenge a number of assumptions about "Westernization" that are used to de-legitimize such criticisms. However, problematic pictures of "national identity" and "cultural authenticity" do not pose challenges exclusively for Third-World feminists. Dangerous visions of "Nation" and "national culture" seem ubiquitous across a range of nation-states in various parts of the world. I would like to end by examining the import of such views of "Nation" and "national culture" for feminist political contestations within Western as well as Third-World national contexts.

I am arguing that, instead of locating ourselves as "outsiders within" Third-World national contexts, Third-World feminists need to challenge the notion that access to "Westernized educations," or our espousal of feminist perspectives, positions us "outside" of our national and cultural contexts. We need to problematize aspects of pictures of "our Culture and Traditions" that are deployed to de-legitimize our politics, and to insist that our views be accorded the privilege of substantive criticism rather than be subject to such dismissal. We need to insist that what divides us from those we oppose is not their "cultural authenticity" and our lack thereof, but differences of *ethical and political vision* about what sort of political entities our Nations should be and how they should treat their different members

Given the interpenetration of "Western" values and institutions with the national political and cultural landscapes of "home," and the way that "Western" and "local" elements mesh in the geography of our lives, as well as in the lives of those in the Third World who do not share our cultural critiques, I believe many Third-World feminists would do better to insist that our voices are neither more or less "representative" of "our cultures" than the voices of many others who speak within our national contexts. In Third-World contexts, as elsewhere, feminist perspectives, like any political perspective, should not be considered valuable only if they accord with prevailing or dominant views and values. Political perspectives are often valuable precisely because they constitute new ways of seeing, fresh modes of reflection and assessment. New modes of assessment might well turn out to be as problematic as the older modes they critique, but that is a matter for sustained political discussion within a political community. What feminists everywhere need to insist on is not immunity from criticism but on the problematic nature of forms of dismissal that seek to undercut their very entry into such political dialogue.

We all need to recognize that critical postures do not necessarily render one an "outsider" to what one criticizes, and that it is often precisely one's status as "inside" the nation and culture one criticizes that gives one's criticisms their motivation and urgency. Third-World feminists are "insiders" in the sense that they are often both familiar with and affected by the practices, institutions, and policies they criticize. They are also active citizens within their respective national landscapes, whose political analyses and protests have been crucial to making issues affecting women into matters of national awareness and concern.

We need to move away from a picture of national and cultural contexts as sealed rooms, impervious to change, with a homogenous space "inside" them, inhabited by "authentic insiders" who all share a uniform and consistent account of their institutions and values. Third-World national and cultural contexts are as pervaded by plurality, dissension, and change, as are their "Western" counterparts. Both are often replete with unreflective and self-congratulatory views of their "culture" and "values" that disempower and marginalize the interests and concerns of many members of the national community, including women. We need to be wary about all ideals of "cultural authenticity" that portray "authenticity" as constituted by lack of criticism and lack of change. We need to insist that there are many ways to inhabit nations and cultures critically and creatively. Feminists everywhere confront the joint tasks of selectively appropriating and selectively rejecting various facets of their complex national, cultural, and political legacies, a critical engagement that can alone transform one's inheritances into a "culture" of one's own.

I believe that Third-World feminist political contestations highlight certain features that are crucial to feminist agendas in a variety of national contexts. Feminist attempts to call political attention to the problems of women and members of other marginalized groups are not projects of drawing attention to simple "matters of fact" that become easily "visible" when attention is drawn to them. They involve *normative contestations and re-descriptions* of the ways particular institutions and practices adversely affect groups of people. They also involve calling attention to "matters of fact" that are often overlooked or explained away, and making the case for the pervasive and systematic nature of certain problems that may be perceived as occasional and random. They involve challenges to widespread unreflective assumptions about what national "culture" and "values" are, how important institutions function, and how various groups of people fare as a result of existing arrangements of national life.

These political tasks are hardly unique to Third-World contexts, but seem crucial components of political contestations everywhere. It is important to insist that problematic pictures of Nation, Culture, and History of the sort I have discussed are not unique to India or to Third-World contexts. An investigation of past and present visions of the United States, of "American culture" and "the American way of life," reveal the same sorts of problems. They often both obscure the contributions and problems of members of marginalized and powerless groups and suggest that feminist political commitments are unpatriotic and "un-American." They function to stigmatize the predicaments and choices of single mothers, women on welfare, gays and lesbians, immigrants, and members of the "underclass" as "un-American."

Totalizing and dangerous views of "American culture" and "nationhood" can be found in current attempts to portray "Christian values" or particular constructions of "family values" as constitutive of "American culture" and "the American way of life." Views of "American culture" that picture American society as comprised of "free individuals," and of American institutions as already fair and egalitarian, obscure the ways in which various forms of institutional discrimination impede the entry and flourishing of members of marginalized groups. This results, for instance, in widespread perceptions of affirmative action policies as constituting "reverse discrimination" or "preferential treatment" inimical to equality rather than as attempts to equalize opportunity.[63] Pictures of America as a "land of opportunity" where initiative and hard work guarantee economic flourishing, and where poverty is attributed to moral failings rather than to structural constraints, contribute to popular support for eroding state provision of welfare. Welfare recipients become objects of resentment rather than of concern, a process exacerbated by using stereotypes of Black teenage single mothers as the paradigmatic welfare recipient.[64]

Ongoing versions of U.S. nationalism continue to function to marginalize a great many members of its national community, even as American nationalism continues to be deployed to justify problematic economic and political interventions in other parts of the world. And, as the visible presence of many Christian groups on the right wing of the American political spectrum makes amply clear, religious fundamentalist politics are not a phenomenon unique to Third-World contexts. Furthermore, problematic views of women's roles and social place have an important place in all these religious fundamentalist political agendas.

Feminists all over the world need to be suspicious of locally prevalent pictures of "national identity" and "national traditions," both because they are used to privilege the views and values of certain parts of the heterogeneous national population, and because they are almost invariably detrimental to the interests and political standing of those who are relatively powerless within the national community. However, I do not think suspicion and criticism are sufficient; nor do I believe that feminists can escape the predicaments of nationalism, in Western or in Third-World contexts, by appeals to an "international sisterhood of women." If nations are "imagined communities,"[65] then bigoted and distorted nationalisms must be fought with feminist attempts to *reinvent* and *reimagine* the national community as more genuinely inclusive and democratic.

Feminists need to insist that *all* visions of "Nation" are constructs of political imagination, even though many of these visions see themselves as describing the "Truth" of some "National Essence." This does not, however, render all competing visions of "Nation" in any particular context morally equivalent, or leave us without ethical and political reasons for supporting some visions over others. We need to recognize that many seeming conflicts over the definition of "National Culture" are in effect political struggles over visions of the national community and over the justice of various national policies. Finally, even as we struggle to invent and endorse more inclusive and equitable visions of our national communities, national boundaries should not define the bounds of feminist imaginations that care about a more equitable and just global and international order. Justice within nations and saner forms of nationalism seem closely connected to our hopes for justice across nations at an international level.

Just as feminists have a stake in redefining prevailing notions of "Nation," feminists in various parts of the world often have an important stake in redefining a number of "religious traditions." Just as it would be dangerous for feminists to cease contesting problematic prevailing views of "Nation" to embrace an imagined "international sisterhood of women," it would be dangerous for feminists in a number of contexts to attempt to challenge prevailing views of "religion" and "religious tradition" purely by resort to "secularism." Many religious traditions are in fact more capacious than fundamentalist adherents allow. Insisting on humane and inclusive interpretations of religious traditions might, in many contexts, be crucial components in countering the deployment of religious discourses to problematic nationalist ends.

Political challenges to the status quo, feminist challenges as well as others, are calls for critical reassessments of prevailing understandings of important institutions and practices. The rethinking and revisioning they call for are often difficult and painful, since prevailing pictures of one's Nation and History, of one's cultural traditions, of important social institutions such as marriage and the family, are tied to one's picture of oneself as a social individual and as citizen. Although I believe rational argument and persuasion have a crucial role in politics, politics is also about deep emotional loyalties and attachments, and about self-constitutive understandings inherited from a number of sources.

Visions of one's nation, one's national history and community, are deeply tied to one's sense of place, to one's sense of belonging to a larger community, to one's sense of heritage and loyalties. Inherited pictures of gender roles and family and social arrangements are often central elements both to one's sense of self and to one's sense of one's social world. This is often true even when these roles and arrangements are, and are even experienced as, oppressive and restrictive. Rethinking them, and opening oneself to the process of collectively transforming them, is often likely to be an emotionally painful process. It is hardly surprising, therefore, that feminist political movements that call for emotionally difficult rethinking on such a variety of matters important to people's sense of self are met with attempts at delegitimization and dismissal. A critical feminist politics is thus confronted with the tasks not only of resisting dismissal but also of making its political vision widely understandable as well as morally appealing.

I am suggesting that critical political contestations, including feminist ones, are often at an emotional disadvantage, even if they have more rational, better-supported perspectives, since they call for painful reassessments. It is not difficult to understand the seductiveness of conservatism and fundamentalism, and the political nostalgia for mythic national and cultural pasts, in a global period where the shapes and structures of life are changing rapidly all across the world, with attendant dislocations and profound uncertainties. I believe we need to reckon with the fact that, in such periods, critical social theories, including feminisms, that seem to call for even more change will face a difficult and uphill battle. Such acknowledgment demands that we not only attempt to make our critiques and political agendas widely understandable, but also that we provide arguments that explain why the changes we seek are morally and politically appealing.

Feminist political movements, across the world, confront a variety of urgent tasks. Those of us who are part of such movements need to explain in accessible and understandable ways why our inherited pictures of "Nation, Culture, Traditions" and of a variety of important social institutions and practices are flawed and partial. We need to make clear how the distortions and exclusions of these inherited pictures have adversely affected the lives, prospects, and interests of many members of our national and global communities. We need to clarify the ways in which these inheritances have been burdensome, linked as they are to many ongoing national and international disparities and problems. Finally, we need to begin, with caution and openness to criticism and self-criticism, to argue for more just, equitable, and inclusive institutions and practices at national and international levels, and to convey a vivid positive sense of the stakes we have in these changes.

In addition, we need to try not to replicate the limitations of previous emancipatory theories, which constructed their emancipatory projects and subjects as Universals, even as they excluded many groups of people from their political vision. We need to remember that many political projects that sought to redefine and empower marginalized groups constructed their own forms of exclusion and marginalization. I am not sure there are any *methodological* guarantees that can ensure that feminist politics do not create their own misrepresentations and marginalizations. Trying to make sure that we do not claim to speak for or represent "all women" is certainly to be recommended, but that move does not in itself guarantee that those for whom we do not claim to speak are ensured access to the means of public articulation of their own positions and interests. Our best hope, I would argue, lies in striving to make political and civic institutions as open as possible to everyone, especially to all those who are socially marginalized and powerless, so that they may become active participants in articulating their interests, commitments, and visions for justice.

Neither Western feminists nor Third-World feminists can simply sidestep their complex insertions into national political contexts, but rather they need to be alert to the fact that "the nation cannot be taken for granted."[66] I believe it is time to rethink Virginia Woolf's antinationalist assertion when she wrote in 1936 in *Three Guineas* that, "As a woman I have no country. As a woman I want no country. As a woman my country is the whole world."[67] I would argue to the contrary that, as feminists, we indeed have many countries where the fates of a great many women and men call out for critical political perspectives and action for change. At this historical juncture, I believe that any feminism that simply dismisses the idea of "Nation" and the discourses of Nationalisms as "patriarchal constructs" will only contribute to their remaining dangerously so, marginalizing progressive and feminist voices whose critical political interventions into the discourses of nationalism seems increasingly crucial. In addition, for many Third-World feminists, failing to intervene in these discourses of Nation and nationalism is also to undercut our political agency and legitimacy within these national contexts, and to accede to our dismissal as "inauthentic" cultural Quislings whose politics constitutes a betrayal of "our" Nation and Culture.

Feminist intervention in these discourses of nation and nationalism is also important to the degree that feminist political agendas in any national context need the cooperation of the State. Feminist politics has almost always had an ambiguous relationship to State institutions and power. While feminist political movements have often been very critical of the laws, institutions, and policies of various nation-states, they have also often politically appealed to the state to change these laws, institutions, and policies in ways that better guarantee fairness, equality, opportunity, protection, and provision for women, and for other marginalized groups, within various national communities. Our very abilities to engage in the speech, action, and organization necessary for feminist political contestation are dependent on the nature of the institutions and policies of the states under which we live. The political nature of a particular state radically affects the degree to which political movements and challenges meet with responsiveness, or with state repression and reprisal. While the "imagined Nation" is not the same thing as the state, it is increasingly clear that the scripts of Nation and Nationalism have serious effects on the political institutions and agendas of the states we live under, and on the prospects for feminist political movements within them.

To accept that, as feminists, we need to intervene critically in discourses of Nation and Nationalism is not, I would argue, to surrender "the whole world" that Woolf hopes to claim by repudiating nationalism. National contexts, although important sites for feminist struggles, are increasingly just one among others that require our intervention. Increasingly, transnational economic structures adversely affect the lives of many different groups of people scattered over a multiplicity of nation-states, reinforcing structurally asymmetrical linkages between nations, as well as radical inequalities within and across nation-states. As Inderpal Grewal and Caren Caplan put it:

> We know that there is an imperative need to address the concerns of women around the world in the historicized particularity of their relationship to multiple patriarchies as well as to international economic hegemonies. . . . We need to articulate the relationship of gender to scattered hegemonies to such as global economic structures, patriarchal nationalisms, "authentic" forms of tradition, local structures of domination, and legal-juridical oppression on multiple levels.[68]

It is not issues of economic justice alone that increasingly cross national boundaries. There is growing feminist interest, both positive and critical, in the mechanisms and practices of international human rights law and its potential for protecting the interests of women and other marginalized groups. There is increasing feminist cooperation with respect to the transnational facets and effects of religious fundamentalism. I will cite just two very different examples of such transnational political possibilities. The international coalition, Women Living Under Muslim Laws, is engaged in collecting information about the implications of Islamic law, for different groups of women in particular, in various countries.[69] There is increasing attention to the *international effects* of U.S. Christian fundamentalism, ranging from aid to the contras in the 1980s to its deleterious effects on U.S. funding for development, health care, and reproductive institutions in Third-World nations.[70] In short, as feminists we need to attend both to issues within particular nations and to urgent transnational or international issues if we are to achieve greater justice within particular nations, and greater global justice in an increasingly interdependent world.

Two /

Restoring History and Politics to "Third-World Traditions"

Contrasting the Colonialist Stance and Contemporary Contestations of *Sati*

If feminism is to be different, it must acknowledge the ideological and problematic significance of its own past. Instead of creating yet another grand tradition or a cumulative history of emancipation, neither of which can deal with our present problems, we need to be attentive to how the past enters differently into the consciousness of other historical periods and is further subdivided by a host of other factors including gender, caste, and class.

—Kumkum Sangari and Suresh Vaid[1]

Introduction /

My aim in this essay is to explore representations of "Third-World traditions" that seem to replicate what I shall call a "colonialist stance" toward Third-World cultures, to explain why these representations are both problematic and "colonialist," and to describe other representations of "Third-World traditions" that present a very different picture of what these "traditions" are. To make my task of exploring "colonialist representation" manageable, I shall confine myself to a close examination of the discussion of the "Indian tradition" of *sati* or widow-immolation in Mary Daly's chapter on "Indian Sutee" in her book *Gyn/Ecology: The Metaethics of Radical Feminism.*[2] The first section attempts to show both what is wrong with Daly's representation of *sati* and how these problems replicate a "colonialist stance." In the second section, I attempt to contrast the notion of "tradition" that is operative in Daly's chapter to a more *historical* and *political* understanding of "tradition" that is at work in recent historical work on *sati* in the colonial period. I wish to argue that these historically and politically grounded understandings of Third-World "traditions" avoid "colonialist" representations of these "traditions," and provide an analysis that is more useful for a feminist understanding of the issues raised by such "traditions." The third section explores contemporary Indian feminist contestations around *sati*, with the aim of showing that the political issues raised by *sati* are far different from, and more complex than, the picture suggested by a reading of Daly's text. In the concluding section of the essay, I look at some of the broader implications of these contemporary Indian feminist contestations of *sati* for feminist politics, both in Western and Third-World national contexts.

While I focus on the problematic representations of one particular "Third-World practice" in one specific Western feminist text, my analysis of the representation of *sati* in Daly's chapter is motivated by the belief that similar problems occur in other Western feminist representations of issues affecting women in Third-World contexts. Ahistorical and apolitical Western feminist understandings of "Third-World traditions" continue to appear, for instance, in more contemporary work on issues such as *sati* and dowry-murder, and in discussions relating to human rights–based interventions into "cultural practices" affecting Third-World women.[3]

I have no desire, however, to suggest that these problems are characteristic of *all* work on Third-World women done by Western feminists, or are somehow "representative" of Western feminist work on Third-World women. Understanding the nature of the "colonialist stance," with respect to representations of "Third-World traditions," is additionally important because these problems are, I believe, not exclusive to academic feminist writing but perhaps even more common in general Western public understandings of "Third-World cultures," "Third-World traditions," and "Third-World women's problems." I approach my project in this paper both as someone who has learnt a great deal from many Western feminist works, during my time in India as well as my years in the United States, and as someone who has had problems with some Western feminist analyses and perspectives. I also approach this task as someone who is particularly indebted to the critiques of mainstream Western feminism generated by feminists of color.

Colonialism as an historical phenomenon does not only connect and divide Westerners from subjects in various Third-World nations in a series of complicated and unequal relationships. It also connects and divides mainstream Western subjects from Others in their *own* societies whose unequal relationships to the mainstream are themselves products of Western colonial history. Colonial history is not only the history of Western domination of "non-Western" populations, but is also a history of the creation of racially distinct and oppressed populations within Western countries such as the United States. Thus several aspects of "colonialist" representation that I analyze are, I believe, potentially applicable to mainstream Western feminist representations of the "cultures" and "traditions" of Third-World nation-states as well as to representations of the "cultures" and "traditions" of Third-World communities in Western contexts. However, this paper is an attempt to illuminate aspects of "colonialist representation" by focusing on the colonialist representations of the *specific* practice of *sati*. I leave to my readers the task of assessing whether my analysis of colonialist representation helps illuminate similar problems in other Western and Western feminist representations of different "cultural" practices pertaining to Third-World women.[4]

Many mainstream Western feminist perspectives have been criticized by Third-World feminists for excluding or marginalizing from their analyses and agendas the interests and concerns of women who are additionally marginalized in terms of class, race, ethnicity, and sexual orientation. It has been argued that such exclusions not only generate inadequate feminist theories but also result in political agendas and public policies that fail to be adequately responsive to the interests of women from these marginalized groups.[5] However, exclusion, marginalization, and lack of attention have not been the only source of unhappiness with the projects and perspectives of such mainstream Western feminist analyses. In this essay I wish to focus on a different set of problems, ones that have less to do with *exclusion* than with the manner and the mode of *inclusion*.

The terms "exclusion" and "inclusion" are not, in one sense, pure opposites. Since feminist analyses that did not explicitly concern themselves with the applicability and relevance of their analyses to "women on the margins" often perceived themselves as applicable to *all* women, that form of "exclusion" was simultaneously a problematic form of "inclusion." Attending specifically to problems affecting women in Third-World contexts, as Daly does, is a *form* of "inclusion" and is, in one respect, preferable to simply *assuming* that one's feminist perspective applies to *all* women. However, the terms in which such analyses are carried out might still be embedded in theoretical frameworks and conceptual assumptions that have problematic implications.[6] Thus, while Daly's work addresses "Third-World women's issues," I shall argue that it does so in a manner that misrepresents what is at stake, and that these misrepresentations replicate some common and problematic Western understandings of Third-World contexts and communities.

While I focus on "colonialist representation" in one Western feminist text, I would like to insist that the characteristic of "being a colonialist representation" does *not* require that the representation be "produced" by a Western subject. A representation that is "colonialist" would be so when produced by anyone, including Third-World men or women. A "colonialist representation," as I wish to use the term, is one that replicates problematic aspects of Western representations of Third-World nations and communities, aspects that have their roots in the history of colonization. Precisely because of this history and its complex effects on Third-World subjects, it is hardly surprising that one can find "colonialist representations" produced by members of Third-World communities, a point I shall return to. Why then do I focus on colonialist representations in a Western feminist text? The answer is simple. I believe that "colonialist representation" by Western feminists poses an obstacle to the urgent need for feminists to form "communities of resistance"[7] across boundaries of class, race, ethnicity, and national background.

I turn to a critical examination of Mary Daly's chapter on "Indian Suttee" to show how Daly's misrepresentations of the practice of *sati* replicate aspects of a "colonialist stance" toward Third-World contexts. I have chosen to use this particular text for two reasons. It is a text that both provides good examples of various facets of a "colonialist stance" and that sharply contrasts with representations of *sati* in recent work by feminists of Indian background. My choice of text is *not* driven by a desire to "attack" Mary Daly in particular; that these problems are *not unique* to Daly's work is precisely why they are worth discussing.

Like a good deal of Western feminist writing on Third-World women, Daly's chapter on *sati* is both directed at, and likely to be predominantly read by, Western readers unfamiliar with the historical, social, political, and cultural contexts of the practice being discussed. Such contextual unfamiliarity is likely to enable problematic representations to be accepted uncritically and without awareness that the text contains an interrelated cluster of misrepresentations that collaboratively constitute a "colonialist stance." Understanding various facets of what a "colonialist stance" involves might help readers approach such texts more cautiously and critically. I invite readers who are ignorant about the Indian context to read Daly's chapter on *sati* before proceeding to read the rest of my analysis, so that they may judge for themselves the difference that such awareness might make.[8]

Before I proceed to a critique of specific facets of Daly's representation of *sati*, I would like to say a few things about the chapter as a whole. The chapter is approximately twenty pages in length. Daly's discussion aims to criticize both the practice of *sati* and "patriarchal scholarship" on *sati*. The description and analysis of the practice of *sati* itself occupies less than half of the chapter. Three pages are taken up by an aside on child marriages, four pages are devoted to a vindication of the work of Katherine Mayo, and the last three pages are primarily devoted to a general analysis of "sado-rituals." In the critical discussion that follows, I neither claim to provide a thorough account of all facets of Daly's discussion of *sati* nor an exhaustive account of my critical responses to all aspects of the discussion. I focus on only those problems that I see as importantly connected to "colonialist representation."

The Limitations of the Missionary Position: The 'Colonialist Stance' in Mary Daly's Discussion of "Indian Suttee"

1. The 'Colonialist Stance' and the Erasing of History /

Daly's chapter on "Indian Suttee" begins by excluding the issue of history and historical change. After four lines of text that seem intended to introduce the practice of *sati* to Western readers,[9] the rest of the first page of this chapter consists of an extended footnote that also takes up a third of the next page. In this footnote, Daly begins by saying, "Although suttee was legally banned in 1829 . . . it should not be imagined that the lot of most Indian women has changed dramatically since then." Daly's footnote goes on to refer to contemporary incidents of the ill-treatment of Indian widows, dowry-harassment and dowry-murders, high rates of female malnutrition and female maternal mortality, and higher mortality rates for Indian women in general, and cites recent Indian publications and newspaper reports as sources for her information.[10]

What do I find problematic about this introduction? Daly's introduction leads readers to believe that all of the several problems mentioned in the footnote exist in the same "temporal frame" as the problem of *sati*, which is the central topic of Daly's chapter. The footnote conveys the impression that *sati* as well as the various problems mentioned in the footnote, have all afflicted "Indian women" in the past and that each continues to afflict them today. What tend to vanish in Daly's introductory framing are the specific historical contexts and time frames of the various problems strung together on this list as "problems affecting Indian women." Neither in the introduction nor in the rest of the chapter is the reader informed that the practice of *sati* was never a widespread practice in all "Hindu" communities, let alone "Indian" communities. Neither is it made clear that incidents of *sati* were more common in the *past* than they are at present,[11] or that incidents of *sati* were *extremely rare* by 1978, when Daly's book was published. Although there have been a few incidents of *sati* recently, incidents whose political import I will discuss later in the essay, Daly's chapter is highly misleading in creating the impression that widow immolation is a widespread and ongoing practice that threatens the lives of many Indian women today.

There is an interesting contrast between the absence of vital historical information with regard to the time frame in which *sati* was an ongoing practice, and the presence of such information in Daly's chapter on "European Witchburnings," where Western women go up in flames.[12] In the very second sentence of this latter chapter Daly informs the reader that this phenomenon occurred in Europe during the fifteenth, sixteenth, and seventeenth centuries. A footnote on the preceding page informs the reader that "it is claimed that the final execution of a witch in an English speaking territory was in 1730 in Bermuda."[13] I find the discrepancy between the presence of an historical frame in the chapter on "Witchburning" and its absence in the chapter on "Suttee" particularly disturbing, given that readers are unlikely to imagine witchburning to be a contemporary European problem even in the absence of an historical frame, while many readers are only too likely to believe that *sati* is a ubiquitous contemporary Indian phenomenon.

Daly's failure to historically contextualize the practice of *sati* is compounded by her linkage of *sati*, in her footnote, to contemporary phenomena such as dowry-murder, producing a problematic effect that I call an "erasing of history." This linkage of *sati* and dowry-murder has the effect of simultaneously suggesting that the *historical* phenomenon of *sati* is an ongoing "Indian tradition" and that the *contemporary* phenomenon of dowry-murder is a longstanding "traditional" practice. As a result, two historically distinct phenomena are *each* misleadingly portrayed in a manner that suggests that they are both instances of "traditional practices that afflict contemporary Indian women." (Even though dowry itself is a "traditional" institution of longstanding, dowry-murders seem to be a fairly recent phenomenon, one where the number of incidents seem to be *increasing*. Dowry-murder is thus not a "traditional" practice, neither being endorsed by "tradition" nor seeming to have taken place in noticeable numbers until recent times.)[14] Daly's juxtaposition of *sati* and dowry-murder suggests a common temporal framework that these phenomena do not in fact share, since one is a virtually extinct practice and the other a fairly recent problem.

I have argued that Daly's introduction to her chapter on *sati* is misleading in its "erasing of history." However, while misleading representations of phenomena are always problematic, not all misleading representations necessarily constitute a "colonialist stance." In what ways, then, do Daly's failures to provide an historical frame for *sati,* and to distinguish its temporal frame from that of contemporary phenomena such as dowry-murders, constitute misrepresentations that can be seen as connected to a "colonialist stance?"

Daly's introduction operates to convey an impression of the "Duration" of the practices of *sati* and of dowry-murder without any attention to "Change"–to the historical contexts of their emergence or decline. Daly's "erasing of history" hence contributes to reinforcing problematic colonial (and still persistent) Western pictures of Third-World countries as "places without history."[15] The only function of the Present in such representations of Third-World contexts is to testify to the stubborn persistence of the Past in the guise of "unchanging traditions." Daly's discussion suggests an India whose present is possessed by the past, a place whose contemporary reality is neither one where past practices yield to the effects of political contestation and social change, nor one that generates new and complex problems of its own. All patriarchal practices in the Indian context seem *perennially in place*–Unchanging Legacies of the Past. One does not get the sense that some historical practices have virtually disappeared (as with *sati*) nor the sense that new problems, such as dowry-murders, have arisen in the course of modernization and social change. Given Daly's framing, Indian women seem to go up in flames–on the funeral pyres of their husbands and in the "kitchen accidents" that are the characteristic mode of dowry-murder–without historical pause.

Daly's representation of *sati* replicates a "colonialist stance" because it reproduces a Western tendency to portray Third-World contexts as dominated by the grip of "traditional practices" that insulate these contexts from the effects of historical change. I am *not* arguing that Daly *deliberately intends* to collude with this colonialist picture of Third-World contexts. Daly's mode of representation in her chapter on *sati* is in keeping with the overall project of her book, which seems motivated by a desire to testify to the transhistorical and global persistence of patriarchal institutions and practices. However, while her overall discussion of patriarchy in Western contexts tends to convey the picture that "practices change but Patriarchy goes on," the discussion in her chapter on *sati* suggests that Third-World patriarchy goes on differently, without any substantial historical changes in the practices that guarantee its regime. In short, Daly's overall picture suggests that Western patriarchy persists within and despite historical change, while Third-World patriarchy seems to persist without significant historical change. Especially when framed by Daly's astonishing suggestion that "the lot of Indian women" has not changed substantially since 1829, *sati* and all the other problems affecting Indian women that Daly mentions seem to be problems rooted in "Ancient Indian Patriarchal Traditions," which have somehow managed to remain entirely insulated from the tremendous changes of the last hundred fifty years.

2. Dangerous Lacks of Detail and the Politics of Specificity /

Daly's account of *sati* not only erases its *temporal* context but also blurs other important *contextual* features of the practice with respect to its variations across class, caste, religion, and geographical location. Alternately characterizing *sati* as a "Hindu rite" and as an "Indian rite," Daly notes that "at first, suttee was restricted to the wives of princes and warriors" and goes on to cite a Western scholar on its spread to "others of lower caste."[16] This facet of her discussion has the effect of suggesting that although *sati* had its origin in a particular social group,[17] it eventually spread widely so as to become a practice prevalent virtually across *all* Indian castes. What Daly fails to mention is that *sati* was a practice limited to particular castes and specific regions of India, and a practice unknown in many Indian communities. Daly completely fails to make clear that *sati* was not practiced by *all* Hindu communities, and was never practiced by various non-Hindu communities in the Indian population.[18] (Nor does Daly seem to register that if in fact the practice began among communities of "princes and warriors," it must have also "spread to those of higher caste" given that a large number of *satis* in British colonial times took place among the *Brahmin* community of Bengal!)

My motivation in stressing the fact of 'limited practice" is not to vindicate "Indian Culture" by pointing out that not all Indian communities immolated widows. I believe that these contextual features of incidence are important for quite different reasons. Attending to these specificities of incidence serves to counter a colonialist Western tendency to represent Third-World contexts as uniform and monolithic spaces, with no important internal cultural differentiations, complexities, and variations. While Western contexts are represented both as spaces of historical change and internal complexity, Third-World contexts tend to be portrayed as places where "time stands still" and where "one culture rules all." The effacement of *cultural change* within historical time, which I previously discussed, collaborates with the effacement of *cultural variations* across communities and regions to suggest a "Third-World culture" that is "frozen" with respect to both Space and Time.[19]

Failure to attend to features of contextual variation and heterogeneity within Third-World communities produces two sharp contrasts between how Western women and Third-World women are often represented by Western feminists. First, largely as a result of critiques of mainstream Western feminism by feminists of color, there is a great deal more caution about generalizing about categories such as "American women" or "European women" without attending to specificities such as class, race, ethnicity, sexual orientation, and religion. However, this lesson of caution about generalization is often quickly forgotten when it comes to "Third-World Women," a point forcefully made by Chandra Mohanty with respect to a recent publication entitled *Women of Africa: Roots of Oppression,* when she asks, "In the 1980's, is it possible to imagine writing a book entitled *Women of Europe: Roots of Oppression*?"[20]

The second difference is that problems that affect particular groups of Third-World women are more often assumed to be primarily, if not entirely, results of an imagined and unitary complex called "their Traditions/Religions/Cultures"—where these terms are represented as virtually synonymous with each other. As a result, problems that have very little to do with traditions, religions, or culture are represented as if they are the effects of this imagined complex, reinforcing "ethnic" stereotypes and completely misrepresenting the real nature of these problems. An interesting example of this phenomenon is provided by Radhika Parameswaran's discussion of the *Dallas Observer* coverage of the murder of an Indian Christian woman, a member of the diasporic Indian community in Texas, who was set ablaze by her husband after a bitter family dispute. According to Parameswaran, the coverage was studded with references to both *sati* and dowry-murder, with a headline that indicated Aleyamma Mathew to be a "victim of her culture."[21] What is astounding about the *Dallas Observer* coverage is that the references to *sati* and to dowry-murder were entirely gratuitous, given that

Aleyamma's death had nothing to do with either sati or dowry, and everything to do with her husband's alcoholism, history of abusiveness, and family conflicts over whether to return to India!

Thus, Daly's blurring together of the phenomenon of *sati* and dowry-murder, and her failure to attend to contextual variations in the practice of *sati*, both contribute to, and are instances of, this repeated Western construction of Third-World "Traditions/Religions/Cultures" that victimizes "Third-World women." The deployment of this construction produces a multiple metonymic blurring in which every phenomenon of an Indian woman being burnt to death is confused with every other, even when they are instances of very different phenomena. Parameswaran's discussion of the *Dallas Observer* article reveals that the blurring together of *sati*, dowry-murders, and the case of Aleyamma's murder extended far beyond the coverage in this newspaper article. She indicates that defense attorneys suggested that "the woman's death might have been suicide, based on the ancient Indian custom of immolation" and that "the prosecution summoned an expert in Indian culture to testify about the prevalence of wife burning in India." Thus, the defense suggested that Aleyamma's death was an act of *sati*, while the prosecution suggested that her husband's culpability had to do with dowry-murder, even in the complete absence of any evidence connecting *sati* or dowry-murder with her death. What does result however, as Parameswaran points out, is an "overwhelming consensus among the media and in the courts regarding the roles of Indian tradition in . . . the murder of Aleyamma."[22] Aleyamma's murder had as much, or as little, to do with "Culture" or "Tradition" as the murders of many battered white U.S. women, whose murders, however else they are reported, are not usually represented as victimization by "American Culture."[23]

Daly's unnuanced and totalizing picture of "Indian culture and traditions" contributes to an ongoing practice of "blaming culture" for problems in Third-World contexts and communities, a practice that sharply contrasts with "noncultural" accounts of problems where mainstream Western subjects bear culpability. An interesting contrast to the *Dallas Observer* article is provided by a recent *New York Times* article on a very different set of burnings, the recent spate of burnings of predominantly black churches in the United States. While these burnings are attributed to "hate radio" and to racial hostility, and reference is made to black churches being targeted for firebombing during the civil rights years, there is no representation of these burnings as symptomatic of "American Culture" or "American Traditions." Nor is there any allusion to other forms of white racist burnings such as Klan-sponsored cross burnings, even though there is clearly *more ground* for such allusions and connections here than there is in the case of Aleyamma's death and "Indian culture."[24]

Attention to the sorts of contextual variations in the practice of *sati* that Daly overlooks is important if Western feminist scholars wish to avoid what Marnia Lazreg calls "a ritual" in Western scholarship on Third-World women. The ritual Lazreg refers to is "appeals to religions as *the* cause of gender inequality."[25] Neither Lazreg nor I wish to suggest that religious views on the "place" of women, or religious endorsements of particular problematic practices, have *no* role in understanding or explaining gender inequality in Third-World contexts. However, in representing *sati* as a "Hindu practice," while paying no attention to the extremely uneven and limited ways in which *sati* was practiced across different Hindu communities, Daly's discussion suggests that *sati* is a practice endorsed by all versions of Hinduism and engaged in by all Hindus. It is a short step from such "totalizing" representations of "religion" to the equation of "religion" to "tradition" and "culture" that I mentioned previously.

"Religion" appears in such analyses as a relatively unchanging body of beliefs and practices shared by all its adherents, rather than as a cluster of beliefs, practices, and institutions, historically constituted, traversed by change, and affected by interpretative and political conflicts about its values and commitments. "Religion" also appears in these analyses as a set of beliefs and practices unconnected to a variety of economic interests and political agendas that might underlie and contribute to changes in its beliefs and practices. What results is not merely an intellectually inadequate picture of religion as an evolving social institution, but a picture of religion that plays an important role in a "colonialist stance" toward Third-World contexts.

A very different picture of *sati* and its relationship to "religion" emerges in Romila Thapar's discussion of the history of *sati*, where she points out that "it was practiced by variant social groups for different reasons at various points in time," that "the controversy over whether or not it should be practiced was articulated over many centuries," and that "it underwent changes of meaning as well as degrees of acceptance."[26] Thapar's analysis suggests that the practice was not constant, but prone to "revivals" in specific communities at particular historical moments, and that although *sati* was inevitably given a "religious justification" in the various communities that practiced it at various historical junctures, these justifications differed across communities and across time.[27] Her analysis also suggests that "revivals" of the practice always served *worldly* economic and political functions, which also differed at various historical moments.[28]

Discussions such as those found in Daly's chapter on *sati* represent Third-World contexts not only as "places without History" but as "places suffused by Unchanging Religious Worldviews."[29] These two axes of (mis)representation are connected to each other in important ways. The portrayal of Third-World contexts as "places without History" proceeds by depicting them as places governed instead by Unchanging Religious Traditions, whose very lack of susceptibility to change appears as a key symptom of the absence of "History." The unnuanced resort to "Religion" as a category of explanation for practices oppressive to Third-World women constitutes part of a "colonialist stance" toward Third-World contexts because of an intimate linkage between such explanatory uses of "Religion" and colonialist depictions of Third-World contexts as "places without History."

Daly's complete inattention to the variations in the practice of *sati* across Hindu communities is politically dangerous in another entirely different way. Such inattention colludes not only with "colonialist representation" but also with contemporary Third-World religious fundamentalist portrayals of the "Religious Traditions" that they claim define women's "authentic" place within "their" culture. Many strands of religious fundamentalism in the Third-World mirror colonialist accounts of Third-World contexts as places culturally defined by "unchanging traditions." While such views were deployed during colonial times to depict the cultures of the colonies as inferior, irrational, and incapable of change, they are put to very different uses by contemporary religious fundamentalists, who use them to construct and justify nationalist visions that seek to confine women to "traditional roles" in the name of religious values and cultural preservation. Daly's representation of *sati* as a "Hindu tradition" colludes with contemporary Hindu fundamentalist representations of *sati*, in much the same way that Lazreg criticizes Western feminist scholarship on Islamic societies when she says, "In an uncanny way, feminist discourse on women from the Middle East and North Africa mirrors that of theologians' own interpretation of women in Islam."[30]

It is important for Western feminists engaged in scholarship on Third-World women to remember that *colonial* discourses that positioned Third-World cultures "outside history" have dangerous echoes in the discourses of *contemporary* religious-fundamentalist political movements, which have their own reasons for misportraying certain practices and traditions as "timeless" elements of "National Culture." They also need to attend to the fact that "an insistence on History" is often crucial to feminists and others in these Third-World contexts who are engaged in politically contesting such fundamentalist views. For example, historical data about *sati*—about its historical origins, the increases and decreases in the practice at various historical moments, the specificities of its incidence in particular classes, castes, and geographical areas—is critical to Indian feminist contestations of Hindu fundamentalist attempts to portray *sati* as an unchanging and widely endorsed "Indian Tradition." Daly-type mis-representations of *sati* are not simple mistakes but constitute *dangerous lacks of detail*. Western feminist analyses that replicate such problems often only add to "the brown woman's burden"—functioning as obstacles rather than as assets to ongoing Third-World feminist political agendas.

3. Overlooking the Legacies of Colonialism /

Daly's discussion of *sati* also suffers serious limitations in the way in which it represents the historical debate on *sati*. Daly's chapter on *sati* mentions only two sets of "positions" on the issue of *sati*. On one side of the issue, Daly quotes the views of several Western schol-ars and of some Indian men (as quoted by these Western scholars), all of whom either justify or express admiration for the practice of *sati*. On the "other side" of the issue, the opposition to the practice of *sati* is presented in just two voices. One voice is that of Daly herself, and the other is that of Katherine Mayo, whose extremely controversial book, *Mother India*, was published in 1927, and who is clearly positioned by Daly as a prede-cessor "Feminist Searcher."[31] Let me try to explain the several things I find wrong with this picture.

While Daly deserves credit for her scathing analysis of the justifi-cations and glorifications of *sati* that are embedded in the writings of the Western scholars she discusses, there is a good deal missing from the pic-ture that emerges in her chapter. Daly's presentation gives no indication of the complex history of critical opposition to practices such as *sati* and child marriage in the Indian context, extending for centuries. In the late eighteenth and nineteenth centuries, criticisms of *sati* were voiced pre-dominantly by two groups of people—British colonialists, and nationalist and reform-minded Indians.

Contemporary feminists might find many limitations in these colonial and nationalist critiques of *sati*. For instance, many of the British colonial critiques of *sati* seem less inspired by a desire to protect the rights of Indian women endangered by immolation than by a desire to justify the "civilizing mission" of British colonial rule in India. Problematic practices affecting Indian women such as *sati* and child marriage were often brought up primarily in order to emphasize the degenerate nature of "Indian culture." Nineteenth-century feminists from colonizing Western nations had their own versions of such colonialist critiques of "native" practices, making the "salvation and uplift" of colonized women a key part of their feminist mission.[32]

Some of the anticolonial nationalist discourses that criticized practices such as *sati* and child marriage were also often motivated by concerns other than the welfare of women affected by these practices. Many of these critiques seem primarily concerned to make the point that "if we can rouse ourselves to reform these problematic practices, we will be morally fit for national self-government." While Daly's failure to acknowledge the existence of these historical critiques of *sati* might be motivated by her sense of the uniqueness of her feminist critique, this uniqueness is not argued for, since these other critiques are entirely effaced. As a result, Daly succeeds in effacing both *sati*'s contentious status as an "Indian tradition" and the historical backdrop that affects the nature of her own entry into this debate.

These debates on *sati* in the context of colonial rule and nationalist struggle have an historical weight and a contemporary salience that Daly does not appreciate. Many contemporary individuals from Third-World backgrounds are aware that Western critiques of their cultural practices, notably practices affecting women, were often generated in a context whereby they functioned as justifications for colonization and oppression. They are aware too of still-prevalent stereotypic views about Third-World cultures as "backward" and "barbaric" that are held by many Westerners, independent of any substantive knowledge about these contexts. Western feminist scholars engaged in analyses of "Third-World women's problems" need to be aware of this historical background and to proceed in a manner whereby they distinguish the terms of their analyses and representations from the terms of colonialist discourses, taking care not to exacerbate the problems set in place by this colonial, political, and discursive background. This is a task that I believe Daly's chapter on *sati* fails in several significant ways.

When Daly criticizes discussions of *sati* by Western scholars, she fails to notice or remark upon the problematic "colonial" terms of their discussion, even as she unerringly spots the "patriarchal" limitations of their scholarship. Let me provide an example. After correctly condemning the "androcratically attached detachment from women's agony" of Joseph Campbell's celebratory description of *sati*, Daly's text reads as follows:

> This devotee of the rites of de-tached scholarship describes the event as "an *illuminating*, though *somewhat* appalling, glimpse into the deep silent pool of the Oriental, archaic soul . . . {emphases mine}."[33]

What I find problematic is not that Daly chooses to emphasize the two words she does emphasize, but that she neither emphasizes nor seems incensed by the bizarre "colonialist" terms that constitute the end of the quote. Although Daly is clearly outraged at a patriarchal scholar who finds the practice of widow-immolation "illuminating" and only "somewhat appalling," there is no discernible outrage in her text directed at Campbell's stereotype-laden reference to the archaic Oriental soul! Daly's lack of response to these overtly colonialist terms suggests either an obliviousness to their existence or a failure to consider colonialist characterizations to be as worthy of feminist outrage as "patriarchal" ones. Daly's lack of responsiveness to Campbell's colonialist characterization is not an accidental oversight but is rather symptomatic of her failure to understand and deal with the role that racist discourses on *sati* played in the context of colonial India. This is painfully illustrated in Daly's unembarassed embrace of Katherine Mayo's *Mother India*[34] as an exemplar of a feminist perspective on Indian women and on *sati*.

Mayo was an American journalist whose book was published in 1927, twenty years before Indian independence, when the nationalist struggle for freedom from colonial rule was well underway. To put it mildly, Mayo's book was not well received by Indian nationalists. Though Daly acknowledges that the book created a storm of protest in India, she seems to attribute the entire Indian protest against Mayo's book to a culturally chauvinistic and patriarchal defensiveness about Indian cultural practices, and an indifference to the atrocities against Indian women that Mayo's book described.

Daly does not seem to know that a significant part of the Indian protest against Mayo was related to the overtly racist terms in which Mayo discussed India, and to Mayo's explicit political intentions to bolster the British colonial case that India was not "culturally fit" for self-rule.[35] Here is a succinct summary of what was problematic about the explicit political agenda of Mayo's book:

> India was then struggling for independence from the British, but Mayo came to the conclusion that the Indians were not ready to rule their own country because, among other things, they overindulged in sex. She asserted that all of an Indian's woes—"poverty, sickness, ignorance, political minority, melancholy, ineffectiveness" and the "subconscious conviction of inferiority"—could be blamed on the widespread effects of child marriage. Mayo argued that men ineptly raised by child brides were physically feeble, given to unrestrained sexual appetites and of morally "bankrupt stock" at an age when "the Anglo-Saxon is just coming into the full glory of manhood."[36]

Indian national independence was a goal that Mayo was openly opposed to, and her book was explicitly intended to suggest that India lacked the civilized habits and practices that Mayo regarded as moral prerequisites to self-rule.[37] There are good reasons to disagree with Daly's judgment that Mayo is "a startling exception among scholars who have written on women in India." Mayo's book is more aptly characterized as a startling exemplar of scholarship on Indian women designed to justify British colonial rule. If "detached" patriarchal scholarship of the sort Daly critiques deserves to be faulted for its blindness to women's interests and suffering, feminist work such as Daly's deserves as strongly to be faulted for blindness to the colonialist implications of its own analyses and of the sources it embraces as paradigms of feminist research.

I believe that the problem with Daly's enthusiastic use of Mayo's work is more serious than is suggested by a recent characterization, which describes Daly as having "blundered into the use of previously discredited sources."[38] Daly might well be excused if the problem were a simple one of her not knowing that Mayo was a "discredited source." However, one would hardly need to know the credibility that Mayo's work was accorded in order to notice the overtly racist terms and analyses that permeate Mayo's text. Daly neither seems to have noticed these terms, nor do they seem to have diminished the adulation she feels for Mayo. Even without knowledge of Indian colonial history and Mayo's place within that history, it takes considerable blindness to read and portray Mayo's text as simply the response of a Western woman outraged by atrocities committed against Indian women, as Daly does. To characterize Daly's breathtaking blindness to the overt racism of Mayo's text, and to its overt procolonial political agenda, as "blunders" minimizes the seriousness of Daly's failure to read Mayo's text with moral and political discernment.

I mentioned earlier that Daly's discussion fails to acknowledge the existence of Indian nationalist critiques of the very practices Mayo criticized, *sati* among others.[39] Daly's lack of attention to Indian critiques of these same practices has the unfortunate effect of suggesting that these practices were only ever found abhorrent and objectionable by Western women, such as Mayo and herself. Daly does not seem to see that many Third-World feminists would find the implicit suggestion that only Westerners are capable of naming and challenging patriarchal atrocities committed against Third-World women to be a postcolonial replication, however unintentional, of the "missionary position" of colonial discourses, including that of "imperial feminism."

In fairness to Daly, I need to clarify my argument at this point. I do not think that Daly explicitly shares a belief that was central to both the patriarchal-colonial and the imperial-feminist critiques of practices pertaining to colonized women: a belief in the moral and cultural superiority of "Western civilization" and its "civilizing mission." Daly is no less scathing in her attack on patriarchal atrocities committed by "Western civilization" than she is of patriarchal atrocities committed in non-Western contexts. Her discussion replicates the missionary position not because of an explicit commitment to the superiority of Western civilization but because it completely erases the voices and political agency of Third-World critics and critiques of the very practices Daly analyzes. The missionary position is replicated by the ways in which Third-World women are positioned in Daly's text either as "victims of Patriarchal Practices" or as "objects of compassion" of white Western women. This may not be Daly's conscious intention, but it is nevertheless an "effect" of her text, making it a problematic text for Third-World feminists.

One reason why some Western feminist analyses replicate the "colonialist stance" may lie in the fact that they have little real understanding of the possibility or the dangers of such replication. In Daly's case, I suspect that she believes that her aversion to "Western patriarchy" immunizes her to every form of participation in problematic aspects of "Western culture." This belief is perhaps a feminist version of a mistaken but commonplace belief, that a deeply critical stance against one's culture places one entirely outside its orbit and influence. Daly's failure to perceive the possibility that Western feminist scholarship might replicate the "colonialist stance" emerges clearly in her response to critics of Mayo. Daly dismisses such critics *en masse* by arguing that feminist work that addresses patriarchal practices in "another culture" is often subject to "accusations of imperialism, nationalism, racism, capitalism, or any other '-ism' that can pose as broader and more important than gynocidal patriarchy."[40]

Daly's defense of Mayo against her critics seems to miss at least two important points. First, she fails to distinguish between a position that might regard the very fact of a Western feminist "criticizing another culture" to be problematic per se, and positions, such as mine, that have specific objections to particular Western feminist representations of "another culture." Second, Daly fails to see that feminist good intentions might fail to insulate feminist critiques of "gynocidal patriarchy" in "another culture" from generating problematic representations of that culture. My critical reading of Daly's chapter on *sati* is intended to drive home the point that when analyzing "patriarchal practices" in Third-World contexts, Western feminist good intentions need to be supplemented by care and attentiveness to avoiding the "colonialist stance."

I would like to distinguish my concerns about "colonialist representation" in Western feminist work on practices affecting Third-World women from two other positions with which they might be conflated. I would distinguish my position from one that sees *all* Western feminist criticisms of Third-World cultures as inherently colonialist or imperialist, and from another that attributes all colonialist Western feminist representations to explicit convictions about the superiority of Western culture. These two other positions seem to capture what are seen as the prevalent reasons for Third-World feminist unhappiness with Western feminist work on Third-World women. For instance, in discussing some of the reasons for Third-World women's negative response to Western feminist work, Sharon Sievers says:

There may be some feminists who exhibit a classic kind of bias engendered by the inability to see anything valuable in another culture. . . . But even though a majority of western feminists may not subscribe to such views, we are indelibly linked to them by our history and culture. . . . To the extent that we in the west symbolize such hegemonic views to women elsewhere, we should not be surprised to find a reverse devaluation of western culture and "feminism" with it.[41]

Sievers's analysis suggests that there are two different types of problems that result in the negative reception of Western feminist work by Third-World women—first, that some Western feminist works suffer from an explicit sense of Western cultural superiority, and second, that all Western views in general are perceived as hegemonic views and hence devalued. I do not wish to deny that both sorts of reasons might account for *some* negative Third-World responses to Western feminism. However, I think it is important not to reduce "colonialist representation" to explicit beliefs in the superiority of Western culture. I think many of the aspects of the "colonialist stance" that I locate and analyze in Daly's work are interesting precisely because they do not seem to necessarily arise from the author's explicit belief in Western cultural superiority.

I also think it is important to distinguish between Western ideas and texts that are "colonialist" and those that are not. Keeping my discussion of a "colonialist stance" concrete seemed a helpful way to distinguish my position from viewpoints that would dismiss *all* Western work on Third-World women as "colonialist," "hegemonic," or "culturally imperialist."[42] I believe that such generalizations fail to discriminate between various kinds of work, and fail to analyze and explicate the specific ways in which particular Western texts replicate a "colonialist stance." I believe that concretely clarifying various facets of the "colonialist stance" might make it easier for Western feminists to avoid replicating it in their analyses of issues affecting Third-World women even as it enables greater clarity among Third-World feminists about features of Western feminist work they find problematic.

Sati as "Tradition": The Colonial Politics of Tradition Formation /

The assumption that "Third-World women's problems" are fundamentally problems of "Third-World women being victimized by Traditional Patriarchal Cultural Practices" not only looms large in Mary Daly's chapter on *sati,* but also seems to be a pervasive assumption within Western public understanding of Third-World contexts, and of women's issues within them. There are several ways in which this assumption is problematic. For instance, it obscures the degree to which many "Third-World women's problems" are rooted in "modernization" and social change—such as those produced by ongoing economic and "development" policies that result in ecological devastation, in reduced access for women to productive resources such as land and employment, in hyperexploitation, and in injurious working conditions on the "global assembly line."

In this section, I am interested in examining one specific way in which this perspective that "Third-World women's problems are fundamentally problems of Third-World women being victimized by Traditional Patriarchal Cultural Practices" is problematic. The problem I am concerned with, one that is well illuminated by Daly's discussion of *sati*, is that this perspective leaves the concept of "tradition" *un*problematized. In so doing, it buys into a simplistic, ahistorical, and apolitical picture of what sort of entities such "Third-World Traditions" are. What results is both a misleading picture of these "traditions" and an effacement of the political struggles that have affected the import and the significance of these "traditions."

I would like to contrast the "unproblematized" notion of "Third-World tradition" found in discussions such as Daly's to a very different view of "tradition" that emerges in recent feminist historical studies of *sati* in Indian colonial times. Setting out the various facets of the colonial emergence of *sati* as an "issue" serves two important tasks in this essay. First, it provides a contrast to Daly's representation of *sati* and allows a development of the critique in the previous section. Second, the colonial history of *sati* helps to illuminate facets of recent Hindu fundamentalist deployments of *sati* that I will discuss in the following section. Understanding the colonial history of *sati* helps reveal the limitations of Hindu fundamentalist understandings of the practice (underscoring the affinities between their understandings of the practice and that of Daly) and also explains why *sati* remains such a powerful symbol for contemporary Hindu fundamentalist nationalism.

The "unproblematized" picture of tradition shared by both Daly and contemporary Hindu fundamentalism assumes that "traditions" are: (1) unchanging practices; (2) of extreme longstanding; (3) clearly recognized as "dictates warranting submission" by virtually everyone in the relevant cultural community; and (4) clearly sanctioned as requirements by religious texts or uncontested customary norms. Not only Daly's chapter on "Indian Suttee" but also her chapters on "Chinese Footbinding" and on "African Genital Mutilation" subscribe to this "unproblematized" view of "tradition." The picture of "tradition," at work in Mary Daly's analyses of patriarchal practices affecting Third-World women, pays little attention to the "politics of tradition formation" that is revealed by historical investigations of these "traditional practices."

Historical work on *sati* in Indian colonial times suggests that *sati*'s status as "an Indian tradition" is a far more complicated matter than Daly's discussion suggests. Lata Mani's essay "Contentious Traditions: The Debate on *SATI* in Colonial India,"[43] which analyzes the historical constitution of *sati* as a Hindu religious tradition in late eighteenth- and nineteenth-century colonial India, powerfully illuminates the "politics of tradition formation" with respect to *sati*. I will use aspects of Mani's analysis in ways that serve my purposes, without attempting to give a comprehensive summary of her interesting and complex article. Mani's analysis usefully highlights the limitations of Daly-type portrayals of *sati* that simply accept it as a pre-existing and widely shared "Indian tradition" or as a "Hindu rite," by uncovering the complex colonial processes by which *sati* came to acquire that status.

Daly's analysis of *sati* does not note, wonder about, or account for, why *sati* acquired the status of a "practice definitive of Hindu or Indian culture."[44] The question it seems necessary to answer is how and why this particular practice, marginal to many Hindu communities let alone Indian ones, came to be regarded as a central Indian tradition. The answer, Mani's work suggests, lies in various complex nineteenth-century negotiations between British colonials and segments of the Indian elite. British colonial interest in *sati*'s "status as a tradition" seems to have arisen in the context of colonial worries about whether the practice could be outlawed without eliciting extensive protests from segments of the Indian population. As Mani puts it, "Official discourse on *sati* was prompted by a deliberation on whether it could be safely prohibited through legislation"[45] and the concern that "interference in a religious matter might provoke indigenous outrage."[46]

Mani's analysis complicates a commonly held picture of colonials as "interventionists contemptuous of aspects of indigenous culture, advocating change in the name of 'progress' or Christian principles."[47] The British colonials in Mani's discussion emerge not as pure "contemptuous interventionists" driven by a morally fervent sense of their "civilizing mission," but as officials for whom the question of intervention in indigenous tradition was always secondary to the question of the import of such intervention for British colonial power. The concern for "the security of the British empire" that some feared legal interference in *sati* might endanger was, understandably, not depicted as a realpolitik consideration. Concern for the security of Empire was portrayed as rooted in the fact that the continuance of British rule was necessary for "the future happiness and improvement of the numerous population of this eastern world."[48]

Thus, the question of *sati*'s status as a "religious tradition" became relevant to British colonials because this status seemed pertinent to calculations about whether it could be safely abolished. This interest then triggered a complicated process by which *sati*'s status as a "tradition" was subject to question, and by which this question came to have an answer. The British colonials proceeded on the assumption that *sati*'s status as a "tradition" could be determined by investigating whether the practice had a basis in Hindu religious scripture. The task of discovering whether the practice of *sati* had any firm basis in religious scriptures was a job the British colonials entrusted to Indian *pundits* (religious scholars) attached to British courts. The underlying British agenda might be summarized as: "If the practice of *sati* has religious sanction, it might be unwise to abolish it. On the other hand, if it lacks religious sanction, we would have the sanction of 'native religious scholars' themselves for the legitimacy of its abolition."

As a result of this process, scriptural sanction became the touchstone for determining whether the practice was "culturally authentic or legitimate," a touchstone that then also became central to various Indian responses to the question of the status of *sati*. While some Indians read passages of scriptural texts to argue that *sati* did have scriptural sanction, other Indians interpreted the very same passages, or various other scriptural texts, to argue against a scriptural basis for *sati*.[49] Thapar's discussion suggests that what "counted" as "scriptural texts" for this purpose ranged from the *Rig Veda* (circa second millennium B.C.) to ethico-legal texts such as the *dharma-shastras*, which include the Laws of Manu dating from the turn of the Christian era, to commentaries such as that of Medhatitthi in the tenth century A.D. Many of these texts were "reinterpretations" of elements of earlier texts. For instance, the *Rig Veda*'s reference to a ceremony where the widow lay on her husband's funeral pyre before it was lit and was raised from it by a male relative of the husband, seems to have been reinterpreted in the sixteenth century as "Vedic sanction" for *sati*, overlooking the fact that the original text endorses *niyoga* or levirate, where the widow is permitted to marry her husband's brother.[50] Given this range of "scriptural texts" and the fact that there was a "debate" on *sati* extending over centuries, it is hardly surprising that a whole range of positions on *sati* could be shown to have "scriptural sanction"!

Mani's analysis suggests that *sati* was constituted as an "Indian tradition" in the process of British colonial attempts to gain "official knowledge" about this practice. The nature of this attempt generated a debate in which both British and Indian participants were led to rest their case for or against *sati* on a discussion of the import of Hindu scriptures. The *pundits* whose views were solicited by the British were oddly and interestingly positioned both as "authoritative interpreters" of these texts and as those whose "authority" was ultimately determined by British colonial officials, whose political authority underwrote the religious authority seemingly accorded to the *pundits*. British officials retained the power to make the final determinations about *which* of the *pundits'* interpretations they would treat as "essential" and which as "peripheral."[51] The project of "discovering the scriptural authority for a Hindu practice" turns out, on closer examination, to hinge on the authority conferred on particular Indian *pundits*, and ultimately withheld from them, by British colonial officials! I suspect that this odd, interesting, and unequal collaboration between British colonials and Indian elites in the attempt to determine the "cultural authenticity" of *sati* can function as an illuminating parable about many other similarly collaborative constructions of "indigenous traditions" in a variety of colonial contexts.

Several interesting problems mark the face of this "debate on *sati*" between the British and the Indians, and among Indians themselves. None of the participants in the debate seem to have raised any serious questions about the importance they were giving to brahmanic scripture in their attempts to determine the legitimacy or illegitimacy of *sati* as an "authentic cultural practice."[52] As a result, all parties to the debate collaborated in constituting "religious sanction" as the fundamental basis for the "authenticity" of indigenous practices. This in turn had the effect of suggesting "Hindu tradition" to be far more uniform, unitary, and scripturally grounded than it actually was. The participants in the debate jointly eclipsed the degree to which law and "traditional practices" in precolonial India were not determined exclusively by interpretations of religious texts, but had other bases for their "authority," such as the customary practices that varied widely across different Hindu communities, which were interpreted and enforced not by priests but by very localized community councils or caste *sabhas*. In making religious scriptural sanction definitive of the "traditional" status of *sati*, the actual attitudes to the idea and practice of *sati* across various castes and segments of the Hindu community were rendered insignificant as indicators of whether *sati* was in fact a central or definitive "Hindu tradition."

British colonial officials and their Indian collaborators thus obscured the degree to which their joint project of "determining the legitimacy of a practice *purely* by scholarly interpretation of religious texts" is a nontraditional procedure in the Indian context, a procedure that hides its "modernity" from itself even as it works at the task of "uncovering tradition." The view of Third-World contexts as "contexts governed by unthinking adherence to unchanging religious traditions" turns out ironically in the Indian case to be a reality that is "fabricated" (in the twin senses of "made by" and "made up by") by the colonial insistence that the colonized give thought to religious scripture alone in determining what constituted "their traditions." The debate over *sati* generated a notion of "tradition," which the colonial British and some of their Indian subjects jointly helped construct, and one which they came to share, but only by avoiding acknowledgment of the ways in which they collaborated in producing it. There is reason to believe that this process of collaboration between colonial officials and local elites—one that was engaged in *inventing* what counted as "authentic indigenous traditions" under the guise of *discovering* it—was a process that occurred in a number of colonial contexts, albeit with interesting differences of detail. Colonialism turns out to be "interventionist" but in a much more subtle and interesting way than is suggested by the image of "colonial interventionists" contemptuous of aspects of indigenous culture and traditions, advocating change in the name of "progress."

The British colonial consultation of religious pundits to determine *sati*'s status as "tradition" relies on an assumption that the practice of *sati* must be grounded either in legitimate understandings or in misunderstandings of Hindu scripture. Historical investigations suggest, however, that distinctly *earthly* considerations may have had a lot more to do with precolonial as well as colonial *satis* than "religious beliefs," scripturally valid or otherwise. Addressing the issue of why there were more *satis* in Bengal than elsewhere in British India, Romila Thapar points out that the Bengali legal system was anomalous in giving women inheritance rights to their husband's property, making *sati* a convenient mode of eliminating an inheritor.[53] Ashis Nandy has argued that there was an "epidemic" *increase* of *satis* in the early period of colonial rule in Bengal, largely confined to "those groups made marginal by their exposure to Western impact," suggesting that colonialism had more to do with *sati* than Hinduism.[54] *Sati* in other parts of India may well have had different but equally nonscriptural roots and causes.[55]

Ironically, twentieth-century Indians seem as prone to making mistakes about the connections between *sati* and Hinduism as were nineteenth-century British colonials. Many Indians, intellectuals and others, assume that the practice of *sati* corresponds to or is an "imitation" of the act of "wifely nobility" depicted in the mythological story of Sati. The mythological figure Sati is the wife of the god Shiva. In a common version of the mythological story, Sati's father insults her husband Shiva by excluding him from a sacrifice, and Sati flings herself into a fire in protest. Driven almost insane with grief, Shiva carries her corpse throughout India, until Vishnu dismembers her body, strewing bits over the earth, each becoming a site of pilgrimage. While this mythological Sati kills herself by fire in "devotion to her husband," there is little else that corresponds to *sati*-the-practice, since Sati acts in defiance of her father to protest his dishonoring of her husband, kills herself in her father's *sacrificial* fire, and pre-deceases her husband, leaving him to suffer over her death. In *sati*-the-practice, the widow immolates herself on her dead husband's funeral pyre as a sign of wifely devotion, but does not act in defense of the husband's honor. If anything, her act brings glory to herself and good fortune to the family. Gayatri Spivak hardly exaggerates when she says that the "story of the mythic Sati [reverses] every narrateme of the rite."[56] It seems that not only Westerners but also Indians have a difficult time noticing the variations between different kinds of cases of Indian women going up in flames.[57]

To return to colonial Indian history, evidence suggests that *sati*'s centrality as an "Indian tradition" was an *effect* of the extensive and prolonged debate that took place over the very issue of its status as tradition. As a result of this debate, *sati* came to acquire, for both British and Indians, and for its supporters as well as its opponents, an "emblematic status," becoming a larger-than-life symbol of "Hindu" and "Indian" culture in a way that transcended the actual facts of its limited practice. This result seems to have been facilitated by the fact that none of the participants on the various sides of the debate seem to have raised serious questions about why this particular practice was receiving such an extensive amount of attention. Other forms of mistreatment of widows that were considerably more widespread—their stigmatized status in most Hindu communities, and the deprived and miserable existence they were confined to as a result of their status—did not become equally important bones of contention between British colonials and Indian elites.[58] They thus did not get constituted as "Indian" traditions in the same manner as *sati*. It is important to note that this "obsession with *sati*" overlooked not only more routine forms of mistreatment of women, but also other important dimensions of ongoing human suffering. While "thousands of pages of Parliamentary papers" were devoted to *sati*, "the mortality of millions from disease and starvation was only mentioned incidentally."[59]

Even from the distance provided by a twentieth-century perspective, it is hard to give a simple or definitive answer to the "why *sati*?" question—to the question of why it was *this* practice, so limited in scope compared to so many others, that was singled out for such extensive debate and constructed as a practice that was deeply symbolic of "Indian culture." I suspect that *sati*'s fascination for the British had something to do with *sati* being simultaneously deeply familiar in its invocation of wifely devotion and womanly self-sacrifice, and deeply alien in endorsing actual self-immolation on the husband's funeral pyre. The reactions of British officials to actual incidents of *sati* reveal horror mixed with admiration for the "courage and devotion" of the women involved, reactions in which their admiration for the woman's "nobility" mixes uneasily with distaste for the "savagery" of immolation.

I suspect that what was arguably a "difference in degree" between British and Indian scripts about women's cultural place had to be converted to a substantive "difference in kind" to support the sense of vast difference between colonizers and "natives" that the colonial project required as moral justification. Colonial encounters seem to instigate a process of defining "the Self in *contrast* to the Other" on the part of both colonizers and the colonized, and practices affecting women commonly seem to become central elements in this project. But it also seems to be the case that not all practices affecting women have the same usefulness for this project. Practices affecting women that involve a significant measure of the "spectacular" (such as *sati*) or a significant measure of "hiddenness" (such the seclusion of women in the *zenana*, *purdah*, and veiling)[60] seem to provoke a special interest and fascination in these projects of contrasting cultural self-definition. (There is, of course, something also deeply "hidden" about *sati*, enveloped as the women is in ritual, crowds, and flames, and something "spectacular" about the seclusion of women.)[61]

The nineteenth-century Indian version of the "obsession with *sati*" seems only partially explainable as simply a response to the British colonial obsession with the practice. *Sati* was clearly capable of bearing a considerable degree of "symbolic weight" for Indian cultural self-definition. Even for many Indian reformers opposed to the actual practice of *sati*, *sati* became a lofty symbol of "ideal Indian womanhood," indicative of attitudes towards husband and family that bespoke a "feminine nobility" and "devotion to family" that were deemed uncharacteristic of "Western women." Ironically, *sati* becomes intertwined with the construction of an "Indian feminine ideal" enshrined within the script of Indian national self-definition in the same historical period in which it was legally abolished. If this obsessive nineteenth-century debate on *sati* had not taken place, it seems extremely unlikely that *sati* would have become a politically salient "Indian" symbol available for deployment by contemporary Hindu fundamentalists.

For the moment, I want to draw attention to one final feature of the colonial debate on *sati* that is crucial to its political deployment by Hindu fundamentalists today—the shared acceptance by British as well as Indian participants of a distinction between "good" and "bad" *satis*. Virtually all participants in the debate, supporters as well as opponents of the practice, seem to have subscribed to a distinction between "good" *satis* (uncoerced acts of voluntary self-sacrifice by devoted wives) and "bad" *satis* (where the woman was either overtly coerced, or more subtly manipulated by scheming and unscrupulous family members who wished to be rid of the obligation of supporting the widow).

Beside the matter of *sati*'s scriptural sanction, much of the colonial "debate" on *sati* seems to have been a debate about the relative proportion of "good" versus "bad" *satis*. While the supporters of *sati* seemed to consider most incidents of *sati* to be "good *satis*," the opponents of *sati* contended that most incidents were in fact "bad *satis*." The final legal decision to abolish *sati* seems to have been based on a sense that "bad *satis*" were by far more common than "good" ones, and that the dangers of coercion and manipulation that led to "bad *satis*" could not effectively be dealt with by state supervision of these events.[62] That the rare "good *sati*" would now be prohibited was the legal "price" of ensuring the demise of "bad *satis*." Support for the legal abolition of *sati* thus remained compatible for many Indians with a worshipful "respect" for the "wifely and womanly ideal" embodied by the "good" *sati*. These contours of the colonial debate on *sati* thus explain why *sati* remains a potent symbol that can be recuperated and politically deployed today.

I would like to suggest that the case of "Indian suttee" is an instance of a more widespread phenomenon whereby local practices and localized "traditions" in Third-World contexts were constructed into "national traditions" at an historical moment when "shared national traditions" taken to be constitutive of the very idea of "nationhood" became crucial components of political struggles for independence from colonial rule. While Benedict Anderson's view of nations as "imagined communities" is often applied to nation-states that have already achieved political existence as "nation-states," I would like to point out that nationalist struggles under colonial rule required even more strenuous acts of imagination, since they were struggles to imagine "not yet existent nations."

Often enough, these "imagined nations" of anticolonialist nationalism were not seen as prospective political units emerging via joint struggle against a shared history of colonial immiserization, exploitation, and political misrule but were imagined rather as returns to a shared past where "we ruled ourselves" and "defined our own culture and values." Shared "national traditions" had to exist in order to assert a national identity that was politically cast not merely as prospective but as a "recovery" of a past nationhood "lost" to colonial rule. Such "national traditions" came into existence by various processes of "nationalizing" the "local," bestowing on the colonized a unified sense of national self that helped conceal their own heterogeneity and hybridity. Even "objectionable" and "contested" traditions such as *sati* served the agenda of nationalist struggle, since their status as "national traditions" was left unquestioned, and in fact was reinforced by heated debates on their "place within national culture." Failures to understand the construction within colonial history of many Third-World "national traditions" facilitates contemporary deployments of such "traditions" by right-wing and religious-fundamentalist political forces. I turn, in the next section, to the contemporary political uses to which the "Indian tradition of *sati*" has been put.

The Contemporary Politics of *Sati* /

While the previous section focused on various aspects of the "politics of tradition formation" that led to *sati* acquiring the status of an "Indian tradition" in colonial times, this section will sketch out some important aspects of the contemporary politics of *sati* in India. I believe that critical attention to the present economic, social, and cultural agendas in which *contemporary sati* is implicated is important for several reasons. First, it facilitates a fuller sense of the inadequacies of Daly-type accounts of "Third-World women victimized by unchanging traditions" by vividly showing the recent attempts at a "revival" of *sati* to be a profoundly *contemporary* phenomenon. Second, and more importantly, it gives a fuller sense of the political stakes between present-day endorsers of *sati* and those, feminists and others, who publicly contest such endorsement. Third, it allows us to see how significantly the terms and contours of the debate on *sati* provoked by contemporary incidents are influenced by the colonial debate on *sati*.

Much of the debate provoked by contemporary incidents of *sati* represents it as a conflict between "traditions" on the one hand and "Westernization," or "modernization" on the other. Fundamentalist groups, understandably, portrayed *sati* as an integral part of "Hindu tradition, culture and religious values." They not only valorized its "traditional" and "religious" status but also declared its significance inaccessible to Westernized urban Indians.[63] Several segments of the media coverage and public outcry from those opposed to *sati* were critical of *sati* precisely on the grounds that it was "traditional," "religious," and "barbaric." Much of this public condemnation did not question or challenge *sati's* status as "Tradition" or as a "Hindu ritual," casting *sati* rather as a "religious tradition" that no longer deserved the endorsement of "modern" right-thinking Hindus and Indians, challenging the practice without challenging the terms in which the practice was represented.

In so doing, I would argue that they contributed no less than Daly's chapter to replicating "colonialist representations" of *sati*. To forcefully reiterate what I mentioned in the introduction to this essay, "colonialist representations" do not necessarily issue only from "Western" subjects. Their status as "colonialist representations" is determined, rather, by their replicating problematic aspects of the representations of "Third-World traditions" that have their historical roots in the colonial encounter, aspects of which the last section of the essay worked to clarify. In the contemporary debate, Indian feminists were an important exception to the trend, resisting and challenging attempts to portray *sati* in terms of a simple opposition between "religion and tradition" on the one hand, and "Westernization and modernization" on the other.

Let me start with a brief account of some pertinent background facts about *sati* in contemporary India. After being outlawed in 1829, "the practice of *sati* faded into a very rare crime; . . . today it is rarer still."[64] In the four decades between 1947, Indian independence, and 1987, the year in which the immolation of Roop Kanwar restored *sati* to an issue of widespread national debate, forty cases of *sati* have been recorded. Two-thirds of these cases occurred in the state of Rajasthan, mainly in and around the Sikar district, the same state where Roop Kanwar was immolated. On the legal front, the Indian Penal Code, revised in the 1950s, dropped explicit reference to *sati* on the understanding that its provisions against murder and against abetment of suicide were sufficient to deal with cases of *sati*.[65]

It is also interesting to note that most of the recent cases in Rajasthan occurred in a part of Rajasthan where widow-immolation was not widely practiced in the past, and in an area that was the first in the region to make it a penal offense in colonial times, with the support of the local princely rulers and the public assent of local chieftains. The prevalent decay and neglect of *sati* temples and memorials commemorating medieval or colonial *satis* "indicate that the social or religious significance attached to the practice had attenuated by the 1950's."[66] If *sati*'s importance as a "tradition" had visibly declined, how might we understand why recent cases of *sati* have in fact occurred, and why these cases have become focal points of attempts to restore *sati* to the status of "a national tradition?" I believe that these recent cases need to be understood both *locally* (by understanding their implications and "benefits" for the widow's conjugal family as well as for sectors of the local community) as well as *nationally* (by understanding the ends to which these incidents are being deployed by recent Hindu revivalist national politics, ends whose scopes extend far beyond the limited area of the actual incidents).

I will start with a brief sketch of the "local" motivations and interests that seem to underlie these recent incidents, drawing on Suresh Vaid and Kumkum Sangari's discussion of the 1980 case of Om Kunwar, and on Veena Talwar Oldenburg's discussion of the 1987 Roop Kanwar case.[67] Economic motivations for *sati*—in particular the widely shared desire to be rid of the financial obligation of supporting the widow, and the desire to foreclose the widow's claim to a share of the husband's property, a claim that existed in some communities—have been recognized since colonial times. These recent cases suggest that *sati* has become a site where new and very "modern" economic motivations are at play.

Oldenburg points out that Roop Kanwar's dowry—consisting of a large quantity of gold, fixed-deposits in her name, and a wide range of expensive domestic consumer goods—was not only a very substantial dowry by Indian standards but also far beyond the assets of her husband's poorer family.[68] Oldenburg also points out that "the custom in the area was for a young, childless widow to return to her parents with all her dowry."[69] That her conjugal family had dowry-related reasons for preferring Roop's immolation to her widowhood is hard to miss. These facts suggest a certain linkage between the contemporary phenomenon of dowry-murder and some *recent* cases of widow-immolation.[70] It is also fairly obvious that recent cases of *sati* have had economic rewards for the widow's husband's family that go beyond dowry. In both the Om Kunwar and Roop Kanwar cases, modest "memorial shrines" were established within the actual dwelling of the husband's family, attracting "pilgrims" and significant monetary contributions in the form of "offerings."

Other members of the community have also benefited from these *satis* in important ways. These immolations have helped turn undistinguished small towns into important places of religious pilgrimage. Large and ostentatious *sati* temples have been erected at the sites of these immolations, ensuring considerable profit for those on the boards that run them. Their conversion into places of "religious tourism," with chartered buses bringing in pilgrims from towns and cities, has generated dozens of new local businesses—selling pictures, icons, and booklets of the *sati*; selling flowers, incense, and other paraphernalia of worship, and selling food and drink. It should not be imagined that such crass economic considerations on the part of the family or community operated only *post facto*—as a cashing-in on the unforeseen lucrativeness of the incident. An eerie similarity between the cases of Roop Kanwar and Om Kunwar lies in the fact that both women were immolated in spots other than the customary cremation grounds. Roop Kanwar's in-laws "arranged for her to be immolated on a plot near their own home rather than on the town cremation grounds."[71] In the Om Kunwar case, "some deliberation had gone into the choice of a site that could become a pilgrimage place," the site chosen being both accessible from the main road and a conveniently unclaimed piece of property.[72] Commercial calculations had clearly entered the picture long before these women went up in flames.[73]

In addition to these directly economic motivations, these incidents also appear to be implicated in the agendas of local caste-politics. The three castes centrally involved in the politics around *sati* in Rajasthan are the Kshatriya Rajput ruling caste, the priestly caste of Brahmins, and the wealthy mercantile Banias. The Brahmins are crucial functionaries in commemorative temples and are important members of the local religious organizations and of the Hindu fundamentalist groups that use these incidents to organize religious events to commemorate and celebrate *sati*. The Rajputs use these events to reinforce their status as a martial race who are historic defenders of "Hindu dharma,"[74] at a time when their power and status is declining. In an interesting shift, Rajputs who once attempted to preserve *sati* as a "privilege" of Rajput women (indicative of a "caste nobility and courage" befitting "mothers of a martial race") now attempt to represent it as also the heritage of several other castes, even as they continue to specially idealize Rajput widows.[75] The Banias, who hail from the region but who have mostly moved away to become prosperous urban businessmen, seem to be the primary source for the funds to build the ostentatious *sati* temples, faith and profit apparently reinforcing each other. By their various modes of endorsement and support of *sati*, each of these castes consolidates its economic, political, and cultural power. Rather than a simple matter of "tradition," Sharada Jain suggests these recent *satis* are a sly revival of a custom by the "three most powerful castes in Rajasthan whose investment in the process of modernization was the greatest."[76]

In pointing to these economic and political motives, I do not wish to argue that "religion" and "tradition" are entirely smoke screens, having no role to play in generating and shaping these recent events of *sati*. I merely wish to insist that one must not fail to attend to the thoroughly modern motivations that underlie their resuscitation and deployment. Local folklore about past *satis* and shared religious understandings of the phenomenon of *sati* (not necessarily scriptural) do play important roles in mobilizing the public turnout to "witness" these events, in shaping what "witnesses" claim to have seen, in making these events of immolation "acceptable," and in generating the flow of pilgrims to these sites.[77]

A few examples of how religious understandings collaborate in this process will suffice for my purposes.[78] A woman who has vowed to become *sati* is understood to be filled with the palpable force of *"sat,"* which endows her with powers to both bless and curse others, and to burn anyone who tries to restrain her.[79] This understanding of *"sat"* provides convenient excuses for noninterference on the part of family and community, for their not attempting to discourage the woman from "her" decision to "commit *sati*." The woman's flailing arms on the funeral pyre are interpreted not as signs of pain or struggle but as her showering blessings on the crowd.[80] The belief that *sat* makes the woman immune to pain works to make the event acceptable to "witnessing" by an audience, erasing the painful horror of a woman publicly being burnt to death.

While there is evidence to suggest Roop Kanwar was sedated by a local doctor,[81] her demeanor was publicly interpreted as evidence of a spiritual trancelike state believed to be induced by *sat*. A variety of beliefs about *sat* thus collaborate in enabling the event to be seen as an act of pure volition on the part of the woman, and in enabling all data to work as confirmations of the religious character of the event.

Discussing the relationship between faith and coercion involved in these events, Vaid and Sangari argue:

> The active pressure of the witnessing crowd shapes the event. . . . The crowds represent a closure of alternatives for the woman, finalise, approve and supplement the machinations of families, priests etc. The widow's immolation becomes a public spectacle, the property of persons of all ages and social groups. The line between perpetration and belief can be thin—perpetration itself both rests on and creates a substratum of belief . . . 'sat' translates and sublimates human agency—the actual social agents involved in invoking 'sat', family, villagers, other women—into something external or beyond control. 'Sat' is manufactured and gains consent because it first elides human participation then 'benevolently' re-includes the participants who can express the pride of participation without feeling the guilt of collusion.[82]

Apart from their "local" effects, these events are deployed by Hindu fundamentalist organizations at a national level to galvanize mass political demonstrations of support and adulation for "Hindu dharma and culture." There is an explicit patriarchal dimension to this politics. The ideal of the self-sacrificing wife utterly devoted to her husband that is allegedly embodied in these *satis* is held up as a definitive and distinguishing symbol of an "authentic Hindu culture" threatened by modernization and "Westernization." Since this ideal of womanhood is in fact widely shared, even by those communities that have never practiced widow-immolation, it can usefully be invoked as a basis for political solidarity across a wide section of Hindu communities. The public and spectacular dimensions of *sati* help to make the devotion and self-sacrifice more routinely expected of wives into a visible political ideal of "Hindu womanhood."

It is not simply that *sati* is used to uphold symbolically an "ideal of womanhood" whose vision of women's roles and place is problematic. This "ideal of womanhood" is further used to depict some women as more "truly Indian" than others. This "ideal of womanhood" is thus politically deployed to stigmatize, denigrate, and challenge the normative status of many different groups of women whose choices and ways of life do not conform to this "ideal." The "ideal womanhood" embodied by these alleged *satis* is thus defined:

Against women who work (in this area women in agricultural labor), non-Hindu women (only Hindu women can be '*sati*'), the popular caricature of the Westernized woman . . . widows who may seek remarriage, divorced and unmarried women, educated women who may seek employment, urban feminists and any woman who challenges her given role.[83]

The immolation of Roop Kanwar in 1987 was the first historical occasion when political contestation of the practice of *sati* was centrally articulated by Indian women. Indian feminist organizations were vitally involved in arousing public protest and concern over this incident. It is interesting to examine how these protests went *beyond* denunciations of *sati* as an "oppressive patriarchal tradition" even as they kept the welfare of women at the center of their politics.

First, these protests were marked by a feminist refusal to conceptualize this issue as a simple opposition of "tradition versus modernity." Part of this refusal operated by challenging *sati*'s status as an "Indian tradition."[84] It is important to clarify the logic of feminist contestation here. The fundamentalist defense of *sati* rests on portraying it both as: (1) an ancient Indian cultural tradition, and (2) an admirable practice that should inspire respect and reverence from Indians. While feminists attacked both of the fundamentalist premises, as it was politically vital that they do, they did *not* imply that if it *had* been an Indian tradition, it would have been morally acceptable. Another part of the feminist challenge was to point to the thoroughly modern economic, political, and patriarchal agendas in which these incidents were implicated. Apart from factors I have already mentioned, feminists insisted on the modernity of the incident by pointing out that Roop was a city-educated woman, that her husband had a degree in science, that her father-in-law was a school teacher, and that the members of the pro-*sati* lobby were predominantly urban, educated men in their twenties and thirties.[85] Second, feminist protests not only denounced the agendas of Hindu fundamentalist groups making political use of the event, but also denounced the national government for massive governmental failures and delays in taking action—both legal action against the immediate perpetrators, and political action to prevent the carefully orchestrated mass demonstrations organized by Hindu fundamentalist groups that helped construct these events into monumental national political events. Third, while feminist protests affirmed the horror of the particular event of *sati*, they refused to see the practice of *sati* in isolation from the much more systematic practices of patriarchal oppression that affect Indian women.

I will now turn to a number of complex strategies used by feminists to address, complicate, and decentralize the "issue of the woman's consent"—an issue that has been central to the debate on *sati* since colonial times. I have argued that virtually all parties to the colonial debate seem to have endorsed a distinction between "good *satis*" that were purely voluntary decisions on the part of the woman and "bad *satis*" that were results of literal physical coercion or manipulation by family members. The "issue of consent" was raised once again as the central issue in the Roop Kanwar case, not only by Hindu fundamentalists arguing that this was an instance of a "good *sati*," but also by many mainstream journalists whose reportage treated this as the most salient question, even as they remained unsure about the answer. Feminist protest around the Roop Kanwar case challenged this dichotomy between "good" and "bad" *satis* and raised complex questions about women's agency, choice, and freedom, questions whose import range far beyond the practice of *sati*. I can discern four different strategies at work in the Indian feminist political response to the "issue of the woman's consent" that both work together and have interesting tensions between them.

The first strategy can be described as a strategy of pointing to "suspicious evidence" pertaining to the particular case, often overlooked by mainstream media reports, that cast serious doubt on the allegedly voluntary nature of the event. Investigative teams from women's organizations uncovered and publicized a "body of evidence" that "would smell foul even to the most credulous of *sati* watchers."[86] These included facts about the sizable nature of Roop Kanwar's dowry, the commercially convenient choice of the site of immolation, evidence of Roop having been medically sedated, and the fact that Roop's parents were, contrary to custom, not informed until after the event had transpired. They also uncovered the facts that Roop had resided for most of her eight-month marriage at her parents' home in Jaipur, spending only twenty days with her ailing husband and rejoining him only a few days before their deaths, facts that raise serious doubt about the existence of a "wifely devotion" strong enough to have generated a desire to commit *sati*![87]

The second feminist strategy can be described as a strategy of drawing attention to a variety of contextual features that make it virtually impossible to determine what did in fact transpire in these cases. Feminists point out, for instance, that "eye-witness reports" are tainted in at least two ways. Given the highly emotional and symbolically charged nature of the event, it is highly likely that even "sincere" reports are tainted by people's abilities to "see" only those things they could square with their participation in the event. Further, those who might have seen evidence of coercion are unlikely to speak out since they are frightened not only of possible legal consequences but also of the ire of locally powerful segments of the community. Such considerations help cast doubt on the "eye-witness evidence" touted by the fundamentalists that unapologetically endorsed the event's voluntary character. Feminists underline the fact that these contemporary cases are like cases of *sati* in colonial times in that there is no "independent" evidence whatsoever about what the woman herself actually felt or wanted—there are only representations by *interested parties* of what she felt or wanted.[88]

The third feminist strategy can be described as pointing to an array of structural features of the lives of women such as Roop that complicate the idea of what it might mean for Roop, or for any woman like her, to have "chosen" *sati*. As one Rajasthani woman put it, "How many women have the right to decide anything voluntarily? If a woman does not choose her husband and does not decide matters such as her own education or career, how can she choose in a matter as imperative as that of life or death?"[89] Pointing to women's social status and the meager options open to them, feminists made the point that many contextual features of women's lives and options complicate attempts to portray *satis* as "pure acts of volition and wifely devotion." These considerations were also used to call attention to the problematic nature of the "ideal of *sati*"—whereby self-immolation is constructed as a "woman's choice" in a context where it remains culturally acceptable to deprive women routinely of choices over large areas of their lives. Pointing out that "when Indian feminists speak of woman as victim it is in a complex material sense," Lata Mani adds, "in emphasizing women's systematic subordination . . . Indian feminists are specifically trying to counter right-wing discourses that falsely propose women's total freedom."[90]

The fourth feminist strategy was to insist on the fact that the issue of the woman's consent was, from a legal point of view, entirely irrelevant. Feminists reiterated and endorsed the legal position of the Indian Penal Code, in which the victim's consent is irrelevant to charges of either murder or abetted suicide. The attempt to make the woman's consent a central issue was criticized on the grounds that it was being deployed to distract attention from the clear fact that this so-called act of tradition was a crime according to existing Indian law, that those who had participated in it had participated in a criminal act, and that those who were making political capital by "glorifying" it were glorifying a crime. Further, arguing that "religion" could not absolve the perpetrators of murder, Indira Jaising declared, "Just as the personal is political, the religious is secular where women are concerned."[91]

Thus feminists insisted in several ways that the "issue of the woman's consent" as articulated in the debate around *sati*, though it is posed as a *metaphysical* question of the true nature of the woman's will and desire, is fundamentally a *political* issue. The issue of "consent" was seen as one that must be understood and fought both on its own terms (by pointing to data that suggest that it was a matter of other people's wills, interests, and desires) and also understood and fought in terms that challenge the salience and centrality of the issue of consent. There might seem to be a certain *logical* tension between the claim, "The woman did not consent to *sati* in this particular case" and the claim, "It is legally and morally irrelevant whether the woman 'consented' to *sati* in this particular case," since making the latter move seems to undercut and call into question the salience of making the former move. However, I believe the joint deployment of both moves by feminist groups makes good *political* sense, since each move has a crucial political role in generating widespread public concern over recent incidents of *sati*.

Failure to make the first move, to address the issue of the "woman's consent" in its own terms, is to risk not calling attention to ample available evidence that suggests the use of coercion, and to risk failing to engage with a very large body of citizens who might endorse the "ideal of *sati*" but who might be open to seeing actual cases of *sati* as deeply problematic. Failure to point to possible mercenary motivations on the part of the woman's conjugal family, and to the self-serving economic and political agendas on the part of powerful community members and religious leaders, would be to leave unchallenged the view of these incidents that was actively promoted by fundamentalist politicians and religious leaders—that of a heroic voluntary act of wifely devotion that spontaneously generated worshipful witnessing and tribute from members of the larger community. Pointing to the mercenary economic and political motivations of many who "assisted" the *sati* suggests reasons to believe that outright coercion of the woman was involved. It helps cast doubt on the "purity" of claimed religious motivations on the part of those whose "assistance" was crucial to the carrying out of a complicated public ritual. Calling attention to reasons that suggest that a particular immolation was a coerced "bad *sati*" does not necessarily imply that one considers so-called good *satis* to be acceptable.

The second sort of move, which challenges the salience of "the woman's consent," is politically essential both in order to criticize state inaction and to challenge the very "ideal" of *sati*. Challenging the "ideal" of *sati* is a more difficult political move, likely to provoke resistance even from those who do not endorse the actual practice of *sati*, and likely to result in feminists being castigated for their "un-Indian" ideas and "Westernized" ways. Despite these risks, I believe this sort of challenge is crucial in order to broaden the contours of the national political dialogue beyond a debate on the "voluntary" character of particular *satis*, and in order to generate a forceful feminist critique of fundamentalist politics. Questioning the validity of the stereotypes of wifely femininity that constitute the content of the "ideal of *sati*" is politically facilitated if the history and politics of *sati*'s tenuous status as an "Indian tradition" can be publicly articulated and widely communicated.[92] However, getting people to think critically and reflectively about the genealogy of ideas and practices they take to be constitutive of their "traditions," and about the political nature and functions of seductive ideas such as nation, culture, and ideals of womanhood, is not an easy project in *any* national context.

Conclusion /

These details of the colonial politics of *sati* and the politics of recent Indian feminist contestations of *sati* strongly reveal the limitations of Daly-type accounts of *sati* in particular and understandings of "Third-World traditions" in general. I believe that the numerous ways in which *sati* fails to be simply a "matter of tradition" are hardly unique, and that many other issues that are often understood to be issues of "Third-World women oppressed by Traditions" will, on examination, turn out to be, in many significant respects, political problems of a very contemporary character.

Feminist analyses of "traditional practices" affecting women should refrain from leaving their status as "tradition" unexamined. Rather, they should investigate how the regional traditions of *particular* groups acquire the status of "national traditions," check the actual vintage of all supposedly longstanding traditions, note how particular practices get singled out for such honor while many other equally customary aspects of local "ways of life" yield with little notice or controversy to social change, and examine what political purposes are served by each of these aspects of tradition-formation, resuscitation, retention and change. Politically astute historical-genealogical investigations of the "constitution" of "national traditions," of declines, revivals, and changes in the practice and significance of "traditions," and of the political agendas behind their deployment at any given time, seem essential to accurately understanding and effectively challenging such "traditions." Understanding "traditions" as constituted and changing practices, as open to contestation, and as serving a variety of functions promotes a less reverential and more critical attitude to them. While some "traditions" might well turn out less problematic along these dimensions than others, many will turn out to be practices of a sort other than they are imagined to be by religious and cultural fundamentalists, who portray them as unchanging elements of "national culture" and "ways of life." My intention is not to argue that there are no "traditions" in Third-World contexts or elsewhere, or to distinguish between "authentic" and "inauthentic" traditions. Rather, it is to argue that there are often good reasons to understand such "traditions" as *entities different from what they are taken to be.*

My analysis suggests that Western feminists who wish to analyze the import of "oppressive indigenous traditions on Third-World women" need to be particularly cautious in their approach to the question of what these "traditions" are. They should be careful not to take their status as "tradition" for granted without going behind them to understand the historical and political processes that enabled them to acquire this status. While Daly-type accounts of "tradition" can and do amply accommodate the insight that such "traditions" paid scant heed to women's welfare (which is certainly an important part of a feminist critique of such "traditions"), they lack awareness of the politically constituted nature of these "traditions" and fail to attend to the complex political dynamics underlying such a constitution. Thus, while Daly-type perspectives provide room to politically challenge such practices on the grounds of their harmfulness and oppressiveness to women, challenges that are not unimportant, they do not provide the tools additionally required to challenge the status of these practices as "indigenous traditions." I believe that a "double strategy" involving the joint use of both forms of challenge are often *crucial* to contemporary Third-World feminist contestations of "traditional cultural practices" in their national contexts. Western feminist work that forecloses the second type of challenge by buying into misleading views of the nature of Third-World "traditions" might, with good reason, appear both inadequate and dangerous to Third-World feminists politically engaged in challenging these traditions.

Daly's understanding of "patriarchal traditions" suffers from another important limitation. Insofar as Daly indicates any *reasons* for the existence of these "traditional practices," she suggests that they are motivated by a diffuse sort of patriarchal desire to "control women," and by a cultural relish in inflicting pain on women, motivations suggested by Daly's naming of these practices "sado-rituals." I would argue that my discussion of the "politics of *sati*" suggests a very different picture—that patriarchal political discourses about "national identity" are always about the control of women but never *only* about the control of women, since they are also deployed both locally and nationally for economic and political ends that work through but go beyond such control of women. While patriarchal structures and discourses help shape these events of *sati* into profitable occasions and into events that can be manipulated to create mass political support for Hindu fundamentalist political groups, the desires for profit and for political power are not simply *reducible* to a desire to control women. Not only is there more to patriarchy than sadistic desires to control women, but also the control of women is often a means to larger, though connected, ends.

While Daly-type perspectives understand that such "traditions" have ideological functions with respect to the oppression of women, they lack an historical and political sense of the complexities involved in the "formation" of ideologies. They therefore tend to lack the sense that these "formations" may have *manifold* functions, not all of which are simply reducible to agendas to "oppress women." These political and economic agendas also aim to control and marginalize many groups of *men*. Third-World feminist contestations of these "traditions" need to discern, explicate, and respond to the multiplicity of agendas served by the deployments of these such "traditions." As Kumkum Sangari sarcastically points out, contemporary Hindu fundamentalists use *sati* to:

> ... maintain the extended family, Hindu tradition, nari-dharma, patti-bakthi, sectional group identities, a fundamentalist yet cross-caste Hinduism, and that 'spirituality' which is the mark of our 'Indianness' and which distinguishes us from the materialistic West. *Sati* will manage the ideals around which our social order coheres, it will not only ward off the fear of death but feminists as well.[93]

The "national and cultural identity" agendas of Hindu fundamentalism aim to marginalize all non-Hindus, male and female, from the status of "real Indians" and are deployed to question the "authenticity" of all Indians who would like to preserve a secular state. If the political agendas of religious fundamentalisms and nationalisms marginalize groups of people along class, caste, or ethnic dimensions, they marginalize substantial numbers of men as well as women, even though women might be specifically affected within these class, caste, and ethnic groups. I believe that feminists in all national contexts who are engaged in confronting "traditions" that are problematically used to define "national identity" and "national culture" need to focus not only on how the interests of different groups of women are affected by such articulations, but also on how the interests of different groups of men are affected by these same processes.

Problematic Western visions of "Nation" and "national culture" also serve to justify a multiplicity of exclusions.[94] Recent political attempts in the United States to present immigrants as a threat to national well-being or to deprive gays and lesbians of their civil rights on the grounds that they constitute a threat to "the American way of life" are attacks on groups of both men and women. I would argue that feminists need to articulate and contest them as such, even as we continue to attend to problems that might affect, for example, immigrant women but not immigrant men. One of the "dangers" of some forms of Western feminism is their all-too-singular focus on "women's interests," even where they recognize that these interests vary according to features such as class, caste, or ethnicity. I would argue that a serious feminist commitment to attending to dimensions such as class, caste, race, or sexual orientation has to be a commitment to caring about how these factors adversely affect the lives of different groups of men as well as women. A widespread and broad-based political opposition to such agendas requires that all these dimensions and their interconnections receive articulation.

Unsurprisingly, Third-World feminists might be better positioned to understand the complicated politics of such complex issues within their national and regional contexts than are Western feminists. This has less to do with Third-World feminists being "authentic" members of their culture, and much more to do with their familiarity with, and access to, various facets of the debates on such issues at the national level. Western feminists interested in Third-World women's issues might do well to learn about the complex "politics of the issue" that are revealed in Third-World feminist contestations as a prophylactic against simplistic and dangerous analyses.

I would argue that understanding colonial history as the context in which many of these ideas of "tradition" and "culture" were formed is a project of political importance to both Western and Third-World feminists. This may well be a project where Western and Third-World feminists have much to learn from each other as we seek to come to terms with a history that connects Western and Third-World women even as it divides them. After all, colonial history is the terrain where the project of "Western" culture's self-definition became a project heavily dependent upon its "difference" from its Others, both internal and external. The contemporary self-definitions of many Third-World cultures and communities are also in profound ways political responses to this history. Working together to develop a rich feminist account of this history that divides and connects us might well provide Western and Third-World feminists some difficult but interesting common ground, and be a project that is crucial and central to any truly "international" feminist politics.

Such a project might help replace "the colonialist stance" with a shared stance on, and understanding of, colonialism and its ongoing legacy. I am suggesting that what Western and Third-World feminists might hope to have in common may be other than "shared interests qua women" or "common forms of patriarchal oppression that cut across national boundaries." They may hope to have a shared and collaborative political understanding of colonial history, its continuing impacts on contemporary economic and political agendas within both Western and Third-World contexts, and its effects on the overall relationship between Western and Third-World nations and communities. This requires, of course, willingness on the part of Western feminists to struggle for "horizontal comradeship"[95] and to let the "Oppressed Third-World Woman as Object of Rescue" yield to the Third-World feminist as intellectual collaborator and political ally on a wide range of issues that mark our common and fractured world.

Three /

Cross-Cultural Connections, Border-Crossings, and "Death by Culture"

Thinking About Dowry-Murders in India and Domestic-Violence Murders in the United States

Introduction /

Dowry-murder is a topic that has surfaced more than a few times during the years I have lived in the United States. The topic's manner of surfacing in social contexts has sometimes left me nonplussed. I remember being disconcerted at a social event, when an American woman I had just met (having learned that I was a graduate student with an interest in feminist issues) said, "I have heard that many Indian women are burned by their families for dowry." I really do not remember how I responded to that particular conversational gambit.[1] I do however remember thinking about it later, and wryly wondering what an appropriate response would be to "I have heard that many Indian women are burned by their families for dowry" in a cocktail situation. I have turned over in my mind the possibilities of a taciturn "Yes," a tart "I'll bet you have," the disconcerting potential of "I've heard about it too," and the quick reprieve that would be made possible by "Nice to have met you. I think I need another drink!"

When the topic of dowry-murder comes up in academic settings, it is, of course, impossible to avoid a sense of pedagogic obligation to engage with the topic. I am, however, often torn between my desire, both as an academic and as a feminist, to answer questions and respond to work on the topic in "informative" ways, and my apprehension that there are a number of problematic assumptions and understandings about the phenomenon in the minds of those I am engaging with on the issue. It often feels impossible to address succinctly the problems I sense behind the very framing of the questions and the discussion, and behind the ubiquitous surfacing of this topic. I have in the last few years come across two unrelated papers on dowry-murder that began, "Women are being burned to death everyday in India."[2] While this sentence has buzzed in my head each time like a bad headache, I have also realized that it is far from simple to describe the problems I have with that introductory sentence.

In these academic encounters with such topics, I have learned how difficult it is to call attention to misconceptions and to alert people to connections that I suspect are not being made. There are several factors that contribute to this difficulty. In cases where misconceptions have not been explicitly articulated, but where one senses their presence, it is not always clear that there are tactful ways of calling attention to them without striking a presumptuous note of, "I know what you are thinking." Even where misconceptions are explicitly articulated, it is not always clear how best to address them. There are the problems of making others defensive; of making them feel "accused" of problematic understandings; of oneself taking on a tone of pompous pedagogic self-righteousness. In trying to shift attention from the content of a conversation or a piece of written work to its underlying assumptions and modes of framing, one risks sounding evasive and "unwilling to engage with the issue," and even defensive in a "culturally chauvinistic" mode that makes one come across as an "Indian woman unwilling to deal with the problems of women in Indian culture."

I have come to the conclusion that there are certain types of problems that are not best addressed in "dialogue" but by trying to write about them more impersonally, and at a distance. Writing about such issues has the virtue of leaving it open to particular members of one's audience to judge for themselves whether the misconceptions and problems addressed seem familiar, whether they were misconceptions they subscribed to as individuals, and whether the analyses and re-descriptions I attempt in order to counter such misconceptions and problems serve to facilitate a better understanding of the issues.

While this essay calls attention to problems I have with the ways in which the issue of dowry-murder is framed and understood in my encounters with the topic in the United States, this essay is not primarily about the issue of dowry-murder. Rather, the central objective of this essay is to call attention to two sorts of problems that often beset the general project of "learning about Other cultures." I am specifically interested in how these problems affect the *feminist* commitment to attend to the problems of women in a variety of cultural contexts, and to "learning about the problems of women in Other cultures." The first cluster of problems has to do with the "effects" that national contexts have on the "construction" of feminist issues and the ways in which understandings of issues are then affected by their "border-crossings" across national boundaries. This first set of problems has to do with features of context that "bring" particular issues onto feminist agendas, mold the information that is available on the issue, and shape as well as distort the ways in which they are understood when the issue "crosses borders." The second problem I am concerned with has to do with the ways in which "culture" is invoked in explanations of forms of violence against Third-World women, while it is not similarly invoked in explanations of forms of violence that affect mainstream Western women. I intend to argue that when such "cultural explanations" are given for *fatal* forms of violence against Third-World women, the effect is to suggest that Third-World women suffer "death by culture." I shall try to show that fatal forms of violence against mainstream Western women seem interestingly resistant to such "cultural explanations," leaving Western women seemingly more immune to "death by culture." I believe that such asymmetries in "cultural explanation" result in pictures of Third-World women as "victims of their culture" in ways that are interestingly different from the way in which victimization of mainstream Western women is understood.

Let me begin with an example that helps illuminate both of the sorts of problems I am interested in—problems of "border-crossing" and problems of "cultural explanation." I have referred in a previous essay to the prevalent confusion in Western national contexts between dowry-murders and sati.[3] This confusion was evident in a dialogue I came across on the Internet, which began with an American man stating that "suttee is the practice of 'bride-burning' or wives being burned in cooking oil fires . . . for having insufficient dowry." This contribution was followed by a man of Indian background attempting to explain the differences between sati and dowry-murder, describing sati as a traditional, but now rare, practice of voluntary self-immolation on the husband's funeral pyre by widows, and dowry-murders as a recent phenomenon of "burning a bride for insufficient dowry."

While I had problems with many details of this explanation, such as its unproblematic construction of sati as "voluntary" and its description of dowry-murders as results of *insufficient* dowry, my biggest worry was that both sati and dowry-murders were to a large degree unexplained even after this "explanation," remaining fairly mysterious and arbitrary practices that seemed to "happen" to Indian women as a result of "Indian culture." This conversation helped me see how conversations describing and distinguishing between institutions and practices that are "culturally unfamiliar" might result, often unintentionally, in an understanding of forms of violence against women "specific" to Third-World contexts as instances of "death by culture."

This conversation also brought home to me the ways in which understandings of issues are shaped by "border-crossings." The conversation illuminated the ways in which recent Indian feminist engagement with the issue of sati seems to have "filtered through" to many members of the American public. It suggested that what often gets edited out when such information engages in "world-traveling" are "facts" well known to many in the Indian context—such as that sati is a virtually extinct practice, that the recent feminist protest was provoked by a single incident and was centrally part of an ongoing political struggle against Hindu fundamentalism. The "information" that does "filter through" into the American context often seems to result merely in a vague awareness that "women are being burned to death every day in India," amalgamating sati to dowry-murders in a construction of "Indian culture" as one beset with a "cultural habit" of burning its women! This Internet conversation thus struck me as capturing both sets of problems pertaining to "understanding issues affecting women in Other cultures" that concern me in this essay.

The first two sections of this essay both explore the ways in which "national contexts" shape feminist issues, and the implications of such shaping for "cross-cultural understanding." The first section of this essay attempts to show how national contexts shape feminist agendas by exploring the differences between the U.S. and Indian feminist agendas around issues of domestic violence. It argues that failures to understand the effects of national contexts on feminist agendas around domestic violence result in failures to connect dowry-murders in India to the general U.S. category of "domestic violence," and in failures to understand the nature of contextual asymmetries in U.S. and Indian feminist engagements with fatal forms of domestic violence.

The second section of the essay attempts to call attention to another, perhaps less obvious, way in which "cross-cultural understanding" of issues is complicated. I wish to argue that the ways in which "issues" emerge in various national contexts, and the contextual factors that shape the specific issues that are named and addressed, *affect the information that is readily available for such connection-making* and hence our abilities to make connections across these contexts. I use the issues of dowry-murders in India and domestic-violence murders in the United States to argue that the project of understanding "cultural similarities and differences" may founder on what phenomena are "visible" and what information is "available" as elements for such "comparative understanding." This section draws attention to the ways in which the very constitution of cultural "similarities'" and "differences" is a politically complicated project.

The third section of the essay explores the effects that traveling across national borders has on the understanding of specific issues. It raises questions about the *sorts* of issues pertaining to Third-World women that predominantly cross national borders, and points to the adverse effects that "decontextualized information" has on the understanding of these issues in Western contexts. While the first two sections argue that failing to understand the effects of national contexts on the construction of feminist issues impedes "cross-cultural understanding," this section argues that information on these issues is significantly "decontextualized" when it crosses borders. It explores the misunderstandings that such decontextualization facilitates, and suggests that problematic "cultural explanations" of culturally alien phenomena are encouraged by such decontextualization.

The last two sections explore "death by culture" and attempt to think critically about *how* "culture" is invoked in accounts of violence against women in Third-World contexts. The fourth section analyzes problematic "cultural explanations" of dowry-murders, showing what is wrong with them and how they perpetuate the tendency to suggest that Third-World women suffer "death by culture." It attempts to outline a different form of explanation for dowry-murders that, while it clearly attends to features of the Indian context, does not suggest that Indian women are "killed by culture." The fifth and final section explores the ways in which domestic-violence murders in the United States seem resistant to problematic "cultural explanations" of the "death by culture" variety. By calling attention to the difficulties in giving "cultural explanations" for violence against mainstream Western women, I attempt to think about the political implications of the fact that "cultural explanations" seem more plausible with respect to violence that affects Third-World women.

There are some important questions that lie beyond the borders of this essay.[4] I focus on only one example of a "border-crossing" issue, namely dowry-murder. I also focus on just one "border" that this issue crosses, attending only to the shaping of this issue in India and to its "reframing" in the United States. While I attend to how the issue emerges in the "general public understanding" that results from its border-crossing into the United States, I do not specifically explore how this impacts on understandings of, and responses to, the issue among members of the diasporic Indian community in the United States. I do not explore how this issue has fared in crossing the borders of other Western nation-states. And while I believe it would be very illuminating to see how particular "Third-World women's issues" are represented in Third World national contexts *other than their own*, and ways in which such border-crossing might be mediated by "Western" and "local" media, I do not attempt to do so in this essay. Another interesting question I do not discuss has to do with the effects of "international circuits of knowledge"—whereby discussion of a Third-World issue in mainstream Western media or scholarship may "travel back" to its original Third-World national context, affecting understandings of, and responses to, the issue in complex ways.

The final limitation of this essay that I would like to mention has to do with the fact that I am focusing on issues crossing national borders. In so doing, I do not examine internal borders between communities within a single nation-state, even though I am aware that such internal borders are often salient to the issues of "cultural explanation" I discuss. To put it bluntly, there is a marked tendency to proffer "cultural explanations" for problems within communities of color within Western contexts more readily than there is to proffer "cultural explanations" for similar problems within mainstream Western communities. For instance, female-headed households, teenage motherhood, and welfare dependency have been attributed to "cultural pathologies" within the African American community,[5] while "white culture" is seldom indicted for these same problems when they occur in white communities.

This essay is strongly motivated by my sense that feminists need to think about the ways in which feminist issues are shaped by national contexts, and further affected by crossing national boundaries and entering the terrain of what Lata Mani calls the "multiple mediations" of an "age of multinational reception."[6] Such issues increasingly cross national borders as a result of at least two different factors. The first is increasing global migration, whereby an issue such as dowry-murder becomes not only an issue for communities in India, but also an issue for immigrant Indian communities in countries such as Britain or the United States. The second is the growing transnational "exchange" of feminist scholarship and information, which seems connected as both cause and effect to increasing academic and pedagogic efforts to "learn about Other cultures" and women's issues within them. While I believe this increasing "multinational reception" of feminist issues is both inevitable and important, these border-crossings are often marked by problematic "mediations." I believe it is important for all feminists to think about the general structures that mediate such "border-crossings" and to critically address the specific problems that arise when particular issues cross particular "borders." This essay is motivated by my belief that transnational cooperation and solidarity among feminists depends on all of us better understanding such issues of "context" and "comparative understanding," as well as on attending to asymmetries in "cultural explanation" that contribute to problematic pictures of "our similarities and differences." I try to address these various issues in a manageable way by talking about dowry-murders in India and about domestic violence in the United States.

Feminist Movements, National Contexts, and the "Making" of Feminist Issues /

The juxtaposition of domestic violence in Western contexts and dowry-murders in India will likely seem odd to some readers, or at least a juxtaposition that is not self-evident. It is precisely the fact that the significance of this juxtaposition will not be self-evident to many that prompts me to start with this "joining together" of two phenomena that are taken by many Westerners to be "unconnected." I know they are often taken to be unconnected because I have had several conversations in which Americans seemed to have been startled by my matter-of-fact claim that dowry-murders are not only often preceded by domestic violence but that they also constitute one extreme form of domestic violence. I no longer make this claim matter-of-factly, since I have become aware of its oddly polemical weight. I have, in turn, been startled by the fact that the proposition that dowry-murders were a form of domestic violence was "news" to members of my audience here. What follows is an attempt to make sense of *why* the connection between dowry-murders and domestic violence is not "visible" to many Americans, as well as an attempt to "make" the connection.

Most Americans that I have talked to about dowry-murder know that many U.S. women are killed by their partners as a result of domestic violence. Given that many members of the U.S. public know that domestic violence has fatal forms, why is it that they make no connection between the "foreign" phenomenon of dowry-murder and the "familiar" phenomenon of domestic violence? What are the difficulties that stand in the way of this connection being made? I believe that part of the answer to this question lies in the ways in which domestic violence agendas have developed in the United States, and their effects on the ways in which the term "domestic violence" is widely understood. Let me explain what I mean.

When I began looking through the articles in my files, and through several books that either wholly or partly address issues of domestic violence in the U.S., I did not come across any book or article that *centrally focused* on U.S. women *murdered* as a result of domestic violence (even though I found a fair amount of writing on legal issues pertaining to women who killed their batterers). In all of the American "domestic-violence" readings I initially went through as I began writing this piece, I found no data about the number of women who are annually *killed* as a result of domestic violence, though I found plenty of other kinds of data on facets of domestic violence such as injuries and homelessness. None of several American feminist friends I called knew off-hand roughly how many women were killed by their partners each year in the United States. Nor could they find this figure easily when they went through their collections of books and articles on the subject. We were all struck by the fact that it was quite difficult for any one of us to find this particular piece of data, and also struck by the degree to which deaths resulting from domestic violence have *not* been much focused upon in U.S. literature on domestic violence.[7] A friend who participated in my search for the numbers of U.S. women annually killed by their partners commented that she was surprised at the difference between the "disappearing dead women" in U.S. accounts of domestic violence and the "spectacular visibility" of women murdered over dowry in India.

Discussions of domestic violence in the U.S. contexts are not lacking in mention of grievous injury to women. Although fatalities are often mentioned along with injuries, most discussions do not centrally focus on the most "extreme cases" where the woman dies as a result of domestic violence. There is a striking contrast between the lack of focus on fatal cases that enters into the construction of the category "domestic violence" in the United States context, and the focus on deadly cases of domestic violence in the Indian context that has given visibility to the category "dowry-murder." I believe that this "asymmetry in focus" contributes to the lack of perceived connection between dowry-murders and domestic violence in the minds of many Americans.

How is this "asymmetry in focus" to be explained? I think these differences in focus are connected to the different ways in which issues of violence against women emerged within, and were taken up by, feminist movements in India and in the United States. In many areas of U.S. feminist effort around domestic violence, such as challenging police nonresponsiveness to domestic-violence complaints, and countering various laws and legal attitudes that trivialized domestic violence or dismissed it as a "private quarrel," there was little reason to single out cases of domestic violence that resulted in death. Rather, the focus was on generating legal and institutional responses that addressed a *wide spectrum* of domestic violence cases, ranging from the fairly minor to the potentially lethal. As a result of U.S. feminist efforts around issues of domestic violence, public attention was certainly drawn to the various ways in which women were often brutally and repeatedly injured in domestic violence attacks, terrorized and stalked, and often additionally endangered if they tried to leave violent relationships. But the bulk of the U.S. feminist responses to domestic violence, quite understandably, seem to have focused on victims who were still alive, who needed either shelters, counseling and assistance, or various forms of legal redress.

While the much publicized trial of O.J. Simpson for his wife's murder has put more of a spotlight on the fact that U.S. women are *killed* as a result of relationships plagued by domestic violence,[8] such deaths have not necessarily been portrayed as the "typical" or "paradigmatic" outcomes of domestic-violence situations. The fact that domestic-violence situations *can* end in death seems to be used as an indicia of its potential seriousness and danger, rather than as an emblem. Let me reiterate that I believe this makes sense, given that there seem few reasons, in the U.S. context, to focus specifically on women *killed* in acts of domestic violence with respect to legal and institutional attempts to address the problem. If anything, feminist efforts on the issue may have had good reason to move in the other direction, away from a focus on domestic-violence-related homicides, since homicides are likely, by dint of their seriousness, to receive police and legal attention where less drastic forms of domestic violence do not. Feminist efforts in the U.S. seem to have moved in the direction of *widening* the scope of what is understood to constitute "domestic violence," pointing out that verbal, emotional, and psychological abuse often constitute components of domestic violence.

If we are to understand the "asymmetry" between feminist engagement with domestic violence in the U.S. and Indian contexts, we also need to understand why the Indian feminist movement focused on domestic violence in the extreme form of "dowry-murder" and did not focus on general issues of domestic violence to the same degree as in the United States. In what follows, I will attempt to provide an answer by giving a brief sketch of the history of contemporary Indian feminist engagement with issues of violence against women. In an article on the Indian women's movement, Mary Fainsod Katzenstein points out that a report on Indian women, commissioned by the government of India in 1974 in anticipation of the International Women's Year declared by the United Nations in 1975, played a "catalytic role in the emergence of the contemporary women's movement in India."[9] Katzenstein adds:

> The report dramatically called attention to existing gender inequality with its documentation of a declining sex ratio (read as an indicator of differential female mortality) and its presentation of evidence of inequalities in education, income, access to health care and political representation. The report galvanized both academics and activists. Not only did it cite patterns of inequality that had not been widely recognized but no less important, the process of preparing the report caused several women members of the commission to redirect their scholarly and activist energies entirely.[10]

Although the report sparked an interest in organizing around gender issues, issues of sexual violence were given little attention at the start, as the movement initially focused largely on economic and demographic issues. Members of committee that wrote the 1974 report have, in retrospect, acknowledged their inattention to issues of violence against women. As one member puts it:

> I realise now that there were other things which we should have investigated. We did not include rape in our inquiry. We took some note of suicides when they were brought to our notice, but no one mentioned a single case of dowry-murder. Harassment, even torture was reported but never a murder. Today I realize that the issue of violence of crimes against women did not feature in our report as we had not investigated it. Even the practice of dowry was not in our initial questionnaire—it was forced on us by the women we met.[11]

However, by the late 1970s issues of violence against women began to move to the forefront of the feminist agenda. Katzenstein remarks that "it was the focus on violence against women, beginning in the late 1970s, that propelled the movement forward and endowed it with much of its strength."[12] The two most "visible" issues initially addressed by women's groups were the issue of dowry-murder and that of rape, especially police rape of poor women held in custody.[13] Many women's groups that addressed the issue of dowry-murders did not address the issue in isolation from the general issue of domestic violence, which was also addressed quite apart from dowry-related contexts. For instance, a number of women's groups addressed wife-beating in the context of male drinking and alcoholism.[14]

Although the issue of dowry-murder was hardly the only issue pertaining to violence against women that was addressed by the Indian women's movement, it has probably had the most widespread impact on public attention in India and received the most sustained media coverage, resulting in dowry-murders being reported in a more ongoing way than many other issues affecting Indian women. I believe that there are a number of reasons for the public attention that dowry-murders have received. While issues such as that of police rape of women in custody primarily affected poorer women, dowry-murders were predominantly a middle-class phenomenon. And although the political energies of the women's movement were crucial in calling a number of issues of violence against women to public attention and to underlining their prevalence, I suspect that issues such as police rape, or domestic violence as a general problem, were not "surprising" to many Indians, while dowry-murders were.

Let me attempt to clarify what I mean by talking about my own experience around these issues. Like many Indians, I was aware of the existence of domestic violence, and of dowry-related harassment of women, long before these became public issues that women's groups organized around. And even before it elicited organized protest, I suspect that there was a fair degree of general awareness that poor and lower-caste women were vulnerable to rape and sexual exploitation. My sense of this is confirmed by one of the members of the commission that wrote the 1974 report on Indian women, who acknowledges retrospective shock at the fact that the commission did not look into the issue of rape, and adds, "I cannot say that I was not aware of rape as an instrument in subjugating the lower classes and lower castes."[15]

In my own case, which I think was not uncharacteristic, one of the two "issues" that I was completely unaware of until they were named, articulated, and publicized by women's groups was the issue of dowry-murder.[16] It took the activism and intervention of women's groups to facilitate the recognition that what lay behind occasional newspaper reports of women dying in "kitchen accidents" or "committing suicide by burning themselves to death" was a quite different and increasing phenomenon—the burning to death of women for dowry-related reasons.

Before women's groups named this issue, demonstrated against it, and drew media attention to it, I believe few Indians were aware that there was a growing pattern of women being burnt to death for dowry-related reasons in "respectable middle-class Indian families." I believe that public unfamiliarity with this issue combined with its heinousness and its predominantly middle-class occurrence to make dowry-murder one of the most publicly visible issues of those addressed by women's groups in India.

There also seem to be contextual reasons as to why some other aspects of domestic violence received less organizational attention and effort from women's groups in India than they did in the United States. A significant proportion of feminist efforts around domestic violence in the United States seems to have focused on publicizing the need for shelters for battered women and in setting up and organizing such shelters. While there have been some attempts by women's groups in India to organize shelters for battered women, there are considerably *fewer* efforts in this direction than has been the case in the United States. Understanding the reasons for this difference is, I think, interesting in its capacity to illuminate the degree to which specific feminist policies and solutions are dependent on the background social, economic, and institutional features of the national landscapes within which feminist groups operate.

Why did organizing battered women's shelters not have a central place in Indian feminist agendas? The answer is not, as some Western feminists seem to have assumed, that the Indian women's movement is "less developed." Madhu Kishwar alludes to these assumptions when she says:

> Over the last decade, innumerable western feminists have asked us: "Do you have battered women's homes in India?" The assumption is that not to have such homes is to be at a lower stage of development in the struggle against violence on women, and that such homes will be one inevitable outcome of the movement's development.[17]

Kishwar goes on to provide a very different kind of account for this difference, pointing to a number of factors that help make battered women's shelters a feasible strategy for affording assistance to battered women in countries like the United States, factors that play out differently in India. Kishwar says:

> Battered women's homes in the west . . . seemed to act as a useful type of short term intervention because of (a) the existence of a welfare system which includes some, even though inadequate, provisions for public assistance, unemployment, benefits, subsidized housing, and free schooling for children; (b) the overall employment situation being very different from that in India; (c) the lower stigma on women living on

their own and moving around on their own; and (d) the existence of certain avenues of employment that are not considered permissible for middle class women here.[18]

Although the situation is far from rosy in countries like the United States, and might conceivably get much worse if current attacks on state provisions such as welfare are successful, it is still feasible for U.S. battered women's shelters to help at least some women leave abusive domestic relationships. Enabling some battered women to secure welfare for themselves or their children, assisting others in securing paid employment, state-funded medical care, and legal aid around custody issues, are all ways in which U.S. battered women's shelters can offer more than temporary refuge. The provision of such services enables at least some women to leave relationships they would not otherwise be in a position to leave. The virtual absence in India of state-provided welfare, education, and medical care, the unavailability of state-provided legal services to deal with custody, and far greater levels of unemployment, render it very difficult for feminists to help generate structures that would enable Indian women to leave the family contexts where they are victims of violence. With the exception of the relatively small group of women who earn enough on their own to support themselves and their children, few women are materially in a position to leave abusive relationships. In addition, as Kishwar suggests, there is much greater stigma in India around issues such as divorce, separation from one's husband, and "women living on their own," factors that might well deter even women who could economically support themselves. Kishwar points out that groups attempting to help battered women often have no resources but to try and persuade the women's marital families to take them back on "slightly improved terms."[19]

In the Indian context, organizing around issues such as shelters for battered women, which require a variety of state and institutional structures that are not readily available, is not highly feasible.[20] In contrast, dowry-murder was an issue around which Indian women's groups *could* effectively organize in a number of ways. Women's groups in India had the resources to publicize cases of dowry-murders and hold public demonstrations and protests, often in the neighborhood where "suspicious burnings" had occurred. Such public efforts to call the phenomenon of dowry-murder to national attention had the important function of alerting Indian families to the potentially lethal situations in which marriage placed some of their daughters. Such efforts also provoked a considerable amount of public "consciousness raising" on the institution of dowry, led to calls for people to pledge not to give or take dowries, and for people to boycott marriages where dowry was involved. Women's groups in India also engaged in pushing for a variety of legal changes that would enable more efficient prosecution of the family members responsible for these murders, and generated debates on possible changes in property and inheritance laws that might ameliorate the problem of dowry-murders.

The preceding account helps explain why general issues of domestic violence have played a bigger role in Western national contexts than in India, and why dowry-murders were the aspect of domestic violence most widely addressed in the Indian context. I believe such explanations are useful in accounting for "asymmetries" in the development of feminist issues in different national contexts. They call attention to economic, social, and institutional features that make certain policies and strategies feasible in some contexts but not in others, features that might be "taken for granted" and remain less visible prior to attempts to account for such differ-ences. They help to make feminists in various national contexts more "contextually self-conscious" about the features of their national landscapes that might shape their engagements with issues of violence against women, and help clarify why "similar problems" might sometimes not permit "similar answers."

The preceding analysis helps call attention to some of the complexities inherent in the project of "learning about issues of women in Other cultures." It challenges the unreflective and naively optimistic view that sees this project primarily in terms of "information retrieval"—as a simple matter of acquiring information and learning "the facts" that illuminate these "problems of women in Other cultures," and then perhaps going on to understand our "commonalities and differences." It suggests that we need to understand the ways in which feminist agendas are shaped by the different conditions that obtain within different national contexts if we are to understand the connections between the "visibility" of dowry-murders in India and the relative "invisibility" of the issue of domestic-violence murder in the United States.

In the absence of such an understanding, it is not surprising that many Americans fail to connect the unfamiliar phenomenon of dowry-murder to the more familiar category of "domestic violence." I have suggested that there were good reasons for feminist organizations in the United States not focusing on domestic-violence fatalities, and good reasons for feminist organizations in India devoting a fair amount of organizational and public effort to the fatal form of domestic violence that is dowry-murder. One "effect" of these contextual differences is that there is a *visible category* of "dowry-murder" that picks out a lethal form of domestic violence in the Indian context, while there is no similar, readily available category that specifically picks out *lethal instances* of domestic violence in the United States. In contrast to "dowry-murder," *fatal* forms of domestic violence in the United States are a problem lacking a term that "specifically picks them out" from the general category of "domestic violence." I believe that this "absence" operates to impede Americans from making the connections that would facilitate their seeing dowry-murder as a form of domestic violence.

The Effects of "Absences" on Projects of Cross-Cultural Understanding /

The preceding analysis suggests that the project of "understanding Other cultures" is made difficult by the problems one often has in "seeing" features of one's "own context" that might be relevant to this project, features that might make a difference to the sense of "similarities and differences" one develops. I think it is quite difficult to "notice" that a term like "domestic-violence murders" is "absent" in the U.S. context, and to perceive how this "lack" contributes to the phenomenon lacking specificity of a sort it might have had if a term had "picked it out" and made the underlying issue the focused subject of public and political concern. The absence in the U.S. context of a term such as "domestic-violence murders," and the lack of focus on this issue in U.S. feminist agendas on domestic violence, only forcibly struck me when I began working on this essay. I believe that the effects of this "absence" go beyond its functioning as an impediment to many Americans making connections between dowry-murders and domestic violence. I would like, in this section, to go on to explore some of the less obvious ways in which this absence works to complicate "cross-cultural understanding" of "similarities and differences" between forms of violence that affect women in Third-World nations and violence against women in Western national contexts.

One of the things I hoped to do when I began this essay was to work on making a stronger connection between Indian dowry-deaths and domestic violence in the United States by comparing the number of women annually killed in dowry-murders in India to the numbers of U.S. women annually killed by their partners. I wanted to make this comparison to see if data would support my suspicion that the incidence of "domestic-violence murders" in the United States was "numerically similar" to the incidence of dowry-murders in India. If I found the incidence of the two phenomena to be "numerically similar," I hoped to argue that, given their relatively equal seriousness as "social problems," it was even more interesting that one phenomenon had a specific name and activist focus and that the other did not. What I completely failed to realize was the degree to which the absence of a term that conferred "specificity" on the phenomenon of "domestic-violence murders" in the United States would affect my very attempt to make this comparison. Let me clarify what I mean.

Setting out on this task, I found it easy to locate recent data on the annual numbers of dowry-murders in India. I discovered the numbers quickly after I started looking, and came across them fairly often. I even found tabulated data on dowry-murders, assembled by the National Crimes Bureau of the Government of India, that not only had figures for the years 1987 to 1994 but also showed the geographical distribution of dowry-murders across various regional states within India. The recent numbers suggest that roughly 5,000 Indian women are killed each year over dowry. On the other hand, in noticeable contrast to information on domestic violence in the United States, I discovered very little national data on other aspects of domestic violence in India. This is not surprising given the lack of infrastructures such as shelters that facilitate in the gathering of such data in the U.S. As a result, I did not find national data on the general incidence of domestic violence, on the numbers of women seriously injured in such incidents, or on how many Indian women are believed to be killed annually for *non-dowry-related* reasons. The conclusion I arrived at was that the construction of "dowry-murder" as a specific public issue had had institutional effects, such as the generation of "official national data" on the phenomenon. On the other hand, the contextual features that work in India to make general issues of "domestic violence" much harder to address institutionally also impede the ability to generate "official data" on the broader facets of domestic violence. One result is that it is easy to find Indian figures for "dowry-murders" but not for the presumably wider category "domestic-violence murders."

Moving on to the "other side" of my attempted comparison, finding the statistics for "domestic-violence murders" in the U.S. was not easy, as I have previously mentioned. In many of the places I searched for this figure, I found a good deal of data on numerous aspects of domestic violence, but not the particular figure for "domestic-violence murders" that I was looking for. There was readily available data on the overall annual number of domestic-violence cases, on the numbers of battered women seeking assistance from shelters, on the numbers of women seriously injured as a result of domestic violence, and on the numbers of women and children who were homeless as a result of domestic violence, but it was difficult to locate the U.S. figure for "domestic-violence murders." I came to the conclusion that the same lack of organizational focus on "domestic-violence murders" that leaves it a "phenomenon with no specific name" in the U.S. also works to make it a phenomenon that is not focused on widely in fact sheets and other public information on domestic violence.

In my search, I first arrived at a "ball-park figure" for U.S. "domestic-violence murders" indirectly rather than finding the figure stated outright. I worked it out through looking at the FBI's Crime Index, which reports the overall number of U.S. homicides for 1994, and states that 79 percent of murder victims were men. I worked out that the 21 percent of murder victims who were women came to roughly 5,000 women. The FBI statistics also said that 28 percent of female murder victims were "slain by husbands or boyfriends," although they did not go on to specify the number.[21] I worked out from the figures that roughly 1,400 U.S. women annually were victims of "domestic-violence murder." When I did begin to find direct information on "domestic-violence deaths" in other sources, the numbers I found varied quite widely.[22]

I decided to work with the FBI figure, a figure eventually confirmed by a couple of other sources, that suggested that roughly 1,400 U.S. women annually were victims of "domestic-violence murder."[23] However, I began to realize that there were all sorts of problems in attempting what I wished to do next—which was to argue for the "comparative numerical seriousness" of U.S. "domestic-violence murders" and Indian dowry-murders. The most obvious problem was that the Indian figures available were for the *narrower* category of "dowry-murder" and not for "domestic-violence murders in India," while the U.S. figures I had worked out were for the *inclusive* category of "domestic-violence murders." However, on closer examination, it also turned out that the scope of the U.S. figure for "domestic-violence murders" might be, in another respect, *narrower* than the scope of the Indian figures for "dowry-murders."

The Indian statistics on dowry-murders, including those put out by the government of India, reflect the number of deaths *suspected* to be dowry-murders, rather than those that have been "proven" to be dowry-murders through the criminal justice process. The "official definition" of a dowry-murder is "any instance where the death of a woman is caused by any burns or bodily injury or occurs otherwise than under normal circumstances within 7 years of her marriage, and it is shown that soon before her death she was subjected to cruelty or harassment by her husband or any relative of her husband for, or in connection with, any demand for dowry."[24] Some of the incidents that are counted as "dowry-murders" might in fact be the "accidents" or "suicides" or "illnesses" they are inevitably claimed to be, though there is no real way of telling how many. There are also likely to be a number of dowry-murders that do not evoke "suspicion" and fail to be counted in the statistics on dowry-murders, though again it is impossible to know how many.

On the other hand, the U.S. FBI statistics on "domestic-violence murders," I believe, reflect only those cases where the partner is *convicted* of the crime.[25] I found out, in addition, that roughly 40 percent of all U.S.

homicide cases remained legally "unsolved," though I did not find any data that specified the percentage of murders involving female victims that remained unsolved. One problem, then, with trying to argue that U.S. "domestic-violence murders" are comparatively as "numerically serious" as dowry-murders in India is that the Indian figures seem to reflect "suspicions" rather than "legal convictions," while the U.S. figures seem to reflect the opposite. While the activism around dowry-murders in India has undoubtedly contributed to the collection of official national data on "suspected dowry-murders," it might well be that the lack of focus on "domestic-violence murders" in the United States has resulted in there being no widely available official data on *suspected* domestic-violence murders, even though domestic-violence activism might well account for FBI statistics now specifying how many female homicides resulted in the convictions of the women's partners.

I am arguing that the complicated factors that have shaped different national agendas on issues of domestic violence seem to exert a considerable amount of influence on the kinds of "official data" that are generated on various aspects of the phenomenon. Given that very different kinds of domestic-violence data seem to be available in the Indian and U.S. contexts, any attempts to "compare" the figures on "domestic-violence murders in the U.S." and "dowry-murders in India" more than hint at comparing apples and oranges. However, working on the principle that there may be a point to comparing apples and oranges if one is interested in understanding some aspects of fruit, I will press on with the "comparison."

The population of India is roughly four times that of the United States. Given that roughly 1,400 U.S. women annually are (known to be) victims of "domestic-violence murder" and that roughly 5,000 Indian women annually are (suspected to be) victims of dowry-murders, it seems as if one could at least safely say that the proportion of the women in the U.S. population who are victims of "domestic-violence murder" seems *roughly similar* to the proportion of women in the Indian population murdered over dowry. These figures at least make plausible the claim that "death by domestic violence" in the U.S. seems to be numerically as significant a social problem as "dowry-murders" are in India. Given that roughly the same proportion of women in the U.S. population are possible victims of "domestic-violence murder" as women in the Indian population are possible victims of "dowry-murder," it is interesting that one of these phenomena is named, noted, and made into a "specific social issue" while the other is not.

I have already given an account of the reasons that may have shaped the U.S. domestic-violence agenda away from a focus on fatalities, and of the factors that led to the Indian feminist focus on dowry-murders. What

I have pointed out in this section is how different kinds of "focus" and "lacks of focus" on various aspects of domestic violence in India and the United States also shape the kinds of data that are readily available in the two contexts. Such differences of data as well as "absences of data" are, by their nature, difficult to see and to make sense of. However, the ability to see them and make sense of them seems to me to be crucial to attempts to better understand "similarities and differences" between problems women confront in different national contexts.

Border-Crossings, Lacks of Context, and the Construction of "Death by Culture" /

My previous analysis pointed to how some of the ways in which issues are "shaped" within different national contexts might affect the project of "cross-cultural understanding." In this section, I will attempt to explore the effects of "border-crossings" on issues affecting Third-World women, and the distortions that accompany such issues in their travels across national borders. I believe that Western feminists interested in the "problems of women in Other cultures" need to think about: (1) the kinds of Third-World women's issues that cross Western borders more frequently than others; and about (2) the effects of the "editing" and "re-framing" such issues undergo when they do cross borders. I will try to address these issues by focusing on dowry-murder.

In thinking about issues of "violence against Third-World women" that "cross borders" into Western national contexts, it strikes me that phenomena that seem "Different," "Alien," and "Other" cross these borders with considerably more frequency than problems that seem "similar" to those that affect mainstream Western women. Thus, clitorodectomy and infibulation have become virtually an "icon" of "African women's problems" in Western contexts, while a host of other "more familiar" problems that different groups of African women face are held up at the border. In a similar vein, the abandonment and infanticide of female infants appears to be the one gender issue pertaining to China that receives coverage. These issues then become "common topics" for academics and feminists, and also cross over to a larger public audience that becomes "familiar" with these issues. It is difficult not to conclude that there is a premium on "Third-World difference" that results in greater interest being accorded those issues that seem strikingly "different" from those affecting mainstream Western women. The issues that "cross borders" then become the "Third-World gender issues" that are taught about and studied "across the border," reinforcing their "iconic" and "representative" status as issues.

My analysis in the first section of this essay suggested that the issue of dowry-murder has "crossed Western borders" in part because this issue occupied an early and visible place on the agendas of Indian women's groups and remains an ongoing Indian feminist issue today. While that *is* part of the explanation, I believe it can only be a very *partial explanation*, since many other issues that have received sustained attention from Indian women's groups have not acquired the same sort of "familiarity" to many Westerners. Thus, I believe that features of dowry-murder that mark it as "Other" also partly account for its "border-crossing." These features of "Otherness" simultaneously operate to cause the phenomenon to receive "notice" and to distort understandings of the phenomenon.

One factor that I believe helps dowry-murders receive Western attention is the history of Western fascination with "the Indian tradition" of *sati* or widow-immolation. This historic association of *sati* and "Indian culture" and "Indian women" results today in a metonymic blurring of *sati* with dowry-murder, generating a confused composite of "burnt Indian women" variously going up in flames as a result of "their Culture." "Women being burnt" thus becomes constituted as a "paradigmatic," "iconic," and "familiar" form of "violence suffered by Indian women." The terms "*sati*" and "dowry-murder" come to have a vaguely familiar ring, even though their exact referents are often not well understood. What is "understood," however, is their "Indianness," their status as "things that happen elsewhere," which in turn suggests that they are unlike "things that happen here."

This effect is only compounded by the fact that there is little "coverage" or information in the United States about the general issue of domestic violence as it affects women in India, and by the fact that reports about dowry-deaths are seldom framed in terms of the general issue of domestic violence.[26] Given that dowry-related domestic *harassment* is far more widespread in India than dowry-*murder*, and that non-dowry-related forms of domestic violence are likely the most widespread of all, this focus on dowry-murders as a paradigmatic case of "violence suffered by Indian women" is one that centers on the most "extreme" and "spectacular" forms of domestic violence suffered by Indian women. Domestic violence against Indian women thus becomes most widely known in Western contexts in its most *extreme incarnation*, underlining its "Otherness."

The "alien" features of "burning" and "dowry" help to further code the phenomenon as "Indian" and "Other" and intersect to expunge any trace of the phenomenon's connection to the more "familiar" domestic category of "domestic violence." Consider the possible effects on Western understandings of dowry-murder of the "lurid exoticism" of fire and of women being burnt to death. Given the lack of contextual information, Indian women's murder-by-fire seems mysterious, possibly ritualistic, and one of those factors that is assumed to have something to do with "Indian culture." While the use of fire as the preferred instrument of dowry-murder does have much to do with details of the Indian context, these details are less "cultural" and "exotic," and more mundane and material, than they are often assumed to be.

Pointing out that fire is chiefly chosen for "the forensic advantage" it has over other methods of killing a wife, Veena Talwar Oldenburg goes on to say:

> It virtually destroys the evidence of murder along with the victim and can easily be made to look like an accident. It is also relatively simple to commit. It occurs in the kitchen, where the middle-class housewife spends a large amount of time each day. Pressurized kerosene stoves are in common use in such homes; a tin of fuel is always kept in reserve. This can be quickly poured over the intended victim and a lighted match will do the rest. It is easy to pass off the event as an accident because these stoves are prone to explode (consumer reports confirm this), and the now ubiquitous but highly inflammable nylon sari easily catches fire and engulfs the wearer in flames. Signs of a struggle simply do not show up on bodies with 90 or more percent third-degree burns.[27]

Oldenburg's account underlines the fact that the use of fire as a murder weapon is far more a matter of expedience than it is a matter of exoticism. Burning a woman to death in the Indian context is no more "exotic" than shooting her to death is in the U.S. context. Conversely, death by shooting in a middle-class domestic context would be rather "exotic" in India, where firearms are not freely available and widely owned, and where widespread ownership of firearms and the prevalence of gun-related violence is often perceived of as "typically American."

I believe that the "exoticizing" features I have mentioned above have both contributed to dowry-murder's popularity as a border-crossing issue and have contributed to popular misunderstandings of the issue. In addition, I also believe that such misunderstandings are facilitated by the fact that certain kinds of "contextual information" are often left behind when issues cross national borders. For example, many Indians have sufficient "contextual information" to know that dowry-murders are just one extreme and specific form of domestic violence directed against Indian women. They are likely to know that mistreatment and harassment of Indian daughters-in-law by their marital families is widespread, that many women are harassed over dowry-related reasons even when they are not murdered, and that Indian women are also abused and mistreated for a range of reasons that have nothing to do with dowry. They are also likely to know that dowry-murders seem to be a fairly *recent* phenomenon that seem to have come into "systematic" existence in the last three decades, and that seem to be on the increase.

When the issue of dowry-murders "crosses national borders" and becomes "known" in Western national contexts as an "issue affecting Indian women," it becomes known "out of context" because many Westerners lack these forms of "contextual information." In traveling across national borders unaccompanied by such contextual information, "dowry-murder" loses its links to the category of "domestic violence" and becomes transmuted into some sort of bizarre "Indian ritual," a form of violence against women that surely must be "caused by Indian culture." The category "Indian culture" then becomes the diffuse culprit responsible for "women being burned to death everyday in India," producing the effect that I call "death by culture."

My analysis suggests that a variety of factors, ranging from the innocuous to the problematic, work together to engender distortions and misrepresentations as "Third-World women's issues" travel across Western national borders. It is understandable for Western media to report on social issues that are receiving attention in other national contexts. But the sorts of contextual information that get "left out" in this process often leave the issue vulnerable to misrepresentation. Cultural and ethnic stereotypes, as well as prevalent limitations in Western understandings of Third-World communities, then add to the ways in which the issue is misframed and misunderstood.

There is often no vantage point from which many members of the American public can "see" some of these factors that contribute to information distortion. To understand, for instance, the different ways in which feminist agendas have shaped the issue of domestic violence in the U.S. and Indian contexts would require historical and political knowledge about India and the Indian women's movement, which is often precisely the kind of knowledge that does not readily travel across borders. The fact that Western reports on "Third-World issues" often refer to these issues being matters of public concern and political engagement within Third-World nations often only serves to enhance these issues' status as "authentic Third-World issues." Thus, "Women are burned to death everyday in India, victims of their culture" appears to Western audiences as simple, solid, incontrovertible information, whereby the real *factual weight* of Indian women being murdered for dowry operates to eclipse critical attention to the ways in which the border-crossing information on the issue is *framed*.

While the factual weight of the information testifies to the "reality of the problem," the references to "culture" commonplace in these reports serves to "render intelligible" everything that might otherwise remain "puzzling" to the audience. Thus, while many Western readers might not know exactly what dowry is, or the factors that lead to dowry-murders, or the exact nature of the relationship of either dowry or dowry-murder to "Indian culture," the presence of references to "Indian culture" can provide a swift and convenient "explanation" for what they do not understand. The references to "culture" in these reports can then combine with more "free-floating" ideas of "Third-World backwardness" and the tendency to think of Third-World contexts as realms of "Very Other Cultures" to make "foreign phenomenon" seem comfortingly intelligible while preserving their "foreignness." Members of the Western audience are often left "feeling solidly informed," with nothing "in the picture" that suggests any need to re-examine the picture.

I am suggesting that the "distortions" that occur when "Third-World issues" cross over into Western national contexts are not reducible to "ethnocentrism" or "racism." While forms of ethnocentric and stereotypic thinking about "the Third World" do play a part in the perpetuation of such "distortions," there are also other different factors at work. One has to attend to the "multiple mediations" that occur between: (1) the ways in which "related" issues have been shaped in Western national contexts; (2) the "life" these issues have in Third-World national contexts, where their coverage and reception occur in a space where members of the national public have a variety of contextual information that puts such issues "in perspective"; and (3) the decontextualization and recontextualization that accompanies these issues on their travels across national borders.

Critical attention to the complexities of the "multiple mediations" that work to "shape" issues in different national contexts, and to "filter" the information that crosses national borders, is vital to all of us who are participants in the project of making both academic curricula and feminist agendas more responsive to "Third-World issues" or problems affecting "Other women." Multicultural education cannot be seen as a simple task of replacing "ignorance about Other cultures" with "knowledge," since problems of the sort I am talking about are precisely not problems of "ignorance" *per se*, but problems related to understanding the "effects" of contexts on issues, and of decontextualized, refracted, and reframed "knowledge." These features of "context" as well as of decontextualization and refraction are, by their very nature, difficult to see and to call attention to, as are their "effects."

Such difficulties complicate the project of "understanding Other cultures." I would like to insist that they cannot be "solved" by simply "deploying" Third-World subjects familiar with the articulation of these issues in specific Third-World contexts to "point out" the distortions and problems that occur as a result of these border-crossing "mediations." While Third-World subjects who are familiar with the representations of an issue in both a Third-World and a Western national context might well have a sense of some of the distortions and misrepresentations that occur as a result of "border-crossing," it is hardly *easy* for them to develop a fine-grained sense of the ways in which various "mediations" on particular issues collaborate and cohere to create the widely shared misunderstandings that shape the understanding of the issue in a Western national context.

It has not been a simple task for me to figure out exactly what many Americans "don't seem to get" about dowry-murders, or the structures that might facilitate such "not getting." And this sort of task of "figuring out" what isn't "getting across" seems inevitably a messy, provisional, and uncertain business. One relies on particular encounters and conversations, the impressions and hunches one develops as a result, and a strange assortment of information, impression, and speculation. And, as I mentioned earlier, there is a variety of difficulties in trying to figure out how to "get across" what particular individuals may not "be getting." In short, I am fairly pessimistic about any "quick fixes" for these sorts of problems of informational "border-crossings."

Dowry-Murders and the Limits and Limitations of "Cultural" Explanations /

In this section, I would like to move on to exploring the ways in which "culture" is deployed in explanations of dowry-murders in India and to point out the problems with some of these attempts at "cultural explanation." In doing so, I wish to lead up to thinking about why "Indian culture" is invoked in explanations for dowry-murders in ways in which "American culture" is not usually invoked in explanations for either U.S. domestic violence, in general, or for "domestic-violence murders" in the United States.

What I am calling "cultural explanations" of dowry-murders all too frequently invoke "Hindu religious views on women." I shall begin with an example that helps vividly underline what is problematic about such religious "cultural explanations" of dowry-murder. The example I shall use is a chapter from Elizabeth Bumiller's book, *May You Be the Mother of a Hundred Sons: A Journey Among the Women of India*. I choose this example not because this text is uniquely problematic, but because this is a book whose covers carry glowing review blurbs from *Newsweek*, *The New York Times Book Review*, and the *Philadelphia Inquirer*, all indicating that the book was a "national bestseller." It is a book I have seen in several bookstores, including the bookstore of the college where I teach, and it is a book that a friend of Indian background reports having several copies of, presented to her by friends. In short, I pick it only because it seems to have had a more significant public presence and influence than most "academic" writing, and not because there are no "scholarly" examples of these same problems.

The third chapter in Bumiller's book is (alas all too predictably) entitled "Flames: A Bride Burning and a *Sati*." Opening with the line, "When Hindus look at fire, they see many things beyond flames," Bumiller's first paragraph goes on to describe the use of fire in several Hindu ceremonies and rites of passage.[28] The second paragraph opens with the line, "Fire is also a special presence in the lives of Hindu women" and launches into a narration of the mythological story of Sita throwing herself into a fire to prove her chastity to her husband Rama, in the Hindu epic the *Ramayana*, a story that is continued and concluded in the third paragraph.[29]

The fourth paragraph goes on to say:

> Sita's ordeal has left an indelible mark on the relationship of women to fire, which remains a major feature of their spiritual lives, a cause of their death and a symbol, in the end, of one of the most shocking forms of oppression. What follows is the story of two Indian women, Surinder Kaur and Roop Kanwar, both of them victims of fire and Hindu tradition.[30]

Let me briefly point to several problems with this "framing" of Bumiller's chapter. The mythological story of Sita, which has occupied two paragraphs, is a story about Sita *proving her chastity through an ordeal by fire*, and its deployment in this chapter is completely gratuitous, given that the Sita story is an instance of neither *sati* nor dowry-murder. Further, given that one of the two Indian women mentioned in the quote above, Roop Kanwar, was a victim of *sati*, and that the other, Surinder Kaur, is a survivor of an attempted *dowry-murder*, they are hardly victims of "one" form of oppression, as Bumiller claims. Bumiller's failure to make a clear distinction between *sati* and dowry-murder operates as yet one more example of the tedious "metonymic blurring" of completely unrelated phenomena having to do with "burning Indian women" I have previously discussed, a blurring whose ubiquitousness accounts for the headache that sets in when I read essays that start with sentences like "Women are being burnt to death everyday in India."

Bumiller also characterizes both women as "victims of Hindu tradition," a characterization that creates different kinds of problems with respect to *sati* and to dowry-murder. *Sati*, the immolation of a widow on her husband's funeral pyre, used to be a "traditional practice" in *some* Indian communities, and was the "exceptional" rather than the "routine" fate of widows even in these communities. Its endorsement by "Hinduism" has been a matter of debate for centuries, and incidents of *sati* have occurred only very rarely in the last half-century. Bumiller terms *sati* a "Hindu tradition" without specifying its contested and tenuous status qua "Hindu tradition," and her subsequent discussion of feminist protests triggered by the Roop Kanwar incident fails to emphasize the degree to which *sati*'s alleged status as a "Hindu tradition" was itself an important site of feminist contestation. Dowry-murder is, in contrast, neither Hindu nor a tradition, even in the "qualified" sense in which *sati* might be so characterized. Even in cases where it is Hindu women who are murdered for dowry, Hinduism neither endorses or condones such murders, allusions to Sita notwithstanding. Dowry-murder can hardly amount to the victimization of Indian women by "Hindu tradition" when there is no such tradition of burning women to death for dowry. In addition, the institution of dowry is not a Hindu institution in at least two important ways. Dowry is not a pan-Hindu practice, given that there are Hindu communities, such as the matrilineal Nair community of Kerala, where dowry was traditionally unknown. It is also a practice that exists within some non-Hindu Indian communities, as Surinder Kaur's case reveals.

Surinder Kaur, who is first invoked by Bumiller as a woman who survived an alleged attempted burning by her husband and sister-in-law, is a Sikh, and not a Hindu. While Bumiller mentions that Surinder Kaur is a Sikh, in the very next paragraph and several times later in the chapter, she seems not to notice its implications. None of the fire-related Hindu ceremonies and rituals that Bumiller thinks testify to the "special relationship" that Hindus and Hindu women have to fire, nor the Hindu mythological story of Sita that Bumiller uses to frame her discussion, are related to Surinder Kaur's own religious background. While Surinder Kaur may have been the victim of fire, she could hardly have been the victim of a Hindu tradition as Bumiller insists, given that she is a Sikh! Few Western readers are likely to unravel themselves from the trail of confusion whereby, in two pages, references to Hindu ceremonies, Sita, and *sati* collaborate to construct dowry-murder as "Indian women's victimization by Hindu tradition" to register the oddity of a Sikh woman being victimized by Hindu tradition, or to register the fact that dowry-murder is neither Hindu nor a tradition!

Quite apart from Bumiller's chapter, I would argue that references to Hindu religion, mythology, and "tradition" make very poor explanations for dowry-murders, since dowry-murders have not been a widespread social phenomenon before the late 1970s. Hindu myths and traditions have been around considerably longer. It is therefore hard to see that they have serious explanatory value with respect to the contemporary phenomenon of dowry-murders. Notwithstanding the contemporary nature of dowry-murders, many discussions on the subject besides Bumiller's tend to be replete with references to Hindu mythology and to texts such as the *Vedas* and the Laws of Manu, which are separated by centuries from the problem they are used to "explain."[31] The tendency to explain contemporary Indian women's problems by reference to religious views is by no means a tendency exclusive to Western writers, but crops up quite frequently in writings by contemporary Indians. In a context where she is talking about both dowry and dowry-murders, Sushila Mehta asserts, "If the scriptures propound that a woman is a man's property, it is axiomatic that a woman has less value than a man. To compensate she must, therefore, bring something of value along with herself for her husband and his people taking the trouble of marrying her!"[32]

Mehta's discussion exemplifies a common tendency to muddle together discussions of dowry (a traditional practice in some Indian communities) with discussions of dowry-murders (neither a traditional practice nor a historical phenomenon of long standing.) Such muddling frequently results in a failure to register that what the scriptures propound may have little explanatory power with respect to the more contemporary of the two phenomenon, dowry-murders, even where they have some connection to the traditional practice of dowry. (I also believe that Mehta misrepresents the institution of dowry, a point I will return to.) I wish to argue that Mehta's discussion is only a very mild example of a "problematic genre" of work on India and Indian culture, written by Indians. Such work frequently equates Indian culture to Hindu culture, Hindu culture to Hindu religious views, and Hindu religious views to views propounded in various Hindu scriptures, without any registering of how extremely problematic every step in this equation is.[33]

I believe that the historical genealogy of these several equations lies in the pictures of "Indian culture" generated by both British colonial and Indian nationalist writings of the nineteenth century. Failures to be self-conscious about the existence of such problematic "genres of writing" often result in less-than-lucid explanations of contemporary Third-World problems and institutions by Third-World subjects themselves. In addition, failing to be aware of the existence of such problematic modes of writing about "Third-World cultures" by "native subjects" is an additional handicap to the project of mainstream Westerners "understanding Other cultures" given that such writing then tends to be uncritically quoted, referenced, and "assimilated" by some Western scholars.

Given that dowry-murders are a *contemporary* phenomenon, it seems fairly obvious that explanations for the phenomenon must be sought in the ways in which the "traditional institution of dowry" has changed in recent times. Invoking the "Indian tradition of dowry" does not by itself provide a plausible explanation for dowry-murder, since the "tradition of dowry" has been around a great deal longer than have dowry-murders. I believe that a plausible explanation for dowry-murders must refer to the significant changes that the institution of dowry has undergone in recent decades, changes that have rendered it murderous.

Let me suggest a brief sketch of what this sort of explanation might amount to. I will begin by setting out what appear to be the three major explanations of the traditional institution of dowry: dowry as "gift," dowry as "compensation," and dowry as "premortem inheritance." The first explanation regards dowry as the material accompaniments of the symbolic "supergift" of the virgin daughter in marriage *(Kanyadaan)*, where the giving of these conjoined "gifts" is read as an attempt to convert material wealth into spiritual wealth.[34] The explanations of dowry as "compensation" either take an "economic" form, explaining dowry as compensation paid to the groom's family for taking on the economic burden of a wife whose contribution to the family income is negligible,[35] or a "religious" form, such as is found in Mehta's view of dowry as an institution that compensates a man and his family for marrying a creature to whom the scriptures have assigned "less intrinsic value."[36] The third explanation sees dowry as a form of premortem inheritance, reflecting daughters' rights to a share of family property.

Leaving aside the question of whether any of these three explanations adequately accounts for the traditional institution of dowry,[37] I will argue that none of these explanations seem to account for important features of the contemporary institution of dowry. In contemporary dowry, there seems to be little sense of attempting to "convert material wealth into spiritual wealth." The "satisfactions" provided by the contemporary giving of dowry seem entirely "this-wordly"—such as maintaining the family's social standing and securing a "good match" for one's daughter. Views of dowry as "economic compensation" fail to account for the fact that daughters with professional qualifications and jobs are not exempt from expectations that their family will provide dowry on the occasion of their marriage. Mehta's view of dowry as "compensation" for women's scripturally assigned inferiority cannot account for changes in contemporary dowry, since the scriptural views are not of recent vintage, while the changes in dowry are.

I find the explanation of dowry as a form of premortem inheritance that gives daughters a share of family property to be the most plausible explanation of dowry, both traditional and contemporary, even as I think it is only a *partial* account. This explanation regards dowry as an institution that gave daughters a share of the paternal estate at the time of their marriage in the form of "movable property" consisting of gold jewelry and household items, while it simultaneously foreclosed them from inheriting "immovable property" such as land. Oldenburg endorses the view that traditional dowry was a form of premortem inheritance, adding:

> In the late nineteenth and early twentieth century, dowry was not the
> enemy but rather an ally of women, acting as an economic safety net in
> a setting where women always married outside their natal villages . . .
> and where they did not normally inherit land . . . the resources that
> were given to women were substantially under their direct control. . . .
> The dowry was the only independent material resource over which
> women had partial, if not total, control.[38]

I think the view of traditional dowry as premortem inheritance is only
a *partial* explanation, since it accounts for what was given to the woman,
but does not account for that part of dowry that consisted of gifts to members of the groom's family. And while I believe Oldenburg is correct in
pointing out that significant components of traditional dowry remained
substantially under the control of women, it was also not property that
was theirs to alienate or dispose of *at will*. There were strong normative
expectations that women preserve their dowry assets such as jewelry for
their own daughters' dowries, and that such assets not be alienated except
in case of serious financial emergencies.

I would like to briefly mention a number of changes that the institution
of dowry has undergone as it has come to exist within an increasingly
market-dominated modern economy and become increasingly "commercialized." Where dowry used to be something whose components and
worth were largely left to the discretion of the woman's parents and their
own sense of their social status, these components are increasingly matters of *explicit bargaining* by the parents of bridegrooms.[39] Traditional
dowry consisted of three broad sorts of components—clothes and household items for the use of the daughter, household items for the *common
use* of the household into which the daughter married, and assets mostly
in the form of gold jewelry that belonged exclusively to the daughter.
Contemporary "demands" for the latter two components of dowry have
escalated due to the emergence of "dowry-bargaining." A huge array of
consumer items, ranging from televisions and refrigerators to scooters
and cars, items that are significantly expensive in the middle-class Indian
context, are increasingly "expected" to be among the items the bride
"contributes to the husband's household." Demands for large amounts
of expensive jewelry and, increasingly, large sums of outright cash, are
part of the new "commercial face" of dowry.[40] If cash is given, it seldom
remains in the daughter's control. The jewelry component of dowry,
which traditionally used to be understood to be something the daughter
retained control of, to be sold only in dire emergencies, now functions
virtually as another form of cash, often taken away from the woman with
little say-so. Paradoxically, the cash and gold jewelry in women's dowries
seem to have become a more "versatile" form of capital than the land and

immovable properties traditionally inherited by men. Gold jewelry can often be more easily converted to cash than land, and gold and cash can be more expeditiously used as collateral for commercial or agriculture-related loans and mortgages, providing a variety of "new" reasons for expropriating them from the women who receive them as dowry. In short, as dowry has become "commercialized," both traditional norms pertaining to women retaining control over their dowry assets, and norms that prescribed that these assets be alienated only in financial emergencies, seem to have significantly eroded.

In addition, where dowry traditionally used to be more or less a "one-shot deal," it seems to be changing into something more like "dowry on the installment plan." Demands for goods and cash nowadays seem to continue for several years after the marriage has taken place, the wife's harassment providing her with an "incentive" to pressure her parents to meet continuing dowry demands by her husband and in-laws. Families that are under pressure to provide large dowries for the marriages of their own daughters have additional incentives to "exploit the daughter-in-law," since the cash and jewelry they obtain from her parents could be used as components for the dowries of their own daughters. If a woman's parents are unwilling or unable to meet these ongoing demands, the woman's "utility" is reduced, making it expeditious to murder her. I am arguing that dowry-murders are, in large measure, the killing of women for outright economic gain. Having expropriated as much money and material goods as they can from the woman's parents, the husband and his family murder the daughter-in-law to facilitate the son remarrying and securing yet another dowry.

The sort of explanation for dowry-murders I have sketched refers to the "traditional institution" of dowry, but recognizes that the changing modern context of this institution must help account for its contemporary murderous effects. While it makes reference to several features of the Indian context, it is not a "cultural explanation" of the sort that alludes to Hinduism, Sita, *sati*, or the Laws of Manu, none of which strike me as adding illumination to the sort of explanation I have offered. I can therefore only note with irritation the tendency of many discussions of dowry-murders, both by Westerners and Indians, to be sprinkled with such "religio-cultural explanations" *even when they go on to also provide the sorts of social and economic explanations* I have sketched. There seems to be a fairly widespread tendency in discussions of "Third-World issues" to engage in what I increasingly think of as a "schizophrenic analysis," where religious and mythological "explanations" must be woven in willy-nilly, even if they do no real "explanatory work."

It is precisely this sort of "schizophrenic analysis" that enables Bumiller to start her chapter with a disquisition about the special relationship that Hindus and Hindu women have to fire, while acknowledging a few pages later the mundane material reasons for the choice of fire as a means of dowry-murder. Later in the same chapter Bumiller suggests an understanding similar to Oldenburg's when she says:

> Bride burning is also grimly expedient . . . kerosene exists in every Indian household and rarely leaves a trail of sold evidence. Prosecutors find it hard to disprove the usual argument made by the in-laws, who testify that the burning was a stove accident or a suicide. Since it has taken place behind closed doors, there are no witnesses.[41]

However, the effect of this subsequent analysis is highly attenuated, if not completely effaced, by the beginning of the chapter where religion, ritual, fire, Hinduism, and burning Indian women are all woven into a very "special" relationship. What I find fascinating and puzzling is the persistence of "exoticising" and "ritualistic" and "religious" elements in accounts where the author knows and acknowledges the quotidian expediencies involved in the use of fire for dowry-murder. Attempts at "cultural explanation" that "weave together" the mundane reasons for the use of fire as a murder weapon with the "spiritual significance of fire to Hindus" end up as "explanations" that need more explanation than the issues they are trying to address. I suspect that Bumiller's ability to remain unaware of the significant tensions between the opening frame of the chapter and her subsequent explanation for the use of fire in the commission of dowry-murders is connected to the widespread tendency to see Third-World women as suffering "death by culture" or "victimization by culture."[42]

In the "explanations" that generate "death by culture," religious views or "traditional values" often become virtually synonymous with "culture." While the institution of dowry can certainly be meaningfully connected to "Indian culture" it is not, I think, given a satisfactory "explanation" by references to "religion." The fact that, for instance, the Laws of Manu (dating to the turn of the Christian era) endorse marriage involving dowry over other forms of marriage, such as marriage by capture or marriage involving bride-price, does little to illuminate the varying considerations about property and inheritance that have undoubtedly contributed to the continuous historical life of this institution.

I do think there are interesting questions (which I am not in the least equipped to answer) about why the institution of dowry has existed in some Indian communities and not in others, and as to why it has persisted in Indian communities when it has disappeared from those Western contexts where it historically existed. While I believe answers to these questions would make reference to many material, social, and cultural aspects of the Indian context, "religious views" alone would hardly suffice as explanation. In addition, while explanations for Indian women's vulnerability to dowry-murder might meaningfully refer to some aspects of "culture," such as underlying marriage and family arrangements that contribute to women's powerlessness, neither dowry-murders nor women's vulnerability to dowry-murder seem explainable as simply the outcome of adherence to a specific set of "religious" views.[43]

My goal here has been to show the significant difference between "death by culture" accounts of the phenomenon of dowry-murder and alternative accounts. One can only speculate about who reads Bumiller-type texts about "women in Other cultures" and the diffuse "effects" of these readings in promoting understandings of "Third-World women's problems" as "victimization by culture." Though Bumiller's book makes no claim to be a "scholarly" work, the book has clearly "functioned" as an academic text, since I have seen it in my college bookstore and in the footnotes of papers, including perhaps those that began with, "Women are being burnt to death everyday in India." I am not sure what to make of the uncanny similarities between the "problematic framing" of Bumiller's chapter on *sati* and bride-burning and the "problematic framing" in a *Dallas Observer's* story about an Indian woman living in Texas who was murdered by being set on fire by her husband.[44] Radhika Parameswaran describes the article as framed by references to *sati* and dowry-murder even though the woman's murder had no connection with either phenomena, and even though, as a Christian, the murdered woman had no "cultural connection" to *sati*, and may well have belonged to a community where marriages did not involve dowry! Reading Parameswaran, one of the first things that came to mind was the thought (wholly unfounded) that the reporter who wrote the *Dallas Observer* article that Parameswaran critiques had read Bumiller's book, even though I know that the ubiquitous "cultural construction" of "burnt Indian women" cannot be explained quite so simply.

Differences of "Culture" and Differences in "Culture as Explanation" /

I would like to end by considering an interesting asymmetry that exists between explanations of violence against women in "mainstream Western culture" and such "death by culture" explanations of violence against women specific to "Third-World cultural contexts." The best way I can think of to point to this asymmetry is the following kind of "thought experiment," which is also a kind of wicked fantasy whose "fantastical" elements are actually more interesting than its wickedness. Imagine yourself meeting a young Indian woman journalist who, after reading Bumiller's book, has decided to retaliate by working on a book entitled, *May You Be the Loser of A Hundred Pounds: A Journey Among the Women of the United States*. The young journalist plans to travel throughout the United States talking to an assortment of American women, trying to learn about "American women and American culture." The chapters she hopes to include in her book include vignettes on American women suffering from eating disorders; American women in weight-loss programs; American women who have undergone liposuctions, breast implants, and other types of cosmetic surgery; American women victims of domestic violence; American women in politics, and American women media stars.[45]

Ask yourself, "What are the structures of knowledge-production and information-circulation that make this book as difficult to imagine as it is impossible to find?" What are the factors that make it unlikely for a young Indian woman to conceive of such a project?[46] What is the likelihood of such a project being taken seriously enough to warrant the various forms of interest that are necessary to enable such a book to be written and published (in the United States *or* in India)? How likely is this book to be considered a serious source of information on "American culture" by the general public, or to appear on the reading list of any course on American culture? How likely is the book to receive reviews that credit the author with having "made the United States new and immediate again" and with being an "Eastern writer who has actually discovered the United States?"[47] What are the factors that make this imaginary book implausible and allow us to feel quite certain that there is no such book?

Pursuing my point about "cultural explanation," I shall continue with my fantasy, and go on to imagine how some of the contours of this Indian journalist's book on "women in American culture" would differ from Bumiller's Indian counterpart. I shall concentrate on her attempts to write the chapter linking domestic violence to American culture. Our intrepid Indian journalist would find it difficult, if not impossible, to account for many "American cultural phenomena" by references to Christian doctrines, myths, and practices. While "Christian values" have probably coexisted with domestic violence, fatal and nonfatal, in the United States much longer than "Hinduism" has coexisted with dowry-murder, one doubts that our journalist would be inclined, either on her own or as a result of her conversations with most Americans, to explain contemporary domestic violence in terms of Christian views about women's sinful nature, Eve's role in the Fall, the sanctity of marriage and the family, or the like.

Permit me to imagine the interesting difficulties that would confront our imaginary journalist as she attempted to write this chapter on "domestic violence and American culture." It just doesn't seem plausible, she has realized, to attempt an explanatory link between the two terms "domestic violence" and "American culture" through references to Christianity. How else, she wonders, is she to link the two terms, enabling her discussion of domestic violence in the United States to illuminate "American culture?" Much of the U.S. literature on domestic violence turns out not very helpful for her particular project, since most of the accounts they give explain the phenomenon in terms of a "non-nation-specific, secularized, general patriarchy," that seems no more distinctively "American" than it is "Christian."

She will find criticisms, most notably by U.S. feminists of color, that the underlying picture of "patriarchy" at work in many U.S. accounts of domestic-violence is often overly generalized. She may find the article where Kimberle Crenshaw argues that strands in U.S. domestic violence discourse have "transformed the message that battering is not *exclusively* a problem of poor or minority communities into a claim that it *equally* affects all classes and races,"[48] and that such views impede attention to the specific needs of battered women of color.[49] She will find that Crenshaw argues that women of color suffer disproportionately higher unemployment, lack of job skills, and discriminatory employment and housing practices, that make it harder for them to leave abusive relationships.[50] She will learn that factors such as being non-English speaking and having an immigration status that is dependent on marriage to the abuser further work to disempower a number of battered women of color in the United States.[51] Through such work, the journalist may develop a better understanding of how American class and race structures, and the outcomes of U.S. immigration policies, affect victims of domestic violence in the United States She will recognize, however, that such references to features of the American context seem quite different from the sorts of "religious" references to "Indian culture" Bumiller's chapter introduction uses to explain *sati* and dowry-murders.

Among the things she will learn in her readings and conversations are that American men batter their partners for "reasons" that range from sexual jealousy, alcoholism, stress, and pure unmitigated rage, to the desire to control the woman or to "prevent her leaving." She will learn that economic dependency, worries about the custody and welfare of children, low self-esteem due to abuse, and the threats and violence that have followed upon previous attempts at leaving are often given as reasons for American women staying in abusive relationships. With the possible exception of "low self-esteem,"[52] these sorts of reasons will seem similar to those that work to keep Indian women in abusive marriages, though they are often eclipsed in explanations that rely on elements such as Hindu mythology or the status of women in the Laws of Manu. She will notice that in U.S. accounts of domestic violence the sorts of reasons mentioned above appear to provide explanation enough, and that there is no felt need to explain why domestic violence in America is "American." None of this, she realizes, is helping her write a chapter that easily links U.S. domestic violence to "American culture."

Suddenly, she has a flash of inspiration! "Guns," she exclaims to herself, "gun-related domestic violence against women is what my chapter should be about. That will provide the tie into 'American culture' I have been looking for, since guns are so quintessentially 'American.' I need to find out how many women are injured annually by guns and how seriously, and how many of these injuries are inflicted by domestic partners. I need to find out how many domestic shooting incidents are claimed to be 'accidents' and how often there is good reason to doubt that they are. I need to find out how many American women are murdered annually by guns, and how many of them by their partners. Finding this information might help me depict guns as an 'icon' of violence against U.S. women, just as 'fire' seems to have become an icon of violence against Indian women."

What our imaginary Indian journalist might run up against as she tries to write this improbable chapter is revealing. Guns and lack of gun control, she will find in her conversations with Americans, are often acknowledged to be fairly distinctively "American" problems. However, in her attempts to relate gun-related violence to women and domestic violence, she will find that gun control and gun-related violence have not widely emerged specifically as "women's issues" or "domestic-violence issues." The journalist will run into difficulties as she tries to find "official data" on the "numbers of U.S. women killed and/or injured by guns in acts of domestic violence." If she starts with sources that have data on domestic violence, she will find figures for the numbers of U.S. women killed and for women injured in acts of domestic violence, but she will find that the sources do not specify how many of these deaths or injuries were gun-related. She will discover that it is not easy to figure out how many of the roughly 1,400 American women known to be killed annually by their partners were killed by guns. When she turns to data on gun-related violence, she will find similar problems. While it is fairly easy to find out that seven out of every ten American murders involved guns, it is less easy to find out whether seven out of ten murders *of women* involved guns. Figures for gun-related murders, she will find, do not often specify how many of these murders were domestic-violence related. While the data on the "handgun victimization rate" (which excludes murder and manslaughter) are broken down by sex, race, and age, they do not often specify how much of the "handgun victimization" suffered by U.S. women is domestic-violence related.[53]

In short, she will predominantly find that figures pertaining to U.S.

domestic violence do not specifically focus on guns, and that data on gun-related violence in the U.S. lacks specific attention to domestic violence. The intersection between "domestic violence suffered by U.S. women" and "American gun-related violence"—which would be the space of "domestic violence against American women mediated by the use of guns"—seems not to be well marked either as an "American" or as a "women's" issue. If she eventually finds the data, she will be struck by the fact that although the majority of women murdered by partners are in fact murdered with firearms, gun control has not emerged strongly as a U.S. feminist issue or even as a "visible" issue in much of the literature on domestic violence.[54] The journalist will discover that her idea about linking "domestic violence" to "American culture" by focusing on gun-related violence against women is not a project easy to carry out, since the two issues seem not to be frequently connected by those engaged with gun-control issues or domestic-violence agendas. She might, however, acquire some interesting "cross-cultural insights" as a result of her frustrations. She might come to see that while Indian women repeatedly suffer "death by culture" in a range of scholarly and popular works, even as the elements of "culture" proffered do little to explain their deaths, American women seem relatively immune to such analyses of "death or injury by culture" even as they are victimized by the fairly distinctively American phenomenon of wide-spread gun-related violence.

Given these difficulties, it is perhaps for the best that this is an imaginary chapter in an improbable book. I would like to end with the suggestion that books that cannot be written and chapters that are oddly difficult to write might have more to teach us about particular cultures and their relationships to "Other cultures" than many books and chapters that face few difficulties in being either imagined or written.

Four /

Through the Looking-Glass Darkly

Emissaries, Mirrors, and Authentic Insiders as Preoccupations

Introduction /

The project of this essay operates at several different but interconnected levels. At one level, I wish to consider some of the problematic roles that are thrust upon Third World individuals when they and their work enter the orbit of certain kinds of Western academic concerns and discursive spaces. At a second level, I want to analyze and discuss these same problematic roles and the attitudes and assumptions that bring them into existence, insofar as they affect discursive encounters between mainstream Western feminists and Third-World *feminists* within Western academic contexts. At a third level, I am interested in these roles as they relate to certain aspects of ongoing academic concerns about muticulturalism and curricular diversity. I write as someone who is strongly in favor of a diverse and multicultural curriculum, but who is worried by some of the understandings and attitudes that seem to shape certain versions of multiculturalism. The three roles I shall discuss are those of "Emissary," "Mirror," and "Authentic Insider."

Since I am centrally interested in roles that individuals from Third-World backgrounds are assigned within Western contexts, the term "Third-World subject" in this essay does not refer to individuals living within Third-World nations. Within Western contexts, I use the terms "Third-World subjects" broadly to refer to individuals from Third-World countries temporarily living and working in Western contexts, to individuals who are immigrants to the West from Third-World countries, to individuals who were born and have lived in Western contexts but have social identities that link them to immigrant communities of color, and to all individuals who are members of communities of color in Western contexts and do not have any sense of an "immigrant" identity. What all these individuals have in common, for the purposes of this paper, is the fact that their communities, achievements, and "culture" have not been regarded as part of "mainstream Western culture."[1] Individuals from all these categories are positioned in interesting ways in projects designed to make the curriculum more responsive to achievements that have been marginal to the pedagogical gaze of mainstream "Western culture," a positioning that accounts for their being assigned the roles I shall discuss.

I believe that the roles of Emissary, Mirror, and Authentic Insider are assigned to a range of Third-World individuals, making them interesting to reflect upon as positions that generally confront people of Third-World background in Western contexts. However, I also believe that the ways in which these positions function with respect to various categories of Third-World persons have interesting differences of detail. For instance, the details of these roles, and the precise contents of the expectations that accompany them, will often differ when they "hail" an African American man, a Native American woman, or a woman who is an immigrant from China. One limitation of this essay is that insofar as I attempt to talk about these roles in a general way, I will be sacrificing attention to these important differences of detail. A second limitation of this paper derives from a different source—the fact that many of the examples I will use are based on my own experiences as an immigrant woman of Indian background. While such examples serve to make the discussion concrete, they will fail to do justice to the details of how these roles position Third-World individuals whose identities differ significantly from mine. I would urge readers to keep these limitations in mind, and encourage reflection about how the details of these roles would differ when assigned to particular members of different Third-World communities.

I reflect upon these positions as a feminist of Indian background who came to the United States as a graduate student in her mid-twenties, and has lived and worked in the United States for over a dozen years now. I write as someone who often finds herself "recruited" to these roles— sometimes as a "person of color," sometimes as an "immigrant," sometimes as an "Indian," sometimes as a "South Asian," sometimes as an "Asian American" and sometimes as a general member of a "Third-World culture." In addition, I am sometimes recruited to these roles as a feminist, and sometimes not. I shall concentrate on these roles as they occur in academic contexts, in part because these are the contexts with which I am personally most familiar, and in part because I am interested in the ways in which these roles relate to academic contexts that are committed to promoting curricular and institutional diversity.

Since an important part of my teaching and writing engages with feminist issues, it is not surprising that, given my background, references to Third-World feminist issues surface in my teaching and writing. What initially led me to attempt to write this paper were some odd responses that my discussions of feminist issues in Third-World contexts seemed often to provoke. The oddness of these responses has suggested to me, in sometimes explicit but often tacit ways, that I was breaching or failing to fulfill roles that had been assigned to me. These responses also helped me see that I had at times played versions of these roles even before I was aware that these were roles I had been playing. As a result of these experiences, I became aware too of the possibilities and the dangers of being taken by, and being taken in by, these assigned roles. Part of my motivation in this paper is to provoke a greater critical self-awareness about the problematic nature of these roles both on the part of Westerners tempted to assign them, and on the part of Third-World persons tempted to occupy them. I would also like to explore how they raise special problems when imposed by mainstream Western feminists on feminists from Third-World backgrounds. In the last part of this essay, I shall try and think through what strategies Third-World subjects, especially feminists, might attempt in order to deal with these roles so as to avoid the problems they pose.

While these roles are often met in a variety of everyday academic interactions as well as in more formal academic settings, they are often not explicit objects of awareness on the part of both those who impose them and those who occupy them. I shall rely on examples and descriptions of these roles, trusting that this will elicit recognition. In describing and naming these roles and their accompanying assumptions, I will undoubtedly present them more cleanly, clearly, starkly, and singly than they often in fact exist and operate. The experience of these roles is often murky, leaving one puzzled and uncertain about what has transpired in an encounter. Often, it is only after repetition and in retrospect that one begins to recognize these roles, and it is only slowly that one begins to be able to articulate what has struck one as problematic about them. By representing these roles and their assumptions vividly, starkly, and perhaps schematically, I hope to make more sense of them, to facilitate their recognition, to show their interconnections, and to subject them to assessment and criticism.

Before I move on to a concrete discussion of the three roles of Emissary, Mirror, and Authentic Insider, let me suggest that these roles can be understood as "Preoccupations," in the dual sense of "concerns" and of "pregiven locations." When individuals from Third-World backgrounds, including feminists, enter the discursive spaces of mainstream Western academic contexts, they enter a field of Preoccupations where a variety of concerns about inclusion, diversity, and multiculturalism are already in place and being played out. These concerns are often strongly shaped by the understandings of mainstream Westerners, who have numerical as well as institutional power in academic settings.[2] These concerns also become Preoccupations in another sense, when they construct roles that function as pre-existing locations within mainstream Western academic settings and discursive encounters that Third-World individuals find themselves occupying. These locations work to shape our entrance, influence what is expected of us, and give us a place that often also puts us in our place. They are Preoccupations in this second sense because they are often occupations assigned to us even before we take up the jobs we are there to do. In referring to these roles as "Preoccupations," I wish to draw attention both to how a set of concerns shapes these roles and to how these roles are often "imposed" on Third-World individuals, defining the locations they "occupy" and what is expected of them.

I have no wish to suggest, however, that these Preoccupations, either as "concerns" or "locations," are only imposed on members of Third-World communities from "without." These roles may become "internal Preoccupations" of Third-World subjects in at least two ways. In the first case, they may be roles that some Third-World individuals "impose on themselves" because of their own concerns and sense of location as Third-World subjects in mainstream Western settings, and due to their own sense of the "cultural politics" of these settings. In the second case, they may be roles neither self-imposed nor embraced without qualification by particular Third-World persons, but nevertheless operate as roles that they must struggle to understand, come to terms with, or subvert, leaving them concerned about, and "preoccupied" by, these roles in this sense.

I do not wish to deny that, in a general sense, all of us are "preoccupied" by concerns, locations, and roles that pre-exist our individual engagements with them. To be thus "preoccupied" is, in this general sense, the mark of being social and historical individuals, persons who must inevitably enter into ongoing social and historical enterprises, and must have a place before we can begin to locate ourselves and name and challenge our place. My interest in this essay, however, is with a limited and specific set of "Preoccupations"–the three roles of Emissary, Mirror, and Authentic Insider. I do not wish to suggest that these constitute anything like an exhaustive list of the roles Third-World individuals, feminists, or others find themselves occupying and confronting. They are, rather, roles I have encountered often enough to have named, and ones that seem worth dwelling upon even as one dwells among them.

Third-World Feminists and Western Anxieties: Confronting the "Anthropological Perspective" /

Before I begin a concrete discussion of these three roles, I would like to address the background of concerns from which these roles arise. Increasing Western interest in "Third-World cultures" has had a noticeable and growing impact on various aspects of contemporary Western academic institutions. For instance, many U.S. educational institutions increasingly offer courses as well as majors in various area studies, such as Asian Studies and Latin American Studies and a variety of ethnic studies offerings. Courses that attend to issues of class, race, ethnicity, gender, to non-Western and postcolonial texts, and to works by Third-World scholars increasingly find room within the curricular offerings of "mainstream" disciplines. Media reports suggest that increasing numbers of U.S. students seem to spend a semester or year abroad, many in a number of Third-World countries. Many of these students are from U.S. communities of color, coming to terms with their multiple identities and cultural locations. There is increasing interest and research in numerous disciplines in topics and issues pertaining to Third-World contexts and communities. My interest is not to analyze these curricular changes and their impacts in depth. It is rather to focus on a certain set of assumptions and attitudes that seems to underlie and shape some versions of this current Western academic interest in "Third-World cultures."

I want to draw attention to what I shall call "the anthropological perspective" with respect to Other cultures—a perspective that seems to shape some aspects of the general commitment to multicultural education and intellectual inquiry, as well as some mainstream Western feminist approaches to "issues affecting Third-World women." The "anthropological perspective" is one whose twin imperatives can be summarized as, "It is important for mainstream Westerners to take an interest in Other cultures," and "It is important that this interest not involve moral criticism of Other cultures by mainstream Westerners." (In naming this stance the "anthropological perspective," I have no intention of imputing this stance to any actual practitioners of the discipline of anthropology, or to suggest it is somehow peculiar to that discipline. I believe the pressures of these imperatives are widely felt and shared in a wide range of academic and disciplinary contexts.)

These dual imperatives of what I am calling the "anthropological perspective" often stem from good intentions, and seem to be responses to problematic aspects of mainstream Western culture's attitudes to Other cultures. The commitment to taking an interest in Other cultures often stems from the recognition that many mainstream Westerners are sadly ignorant about Third-World cultural contexts and thus suffer from parochial limitations of vision. It stems from a recognition that such Western ignorance about Other cultures is not only intellectually confining but also increasingly impractical and imprudent in a world where an increasingly global economy reinforces all sorts of complex interdependencies between nations in various parts of the world. The commitment to learning about Other cultures also stems from a recognition that Western educational curricula have often tended to exclude or marginalize Third-World cultures, both within and outside Western national contexts. The commitment to learning about Other cultures is thus often one part of a larger project of expanding and enriching existing disciplinary canons, curricula, and concerns, to make them more genuinely inclusive, more genuinely representative of the full range of human contributions and concerns.

The second commitment of the "anthropological perspective"—to mainstream Westerners refraining from moral criticism of Other cultures—is rooted in a different, but connected, cluster of recognitions. Among these recognitions are that mainstream Western culture has not simply been inattentive to Other cultures, but has in fact been deeply historically involved in their *representations*, representations that have often been replete with negative stereotypes and imputations of cultural inferiority. This second commitment is often also rooted in the recognition that, as a consequence of colonialism and its aftermath, Third-World cultures and communities both within and outside Western national contexts have been subject not merely to problematic representations and interpretations by mainstream Western culture but also to problematic economic and political interventions, where imputations of "backwardness" and "barbarity" to Third-World communities function to justify their economic exploitation and political domination.

While one does not have to be a feminist to feel the pull of these commitments, I believe that many Western feminists feel the tug of their own specific version of the dual imperatives of the "anthropological perspective." The insistence by feminists of color that mainstream Western feminists attend to differences among women, and to take into account the problems and perspectives of women from minority communities within and outside Western national contexts, has begun to have a growing impact. It has led to the recognition that an adequate feminist perspective and politics must theoretically and practically attend to the problems and aspirations of women in cultural contexts that are different from the "mainstream." Western feminists have often also felt the pressure of the second imperative—that of avoiding negative portrayals and moral criticism of Third-World cultures.

Part of the pressure some Western feminists feel with regard to the second imperative might be rooted in a desire to avoid accusations of racism or colonialism, risks that they not infrequently run if they venture criticism of Third-World contexts. However, I think it is too simplistic to interpret *all* of this anxiety as the result of personal worries about being targets of such accusations. There is often a more principled and less personal anxiety that is at work, having to do with reservations about Westerners in general engaging in negative, critical, or prescriptive judgments about practices and affairs having to do with Third-World communities. These reservations result from the recognition of the fact that such negative judgments have been part and parcel of a Western colonialist approach to Third-World contexts. Given awareness of this history, some Western feminists are concerned, and in some ways rightly so, that they do not themselves subscribe to and reinforce these morally problematic views about, and stances toward, "Other cultures." This desire to avoid contributing to a history of negative stereotypes about Third-World communities and practices, and to avoid normative and prescriptive judgments that seem to replicate a colonialist attitude of "telling the natives what to do," has understandably entered into the range of current Western feminist concerns with power, representation, voice, and marginality.

The three roles of Emissary, Mirror, and Authentic Insider are connected, I believe, to *strategies* that facilitate the "anthropological" project of mainstream Westerners "taking an interest in Other cultures" without engaging in negative portrayals or criticism of the Other culture. In discussing these roles, I will try to show how they can be understood as roles related to different moves employed by mainstream Westerners to comport with the twin imperatives of the "anthropological perspective." I will also try to describe the ways in which these roles assign Third-World individuals, including feminists, interesting, curious, difficult, and problematic places in the service of this "anthropological" project. I would like to describe these three roles one at a time, analyzing the ways in which each facilitates the "anthropological perspective," and exploring the problems each role presents, both with respect to members of Third-World communities in general, and with respect to Third-World feminists in particular.

The first two roles I discuss, those of Emissary and Mirror, seem to be different in one respect from the third role of Authentic Insider. While actual Third-World individuals are often "positioned" as Emissaries and Mirrors, their literal presence does not seem necessary to the versions of the "anthropological perspective" toward Other cultures in which they participate. Those versions of the "anthropological perspective" can, and are, capable of being deployed by mainstream Westerners themselves in their own strategic approaches to Other cultures. In discussing the roles of Emissary and Mirror, I shall therefore address not only the problematics of Third-World individuals actually occupying these positions, but also the problems of the underlying "approach to Other cultures" that go beyond such actual occupations. I shall call the respective "approaches to Other cultures" connected to the Emissary and Mirror positions the "Cultural Riches" and the "Big Bad West" perspectives. The version of the "anthropological perspective" that involves "Authentic Insiders" does, on the contrary, seem to require the actual presence of Third-World persons, and so the problems of the position and the underlying approach to Other cultures coincide more neatly.

Uma Narayan

The "Cultural Riches" Approach
and the "Emissary" Position /

One approach to Third-World cultures
that satisfies the twin imperatives of the "anthropological perspective" is
an approach that concentrates on Third-World "cultural *achievements*"
and avoids issues that constitute Third-World *problems*. I shall call this a
"cultural riches" approach to Third-World cultures. "Taking an interest in
Other cultures" becomes equivalent, in this approach, to learning about
various Third-World contexts and communities in order to appreciate
their myriad achievements as cultures—their complex cosmologies and
metaphysics; the rich details of their religious and ethical beliefs and
social achievements; their various histories, literatures, and philosophies;
their understandings of, and contributions to, the arts; their views about
human relationships to nature and to the social fabric; and so forth.

Such an interest in "Other cultures" is hardly misplaced. Restoring the
achievements of Third-World cultures to their place in the record of
remarkable and impressive human achievements certainly has merit in its
own right. It also serves to undermine the sense that all significant cultural achievements are the achievements of "Western culture," a claim
evidently still fashionable among many of those opposed to multiculter-
alism.[3] On the other hand, there are some limitations that accompany
this "cultural riches" approach to "Other cultures," limitations that have
arguably been part and parcel of Western culture's "cultural riches"
approach to its own achievements. Let me briefly draw attention to some
of these limitations.

What I am calling the "cultural riches" approach has a significant tendency to focus on the texts and artifacts of "High Culture,"[4] the cultural
products of privileged sections of a society, whose social position not only
gave them privileged access to the domains of cultural achievement, but
also gave them the power to constitute these achievements as "definitive,"
"emblematic," and "monumental" aspects of the culture in question. In
many contexts, Western and Third World, these products of "High
Culture" functioned to constitute other aspects and artifacts of local cultures into "folk culture"—into "craft" rather than "Art," into various "peas-
ant" and "lower class" and "women's" practices and achievements—constituted equally as marginal to the "riches" of that particular culture's
"Achievements," as their practitioners were to that particular society as a
whole. My point is *not* that the complex achievements of any High Culture should not be appreciated in all their formal intricacies, aesthetic
richness, and intellectual development. Rather, what worries me is that
versions of such a "cultural riches" approach often tend to be inattentive
to the material, social, and political contexts in which these achievements

were embedded, and to the relationship of these achievements to often-problematic attempts at cultural self-definition.

A "cultural riches" approach becomes problematic in numerous ways if it fails to be self-reflective about its project of appreciation. Let me provide some examples of the sorts of problems I have in mind. In an unreflective "cultural riches" approach, it is likely that the religious or metaphysical views of an elite social group at a particular historical moment may be taken as the defining components of the "world views" of all Hindus or Buddhists or Chinese or Indians.[5] Attention might fail to be paid, for instance, to how the actual religious practices and spiritual understandings of various groups of women, of lower-caste groups, of groups variously socially and culturally marginalized, might challenge and subvert rather than endorse the views found in these documents of "High Culture" or in the doctrines of "High Religion." Finally, such "cultural appreciation" may obstruct understanding the place of these "cultural achievements" within the moral and political fabric of their social contexts, and obscure their ideological functions as justifications for practices or institutions that were unjust and exclusionary and worked to disempower and marginalize a great many of the inhabitants of these "cultural contexts."

These sorts of problems might occur less often with respect to the achievements of Third-World cultures and communities that are not deeply, internally hierarchical or stratified. However, a great many Third World communities and contexts are suffused with enough hierarchy and stratification to make these concerns seriously applicable. It is important to remember that a culture or community's "marginal status" with respect to "mainstream Western culture" does not foreclose the existence *within it* of structures and practices that render some of its own members more marginal to its "cultural self-definition" than are others.

Such "readings" of "Other Cultures" often only serve to replicate a series of problems of the sort that many Western feminists, among others, have found objectionable in Western culture's appreciative encounters with *itself*. For instance, Western feminist philosophers have only recently begun to call critical attention to "readings" of Western philosophical texts (readings that were often important parts of their own training in the discipline) whereby figures as disparate as Aristotle, Locke, or Hegel are portrayed as if they were our liberal contemporaries, whose moral and political theories applied to all members of the community regardless of their social identities with respect to class, race, or gender. Feminists have insisted on the importance of attending to who was included and who excluded by the *actual intended scope* of these theories, and on seeing these theories as politically embedded in specific historical contexts where their doctrines provided intellectual justification for some aspects of the status quo, even as they challenged some others.[6]

Texts and works from "non-Western philosophical traditions" can equally well be read as if they were closer to being our liberal contemporaries than they in fact are. Such problematic readings do not cease to be problematic when carried out with respect to the texts and practices of an "Other Culture." In such a "cultural riches" approach to Nonwestern philosophical texts for instance, the "Wisdom of the East" would only join the "Wisdom of the West" in an acontextual celebratory togetherness that failed to attend to the limitations of such an approach with respect to the complicated task of a genuinely historical and political understanding of *any* culture.[7]

In the context of such a "cultural riches" approach, Third-World individuals are often assigned the "Emissary position" and given the job of conveying the "riches of the Other culture" to an appreciative audience. However, such a "cultural riches" approach to Other cultures does not *necessarily* require a Third-World "member" of a particular culture to be positioned as an Emissary. As even a cursory look at various academic disciplines will reveal, much "celebratory" scholarship on the "riches" of Other cultures is done by mainstream Western academics. However, positioning a Third-World subject as an Emissary might be perceived as having the additional advantage of "authenticity" in being a "representation from the inside." Since I will discuss the problems that arise from assumptions about "authenticity" in a later section, let me concentrate for now on problems arising from such "Emissary" representations.

Let me use as an example a text written from such an "Emissary position" that embodies almost too well many of the problems I previously mentioned with respect to the "cultural riches approach"—Ananda Coomaraswamy's *The Dance of Shiva*.[8] Coomaraswamy's book is also one that well supports my claim that these roles are not always "imposed" on Third-World subjects by Westerners, but are sometimes assumed by Third-World individuals by virtue of their own sense of the "cultural politics" between "Western culture" and their own "home" culture.

Coomaraswamy's book is part of a genre of writing by Third-World subjects that seeks to "validate their culture" in the eyes of Westerners, a project that confirms the "powers of the West" even as it tries to challenge it. The problems with the book's highly laudatory account of "Indian culture" are too numerous to analyze in depth, so I shall content myself with just a few examples. Coomaraswamy not only generally strikes a "holier than thou" attitude to "Western culture," but he also does so quite *literally*, working through clichéd oppositions between "materialist" Western culture and "spiritual" Indian culture.[9] Much of the "Indian Art" he discusses is "High Art," although he does have a brief chapter on "Buddhist

Primitives." He not only unblushingly defends the caste system but also goes on to explicitly give the credit for Indian culture's "riches" to the two upper castes, the Brahmins and the Kshtriyas.[10] The kindest thing I can say about his reverential chapter on the "Status of Indian Women" is that it leaves much to be desired, and reminded me of many syrupy sermons about "Indian culture's respect for women" that I have heard men deliver in India.[11]

One way to summarize the problems with *The Dance of Shiva* is to say that it is a text that provides vivid proof that "Orientals" are as capable of Orientalism[12] as mainstream Westerners! Even as Coomaraswamy attempts to testify about not only the "riches" but also the "supcriority" of Indian culture, he resuscitates every cliché of Orientalism in his portraits of both "Indian" and "Western" cultures. Furthermore, even as he seeks to counter "cultural put-downs" of Indian culture by the West, he is engaged in "putting-down" many groups of Indians who are either entirely absent from the account or whose subordinate status and social positions are reduced to yet more evidence of "Indian culture's wisdom." The book supports my general judgment that the "cultural riches" approach to cultures and representations that arise from the "Emissary position" often result in profoundly distorted and problematic portraits. Not only might many other fellow-members of the culture have good reasons to reject these representations of "their culture," but also such representations constitute more of a handicap than an asset to nonmembers looking to broaden their cultural horizons and understandings.

I am arguing that a "cultural riches" approach to Other cultures might turn out to be problematic for precisely the same sorts of reasons that Western feminists have had problems with idealized and idealizing approaches to the understanding and study of Western culture. However, the imperatives of the "anthropological perspective" sometimes seem to get in the way of mainstream Westerners, including feminists, in seeing this analogy. Where a "cultural riches" approach to other cultures is operative, Third-World individuals who refuse to or fail to cooperate with a "cultural riches" presentation of "their culture" run into problems. I have often encountered a tendency that combines a committed willingness to subject Western culture to a variety of political and critical analyses with an unwillingness to maintain the same stance with respect to Other cultures. This unwillingness then often extends itself and grows from an unwillingness to be personally critical about Third-World cultures to an unwillingness to even engage with such criticisms made by Third-World feminists, criticisms that are met with anxiety or defensiveness.

I do not know how else to account for a number of odd and troubling encounters other than in terms of this sort of anxiety and defensiveness.

For instance, at a dinner conversation in an academic setting, I happened at one point to say something critical about the Indian caste system.[13] I made reference to an Indian creation myth that has male representatives of the four castes emerging from four different parts of the Creator, parts with different symbolic values that correlate to the respective social positions of the four castes within caste hierarchy. A fellow diner, who was a feminist scholar, seemed oddly compelled to suggest that the myth I was talking about was a myth about social "interdependence." This comment was particularly odd coming from someone who would certainly have known better than to say that the biblical myth about Eve's creation from Adam's rib was simply a myth about gender "interdependence." I have had numerous conversations, in classrooms with my students as well as outside the classroom with my peers, where a passing critical remark about some aspect of Indian culture has lead away from a discussion of whatever concrete issue that was the topic of my remark and toward a nervous general discussion about "respect for Other cultures." In two such instances, I remember receiving cautioning inquiries about whether I did not think that my talking about issues such as dowry-murders would reinforce Western stereotypes about Indian culture.

These sorts of anxieties on the part of mainstream Westerners, feminists or otherwise, tend to position Third-World feminists in an odd and disturbing location. In the face of these anxieties, I have often felt as if Third-World feminist criticisms and analyses, including my own, are perceived as impediments, as obstacles, to the "respect for Third-World cultures" that these Westerners wish to endorse and cultivate. I have often felt that the discomfort my criticisms have evoked arose out of a sense that I was not playing my "proper role" as Ambassador and Emissary of my culture, vaunting its virtues, and thus providing an antidote and corrective to Western arrogance and cultural superiority.[14] Despite understanding some of the considerations that motivate these responses, considerations I acknowledged earlier, encountering such mandates to be an Emissary are unpleasant. I have often felt that what both I and "my Cul-ture" were receiving in these encounters was not respect but something that verged on censorship and a condescending form of moral paternalism.

One also meets the "Emissary position" in a different guise, one that has its own sorts of pressures and problems. As an Emissary, Third-World individuals are often expected to be virtual encyclopedias of information on all sorts of different aspects of their complex "cultural heritage." Their encyclopedic expertise is often expected to range from the esoteric to the mundane, from popular to High Culture, from matters of history to contemporary issues. I have, in my fairly short span of time as an academic, been consulted by students working on Indian novels in English, the role of women in popular Hindi films, and Goddess-worship rituals in South

India, none of which remotely fall into my realms of academic expertise, and about all of which I know only a little. While I do not mind being asked for such information, especially by students, I am often taken aback by how much more I am assumed to know about "my culture" compared to what is expected of mainstream Western academics. It has also been instructive to me to learn how oddly flexible the assumed "borders" of "my culture" are. I have, for instance, had more than my share of questions about Tibetan Buddhism from spiritually inclined white Westerners. After several such episodes, I now have a stock answer, which is to point out that I, quite understandably, know as little about it as they probably know about Mexican Catholicism.

I wish next to focus on the specific limitations of the "Emissary position" with respect to the agency and self-articulation of feminists from Third-World backgrounds. I think the "Emissary position" is as problematic in its own way as what I have elsewhere referred to as the "missionary position."[15] While the "missionary position" constructs Third-World women as the "objects of rescue" of mainstream Western men or women or of Third-World men, the "Emissary position" seems to construct Third-World individuals in general *as missionaries*, with the mission of rescuing Westerners from their negative stereotypes and attitudes toward Third-World cultures and contexts. If this description suggests that the "Emissary position" is a simple reversal of the "missionary position", I should point out that it is neither simple nor a reversal. The "missionary position" toward Third-World women, despite its normative problems, was historically at least a successful strategy of political empowerment for some groups of Western women and Third-World men. Antoinette Burton's work shows how, in the colonial Indian context, Indian women became "the 'playing fields' on which Indian men and British feminist women each imagined their own liberation."[16] While the "Emissary position" may be experienced as empowering by some Third-World individuals some of the time, it is seldom, I would argue, politically empowering for many Third-World feminists.

While Third-World feminists undoubtedly have a stake in undoing negative stereotypes of their cultures prevalent in Western contexts and in restoring the achievements of their peoples and communities to view, they also have a political agenda that, broadly speaking, seems to pull in a different direction. As feminists, they have an urgent political stake in calling attention to the norms, institutions, and practices within their contexts that are unjust, unfair, and oppressive to many within their societies, including women. This is not a political agenda that seems compatible with focusing only on the "riches and achievements" of their communities and contexts. Insofar as demands that they occupy the "Emissary position" obstruct this agenda, they weaken rather than strengthen the political agency of Third-World feminists. The demand that they proffer only "positive" pictures of their cultures as a corrective for negative Western stereotypes about the Third-World positions them in the service of others for whom they serve a useful instrumental function, at the cost of fundamentally distorting their own political agendas with respect to their "home" contexts.

While I understand some of the genuine concerns that underlie some Westerners' desire for Third-World subjects to occupy the "Emissary position," I believe this desire traps Westerners who are feminists in a project that is ultimately self-defeating and problematic. In its crudest form, this self-defeating project attempts to conjoin a feminist attention to the problems and political agendas of Third-World women, with a complete lack of criticism of the national, social, or cultural contexts within which these problems and politics exist, a lack of criticism that gets unreflec-tively equated to "respecting that Third-World culture." This project in turn confronts feminists from Third-World backgrounds who seek to discuss feminist issues pertaining to their home contexts before mainstream Western audiences with an impossible task, requiring them to discuss feminist issues within Third-World contexts without saying anything critical or negative about those contexts.

There are a number of things I would like to say that may enable all of us to carry on with our tasks less trammeled by these problems. It seems to me that the project of "cultivating respect for Other cultures" is not a simple one and needs to proceed with discernment and discrimination. Surely, respecting Other cultures (or respecting one's own culture for that matter) cannot mean, and should not mean, respecting or endorsing *every element* of its traditions, values, and practices. After all, the term "respect" has roots in the notions of "looking back at" and "considering"–terms that suggest appraisal and evaluation, not simple acceptance or deference.

It should not come as a surprising revelation to feminists anywhere that a great many cultures have had a fairly poor record when it comes to their treatment of not only their women in general but also large segments of both men and women who constitute the vulnerable, the dispossessed, the disempowered, and marginal members of their society. It should not come as a surprise to any of us that no single "culture" has had a monopoly on values, traditions, and social arrangements that deserve moral criticism, just as no "culture" has had a monopoly on ideas and achievements that are morally valuable. It should come as no surprise that many of our "cultures" are both rich and flawed, in complex and interesting ways.

There is, therefore, no more call for Third-World feminists to treat "our cultures" with hushed reverence than mainstream Western feminists do theirs. What Third-World feminists do when they critique their cultures is not dissimilar to what Western feminists routinely do with respect to their own—they criticize those aspects of their society that are oppressive, unfair, and debilitating to the health and happiness of many of its members, including women. This seems no more than the task that is at the very heart of being a feminist, at the very heart of our hopes and efforts for positive change. To put Third-World feminists in the "Emissary position" is often to impede their feminist analyses and politics, and to fail to recognize the fact that women have good reasons to be disloyal to a multiplicity of "civilizations."

I am aware that many mainstream Westerners have sometimes explicit, sometimes unreflective, assumptions about the superiority of Western culture. I am also aware of the danger that my discussion of issues such as dowry-murders may be heard as nothing more than evidence for the "superiority of Western culture." However, given that these negative attitudes and stereotypes about Third-World communities are produced in a number of powerful institutional sites, I find it unlikely that the solution for "Western cultural arrogance" lies in Third-World feminist silence about the problems women face in their national and cultural contexts![17] Besides, many Third-World feminists have developed strategic skills that enable them to counter "Western stereotypes" even as they continue to develop feminist analyses of problems women face within communities. Two examples of texts that manage to do both, employing a number of interesting strategies that are worth thinking about, are Leila Ahmed's "Western Ethnocentrism and Perceptions of the Harem,"[18] and Nawal el Saadawi's "Dissidence and Creativity."[19]

I often try, when I talk in Western contexts about the problems that affect the lives of Indian women, to point to parallel or related problems in Western contexts. Sometimes I do this simply because the comparisons strike me as interesting. At other times, I am aware that I feel a need to point to the parallels as an antidote to the likelihood that members of the audience might fail to see them, and hence be tempted to engage in culturally arrogant perceptions of Third-World cultures.[20] At these times, I feel resigned to what seems like a necessary though irksome task, recognizing that there are certain historically constituted discursive inequalities that need to be dealt with and cannot be wished away. And I recognize that the nervousness and anxiety that some Western feminists manifest when I fail to be an "Emissary" is also a response rooted in their sense of such discursive inequalities between Western and Third-World feminists, and their respective cultural contexts, even though I think it is not a particularly helpful way to deal with them.

There is yet another danger with respect to the "Emissary position." It suggests that the most urgent political task for Third-World individuals is to valorize Third-World cultures and achievements in order to weaken Western symptoms of cultural superiority. This implies that to engage in *any* negative or critical portrayal of aspects of Third-World cultures is to play into the negative perceptions and stereotypes of mainstream Western culture. These assumptions that help construct the "Emissary position" tend to collude with elements of antifeminist politics in Third-World contexts that attempt to portray feminists as "cultural traitors" who lack respect and appreciation for their cultures because they have critical rather than laudatory attitudes with respect to many institutions and practices affecting women. Third-World feminist failures to occupy the "Emissary position" in Western contexts can then be represented as anti-nationalist or anticommunity betrayals that collude with negative "Western views" about Third-World contexts. Western feminists who are tempted to restrict Third-World feminists to the "Emissary position" need to seriously worry about adopting a stance that has such resonance with right-wing religious frameworks and fundamentalist discourses, much more seriously in my opinion, than they need to worry about Third-World feminists reinforcing "negative Western stereotypes."

Now You See It, Now You Don't: Mirrors, the Big Bad West, and Third-World Disappearances /

I shall move on to discussing another role that sometimes "preoccupies" Third-World individuals in Western contexts, the role of being a Mirror or Looking-Glass to the West. This role too, I believe, arises as a strategic response to the pressures of the twin imperatives of the "anthropological perspective"—that which requires Westerners to take an interest in Other cultures without engaging in negative portrayals or moral criticisms of that Other culture. One strategy to comport with both of these imperatives is to take an interest in Third-World contexts as sites in which Western colonialism, imperialism, economic and political hegemony, and problematic representations of Self and Other have played out. This strategy permits Westerners to take an interest in Third-World contexts, cultures, and communities without engaging in a critical stance toward their indigenous institutions and practices and responses, by confining their critical perspectives to a variety of problematic *Western* agendas, interferences, and self-images that have arisen in the course of Western encounters with Third-World communities.

The positions of "Emissary" and "Mirror" are connected insofar as both function to facilitate mainstream Westerners "taking an interest in their Others" without subjecting these Others to negative criticism. But they differ insofar as the "Emissary position" involves an injunction to provide laudatory accounts of Third-World cultures, while the position of Mirror involves an injunction to sustain, encourage, and provide confirmation for the global predations and depredations of "the Big Bad West."

One place in which this strategy is put to work is in studies of various aspects of colonial history, the history of the West's intrusive entry into Third-World contexts. Let me focus on one example of the sort of work I am talking about, an essay on the role of "magic" in a nineteenth-century European colony in Asia.[21] The paper discusses the deployments of "magic" as a boundary marker between "Europeans" and "natives" from the point of view of Western colonizing powers. The paper does not represent a "Western perspective" in the sense of uncritically endorsing the normative commitments of the colonial Western perspective. It is in fact critical and self-reflective about the self-serving nature of this Western project. However, the perspective of the paper remains Western in another sense—in a manner that I have found to be not uncommon in Western works about colonial contexts. While this essay has rich insights into the complex ways in which "magic" functioned in the Western colonial imagination, it does not theoretically dwell upon the ways in which "magic" might have functioned in "native representations"—as part of their collaborations with, and resistances to, colonial powers, as part of their own race and gender perspectives, as having various boundary-marking and perhaps other sorts of functions both "internal" to "native" society or in their construction of "differences" between themselves and their colonizers. It is not so much that "native" relationships to "magic" are *entirely* absent from the discussion, but that these are minimally represented at a matter-of-fact level of description. They are not subject to the rich range of theoretical readings that the Western deployment of "magic" is subject to. I would have liked to read an equally theoretically and politically rich account of what "native deployments of magic" amounted to—what psychological and political anxieties its deployment functioned to control on *their part*, how it illuminates *their* response to the colonial "encounter."[22]

One reason for such lacks, in this paper as well as others, might be something simple like, "It is not part of the limited project of this paper." I am not at all unsympathetic to this sort of rationale. I am all too aware that papers need to be focused to permit development of trains of thought, that space constraints abound, and that none of us can attend to everything at once. However, I would be a lot happier if the lack of attention to Third-World agents and agency were at least acknowledged and explained, say with regard to the focus of the paper. Otherwise, many such "Western-focused" works on colonialism leave me, despite their merits, with a sinking feeling of watching the West coming back to a focus on *itself*, this time perhaps with more critical self-awareness, but nevertheless with a self-awareness that remains devoted to only understanding itself, even if refracted through the critical lens of its encounters with its "Others."

This focus on the West in colonial studies is clearly an aspect of the disciplinary terrain and not merely the reflection of the "individual" interest of particular scholars. A recent overview of the terrain clearly supports my point (without necessarily sharing the concern that leads me to make this point) when the author observes: "Having focused on how colonizers have viewed the indigenous Other, we are beginning to sort out how Europeans in the colonies imagined themselves and constructed communities, built on asymmetries of race, class, and gender."[23] That, I would argue, is exactly the problem! The "Other" in such texts seems only a "Mirror" that the West uses on its journey of self-discovery, without serious interest in the characteristics of the surface that provides this self-reflection. If colonialism were an "encounter," then in such readings the "Other side" of this encounter often would remain, if not absent, radically undertheorized.

Jane Haggis expresses similar concerns in her critical review of recent studies of white women in British colonies. In reference to one of the texts she analyzes, Haggis points out, "Again and again throughout the text, Fijians and Indians impinge on the tale only in the guise they assume through European eyes."[24] Haggis goes on to add, "Black women are buried deep beneath the weight of white women's vision. . . . Black women are only visible as a reflection of white men's racist and antagonistic sexuality."[25] Haggis then points to a different, less West-focused possibility for colonial studies when she says:

> Rather than forcing ourselves into either/or choices as to which voice dominates and illustrates the world-view, we need to construct our subject in a matrix of voice, action and relation, in order to hint at the tapestry within which they form part and achieve their significance. My own research into the lives of British missionaries in colonial South India has benefited a great deal from talking to Indian people who had dealings with such white women, as well as the women themselves.[26]

In the kinds of work that Haggis and I find problematic, the Third-World context *itself* functions as a Mirror for Western self-reflection. But there are also cases where specific individuals from Third-World backgrounds get similarly "positioned" as Mirrors. I will attempt to illustrate how this works by referring to some of my experiences in discussing issues of contemporary Third-World development. As with some of my experiences with the "Emissary position," these conversations about Third-World development were experiences of discovering myself positioned as Mirror precisely when I failed to live up to the demands of the role.

What I have encountered in some conversations with Western feminists about Third-World development issues is what sounds like a desire to attribute responsibility for Third-World development problems *wholly* to the economic and political agendas of Western nations and to Western-controlled international funding agencies and multinational corporations. I have sometimes tried to introduce a different set of concerns by trying to argue that the economic choices of Third-World nation-states, their local political conflicts and agendas, local mechanisms of exploitation, and local hierarchies such as those of class, caste, or gender, all interact in complex ways to "produce" a number of these problems. I have sometimes also tried to talk about the contributions to these problems made by self-serving and corrupt Third-World governments, and by powerful local elites whose interests are in fact often served by these problematic development policies.

I have seldom succeeded in generating a sustained interest in these concerns. The conversation often deftly moved back to discussing Western contributions to these problems without any significant pause. At other times, my insistence on introducing concerns about Third-World collusion with, and contributions to, problems of Third-World development have led to more overt and explicit "Returns of the West." I have met with rejoinders such as "Third-World nations are after all controlled and dominated by Western powers." I have been informed that corruption and self-enrichment among Third-World politicians, officials, and elites is the result of Third-World countries being sucked into, and corrupted by, "the values of Western capitalism."

I have been forcibly struck by the contrast between the responses provoked by my attempts to introduce concerns about Third-World moral agency and political responsibility and the much more positive and affirmative responses that I have received on occasions when I have criticized Western-inspired development policies or Western political intrusions into Third-World contexts. These sorts of contrasts are responsible for my coming to sense that I was positioned as a Mirror for Western self-reflection. I have come to the recognition that just as many discussions of "the Woman Question" were only tangentially about women, many discussions of "the Third World" are only tangentially about Third-World contexts.

I must emphasize that I am not in the least averse to criticism of Western attitudes and policies in the contexts of colonialism, contemporary development policies, or international politics, either by Westerners or by Third-World individuals. In the context of Third-World development, critical analyses of Western attitudes and policies permit a large measure of (deserved) responsibility for problems to be placed on the Western-controlled global economy, the Western-controlled development policies, and their often tragic impact on Third-World economies. Such a focus has the useful function of challenging self-congratulatory Western perceptions of their "assistance" to Third-World countries or of reminding the West of the degree to which its economic and geopolitical agendas have contributed to the growth of religious fundamentalist movements, say in the Middle East.

In my discussion of the "cultural riches" approach to Third-World cultures and of the "Emissary position," I argued that they served salutary functions in illuminating the achievements of Other Cultures, even as they led to a number of problems if "cultural riches" were *all* one was allowed to focus on, and if an Emissary were *all* one was permitted to be. I would say very much the same sort of thing about approaches to Others that focus on the "Big Bad West." This sort of move is clearly both justified and salutary insofar as the West's record of encounters and relationships with Third-World contexts is often seriously problematic, as is its understanding of the nature and impact of these encounters. To challenge the superior and self-congratulatory attitudes that the West has had with respect to the roles it has played, and continues to play, in Third-World contexts is undeniably important and necessary.

Problems arise, however, when this move, which is useful and important within limits, becomes limitless and occupies all the space of theoretical inquiry and normative appraisal. When this move operates in an unnuanced and totalizing way, what starts as a proper stress upon negative Western attitudes and interferences in the Third World grows into a focus on the Big Bad West, one that operates so as to virtually eclipse the Third World and its agents, institutions, and responses from view. The Third World virtually vanishes, except as a flat backdrop or frame for the Bad Deeds of the West. I have often felt like Alice, watching "the Third World" slowly disappearing from view until it has all the substantiality of the Cheshire Cat's grin.

I am objecting to a focus on Western Bad Deeds that takes up all the available discursive space and that implies that Third-World development problems can all be reduced to the imposition of Western agendas, leaving no room to consider how Third-World economic and political decisions, and local institutions, attitudes, and agendas contribute to these complex problems. I insist that failures to attend to such factors deflect from the agency and responsibility of Third-World nations, institutions, and individuals who get reduced to "Poor Passive Victims of Western Imperialism, Western Capitalism and Western Political Machi-nations." I also insist that such accounts are doomed to inadequacy, at both the causal and the normative levels.

In such perspectives, the Third World and Third-World subjects function as Mirrors in which the West can engage endlessly in the task of returning to itself, even as it believes it is moving its gaze to an Other place. To be a Mirror is different from being a Face that looks back at the West, with a range of expression and responsiveness that, while responses to a Western Other, are also the responses of a Subject-in-Its-Own-Right. To be positioned as a Mirror is to be Put Out of Countenance, to Lose Face. To be treated as a Mirror is to not be treated as an agent capable of "Returning the Gaze," to use Himani Bannerji's apt phrase.[27] A Third-World subject's experience of being positioned as Mirror-to-the-West can perhaps be described as an experience of being blinded by the Unbearable Whiteness of Being!

The Third World as Mirror becomes a reflecting pool that gives a Western Narcissus back his own pale reflection. The Third World plays Echo, without a Voice of its own, with only the power of ventriloquism, hollowly repeating the concerns of the West. The Big Bad West becomes too Big, eclipsing its Other with the Shadow of its Self-Reflection, with its Badness now providing as much of a rationale for its preoccupation with itself as its Goodness did in the civilizing mission of colonial times. As even little children know, Being Bad can often serve even better to secure attention to oneself than Being Good. Finding myself in the Mirror position has more than once reminded me of the joke, where a man says to his date, "Enough about me. Let's talk about you. Whadd'ya think about me?"

I previously argued that the "Emissary position" tends to collude with elements of antifeminist politics in Third-World communities that seek to portray indigenous feminists as "cultural traitors" engaged in antinationalist betrayal. I want to make a similar point about the obsessive focus on the Big Bad West that results when Third-World contexts or subjects are positioned as Mirrors. This focus too tends to collude with perspectives within Third-World contexts that seek to attribute virtually all national problems to the negative impacts of the West, or of "Westernization."

Sometimes these perspectives are explicitly antifeminist, as in the case of Third-World fundamentalisms that not only attribute all national evils to the pernicious effects of "Western influences" on national culture, but also position indigenous feminists as the paradigm embodiments and exemplars of the evils of "Western influence." There are also some more "left-wing" versions of "the Big Bad West" perspective in Third-World contexts that, while not explicitly antifeminist, also constitute obstacles to those Third-World feminist agendas that aim to combine feminist criticism of Western development policies and political intrusions with attention to problematic local structures of class, caste, ethnicity, and gender. Despite significant differences in the understandings and commitments of such right-wing fundamentalist and left-wing political perspectives,

Uma Narayan

deployments of the "Big Bad West" perspective from either side of the Third-World political spectrum constitute impediments to rich and nuanced Third-World feminist analyses, perspectives, and politics.

"Authentic Insiders" and the Perils of Authenticity /

I shall now turn to the role of the "Authentic Insider." The assignment of this position to Third-World individuals is also, I believe, connected to a third strategic response to the dual imperatives of what I have called the "anthropological perspective." Attributing the position of "Authentic Insider" to Third-World persons functions to allow mainstream Westerners to both take an interest in Other cultures and to refrain from criticisms of that culture, since the function of providing a critical perspective on the Other culture is assigned to the "Authentic Insider."

This position is unlike both the positions of Emissary and Mirror in a number of interesting ways. The "Authentic Insider" position permits and sanctions the articulation of political analyses and criticisms of Third-World institutions and practices, while the two others work primarily to deflect and silence them. The underlying strategies involved in the Emissary and Mirror positions can, as I pointed out earlier, be carried out by mainstream Westerners themselves without the actual deployment of Third-World individuals. Unlike these, a strategy that assigns criticism of Other cultures to "Authentic Insiders" needs the actual presence of a member of the relevant "Other culture." The position of "Authentic Insider" is similar to the "Emissary position" in positioning Third-World individuals as "those who speak for their culture" but differs from it insofar as the "Authentic Insider" is *licensed to be critical* in ways that the "Emissary" is not. The position of "Authentic Insider" is different from that of "Mirror to the West" in that it permits more sustained attention to Third-World contexts and cultures without swiftly returning discursive attention to the West. In these respects, it certainly seems to have more discursive latitude and space for Third-World subjects to occupy a range of positions.

The strategy of calling upon "Authentic Insiders" to name and describe the problematic features of their cultural contexts is not without merit. Many Westerners combine ignorance about Other cultures with a "presumption of knowledge." As Leila Ahmed puts it, "Most American women who 'know' that Muslim women in particular are oppressed, know it simply because it is one of those 'facts' lying around in this culture, and most freely admit that they actually know nothing about Islam or Middle Eastern societies."[28] Such presumptive and presumptuous knowledge is also not uncommon among prominent Western male scholars. Allan Bloom and Arthur M. Schlesinger Jr. both provide good examples of "presumptive knowledge" not only of the Indian context but also of Western colonial history when they represent *sati* as an Indian custom that the British ended and were alone concerned to end.[29] Work by feminists of Indian background that gives a very different picture of *sati* as "an Indian custom," and a much more complicated account of the process by which *sati* came to be abolished, provide crucial correctives to such presumptions of knowledge by Westerners.[30] Criticism of Third-World contexts and practices by "Insiders" might often work to ensure accurately critical representations of an Other culture rather than misrepresentations based on "presumptive knowledge."

I argued earlier that both restoring Third-World cultural achievements to view and drawing attention to the West's predations on other parts of the world to challenge its self-congratulatory attitudes have value, and that occupying the "Emissary" and "Mirror" roles, respectively, sometimes has strategic value to Third-World individuals for these reasons, despite their other problems. Similarly, Third-World subjects, including feminists, might find that the "Authentic Insider" role has its moments of utility. It is certainly useful for countering negative portrayals of Third-World communities, practices, and inhabitants grounded in stereotype and ignorance, as a place where a Third-World subject can use her knowledge to point out "what is wrong with Their Picture" without losing space for attending to a variety of things that might in fact be wrong with the institutions and practices of the Third-World context in question.

In what ways does the "Authentic Insider" position become problematic when prescribed or occupied without reflection? The "Authentic Insider" position sets up a "proprietary relationship" between Third-World individuals and the "culture" of their nation or community, in ways that have the potential to function as a set-up. One of the ways in which this happens is when a particular Third-World individual is the *only person* in a particular discursive situation "positioned" to address "Third-World perspectives" or "Indian Women's problems" or the like. This happens not infrequently. When a single voice is positioned as the proprietary "Authentic Insider" with respect to Third-World contexts in general, or to a particular Third-World context, the "singularity" of that voice and its perspective tend to be effaced, and it comes to stand for things like "the Third-World position on human rights" or "the Indian feminist position on development." In such situations, Western perspectives on the issues under discussion emerge with polyphonous richness, with internal divergences, with differences and tensions in evidence, while "the Third-World perspective" appears seamless and monolithic. While there is increasing self-consciousness about assuming that any one position on an issue constitutes "the American position," or "the Feminist position," such awareness sometimes coexists with a failure to see that Third-World contexts and communities are as divided, split, and debate-riven on important issues.[31]

Westerners, including feminists, rarely have to make the qualification that they are not speaking "for the West" or "for all U.S feminists" since it is not frequently assumed they are doing so. Even when they make such disclaimers, the "truth" of their disclaimer is often supported and rendered self-evident by the plurality of positions taken by Western individuals present. When a Third-World subject makes such a disclaimer, the force of its "truth" is rendered relatively inaudible because the discursive context does not bear it out by having a range of Third-World positions actually in evidence. This often positions Third-World individuals in a sort of structural performative contradiction where they have to resort to such disclaimers of "representation" even as they carry out the function of being the sole "representative" from a Third-World background.

Another way in which the "Authentic Insider" position sometimes constitutes a problem is by settings limits on what Third-World individuals are "entitled" to talk about. Even as the "Authentic Insider" is licensed to criticize her own context, she is sometimes deprived of license to critically comment on contexts other than her "own." For instance, to be positioned as an "insider informant from a Third-World nation somewhere else" is to often be denied a passport to address matters of interest or relevance in the West. The injunction to "tell me about your country" can get in the way of what many Third-World subjects could tell about countries other than their "own," and can fail to discern how complicated this "assignment of country" is for many Third-World subjects of diasporic or immigrant background.[32] The assigned "proprietary relationship" between the "Authentic Insider" and "her culture" can therefore function as a threshold of propriety, whereby the "Insider's" desires to talk about contexts other than her "own" acquire the mark of impropriety.

Many Third-World academics in Western contexts are undoubtedly familiar with the experience of being asked to give lectures, or participate in panels, that address "the Third-World aspect" of an issue, even if their interests in, and expertise on, the issue extend beyond that "Third-World aspect." Thus, for a panel on abortion, my presence is much more likely to be solicited to talk about sex-selective abortion in India than to discuss the implications of *Roe* or *Webster*. While I am aware of the importance and interest of addressing the topic of sex-selective abortion in India, and aware too that it is easier for panel organizers to find others who can discuss *Webster*, the "Authentic Insider" position nevertheless works to skew the relationship between the range of interests I have and the range of interests I have occasion to publicly address. The "Authentic Insider " position becomes profoundly limiting for Third-World individuals when they get routinely cast as Native Informants while being denied auditions for other roles they could play just as well.

The imagined "proprietary relationship" between particular "Third-World individuals" and "their culture" often meshes very imperfectly with the range of knowledge and interests they actually have. Sometimes, as I mentioned, it can work to "block" public and professional contributions to interests I do in fact have. At other times, it can result in solicitations to address "Indian" issues or "Third-World issues" where I do not have a shred of expertise in the topics involved. At other times, it results in invitations to address issues that I do happen to have an interest in, but where those who solicited my contribution had no basis for knowing that I in fact have this interest and this knowledge. I have sometimes wondered with wry amusement whether "Third-World individuals" were assumed to have a kind of "knowledge by osmosis" about everything pertaining to "their culture" or to that internally complex entity, "the Third World." I am less amused when I wonder whether the part of my work that pertains to "Third-World issues" might seem like "automatic knowledge" seeping from my Third-World pores, rather than the results of intellectual and political effort!

Another problem with the "Authentic Insider" position has to do with the fact that it is often "conferred" on Third-World subjects by Westerners. The power to confer "authenticity" is also a power to call it into question. The function of the "Authentic Insider" is often to introduce "difference" into the rest of the conversation. While the introduction of "difference" by addressing problems and contexts that would otherwise remain absent from the conversation is pertinent, the "demand for difference" sometimes takes complicated, confused, and confusing forms. People from Third-World backgrounds often disappoint by virtue of being perceived as "Westernized" or "not black enough" or "insufficiently Indian"—as not being "really different enough" to represent "difference," lacking the "real authenticity" of a "true native."

Lata Mani tells an interesting story about such disappointments of "authenticity." The story starts with Mani's visit to a Western acupuncturist, who after finding out that she is writing a thesis on *sati*, first asks her how she understands widow-burning, but swiftly adds, "Of course, you are Westernized and your ideas have probably changed from living here. I wonder what women in India feel about it?" Mani goes on to describe her anger at his "desire for 'true' knowledge, and a demand for authenticity that was impossible for me to meet, given that any agreement between us, however fragile and superficial, would immediately make me 'Westernized': not like 'them' but like 'him.'"[33] The "demand for difference" in such cases seems to run into "supply-side" problems in the "market-place of ideas"!

Feminists from Third-World backgrounds who find themselves positioned as "Authentic Insiders" probably run a greater-than-average risk of causing such disappointment, especially when the terms of their analyses seem familiar to Westerners. Their views, terms, and discourse are sometimes attributed wholesale to a "Westernization" that diminishes their "authenticity." In such encounters, feminists from Third-World backgrounds often discover that they are not "the Real Third-World Woman" who constitute some imagined subsection of the women "back home." However, as Indira Karamcheti usefully insists, "Neither I nor anyone else can deliver a representative, authentic Third-World woman to academia or elsewhere. Even in India, there is no such thing as *the* Indian woman–there are only Indian women. And the individuals are far more interesting than any assumed stories of authenticity."[34]

While seldom explicitly articulated, one consideration behind the disappointed discovery that a particular Third-World feminist is not "the Real Third-World Woman" could perhaps be put thus: "Well, your analysis of *sati*, or female genital mutilation, or sex-selective abortion is the analysis of a Westernized feminist. What are the views of the women who actually undergo, or face the prospect of undergoing, these practices? That is what we really want to know." While this is a pertinent question, it is impertinent in what it misses. Many allegedly "Westernized" Third-World feminists *do* attend to, and reflect upon, the views of the women who actually confront, undergo, or participate in these practices.[35] Sometimes, but not always, they *have* personally confronted an issue, or have relatives or friends who have. But that apart, what they have to offer as feminists is an understanding or analysis of the phenomenon in question, not simply a summary report of what women who are actually subject to these phenomenon think or feel. Western feminists who work on welfare rights or on the issue of funding for abortion are not routinely queried about whether they have been on welfare, or faced difficulty obtaining funds for an abortion, or told that their views do not count since they are not the views of "Real Women on Welfare." While the concern to know the opinions of women directly affected by all these issues is appropriate and legitimate, it is illegitimate to assign those opinions the status of being the *only* things that matter to, or constitute, a feminist political analysis.

I suspect that, some of the time at least, what feminists from Third-World backgrounds are running up against in these cases are "the ambiguities of representation." Any feminist account of an issue constitutes a "representation" in the sense of being an interpretation and analysis of an issue. Such a "representation" is in one sense inevitably the author's own point of view, consisting of her posing of the questions, her marshaling of the evidence, her articulation of what is taking place, and her recommendations for change. Such a "representation" might or might not be "representative" in the sense of embodying assumptions and understandings that are widely shared by other feminists in a particular context or community. Whether a particular "representation" is "representative" in this second sense is an *empirical* question, and is always a matter of aspects, whereby a particular work may embody some widely shared aspects and not others. In any case, the claim that a feminist analysis or point of view is "representative" in this sense does not imply that these shared aspects are common to all feminist analyses in a context or community. The same points apply to whether the assumptions and understandings in a feminist analysis are "representative" of views and perspectives generally held by women or by citizens at large.

There is a third sense of "representation" that pertains to "being a representative of," which refers to whether a speaker or author has authority, or is authorized, to "speak for" a group, institution, community, or nation. It is in this sense of "representation" for instance, that countries have ambassadors and officials who "represent" them in other countries, or in bodies such as the United Nations. "Being a representative" is open to a variety of normative considerations—for instance, it may make an important difference whether such "authority to represent" was dictatorially conferred or democratically acquired. Even where a person's "authority to represent" seems normatively unproblematic, it does not follow that the representative's views are, or always should be, the views of the majority of people in the constituency or group represented.

I believe that one of the dangers of the "Authentic Insider" position is that it risks the conflation of all these senses of "representation." The "Authentic Insider" position on an issue always constitutes a "representation" in the first sense. But the "Authentic Insider" is often confronted by the belief, or the hope, that her views are "representative" in the second and third senses. Part of the value attributed to "insiderness" and of "authenticity" seems to lie in the "Authentic Insider's" capacity to produce accounts that are widely shared by those at "home" and to produce an account that "gives voice to" these shared accounts, thus conferring upon her the authoritative status of "being a representative" of her community or nation. These elements in turn are part of the imagined "proprietary relationship" between an "Authentic Insider" and her "native" cultural context. As a result of these conflations, the "discovery" of the Insider's inability or refusal to "be representative" in the second and third senses of the term works to devalue and invalidate her "representations" or accounts in the first sense.

In these cases, a particular Third-World feminist's voice is first assumed to have value because it is imagined that through her voice "Third-World Women Speak Out" and is then delegitimized *qua analysis*, not for its failures to analyze but for its "failure" to be the sort of voice it was imagined to be! It often fails to be noticed that such "disappoint-ment" is a function of previous "appointments" that were conferred upon a particular Third-World feminist job she neither applied for nor has the "qualifications" to fulfill, since her own understanding of her task is often a more "qualified" and restricted one.

Another problem with the "Authentic Insider" position is that "Authentic Insiders" often seem to be present in order to "speak out" but not necessarily to be "spoken to." What "Authentic Insiders" say is often heard with interest, but they seldom encounter serious criticism or open critical engagement from mainstream members of the audience. Such silence may sometimes well be a result of relative ignorance about the issues and contexts under discussion, and may reflect a choice to focus on trying to understand rather than on trying to respond. But at least some of the time, I believe that the "Insider's" assumed "authenticity" works to intimidate and silence mainstream members of the audience, causing them to refrain from articulating questions or comments that reflect their own critical understanding. There are times when the "authenticity" of the "Insider's experiences" seems explicitly understood to constitute a normative basis for "Outsiders" refraining from critical engagement with the views and viewpoints of Insiders. For instance, Marilyn Friedman says:

> It is most respectful to women in cultures and subcultures other than my own to remind myself repeatedly that they know, as I seldom do, what it is like to live as women in their cultures. Unless very strong rea-sons suggest otherwise, I should, thus, avoid activities and teaching styles that challenge the practices of their lives unless invited or wel-comed by them to do so.[36]

I believe that such normative equations of "respect" with avoidance of criticism handicap rather than aid both the project of multiculturalism and the prospects for feminist solidarity across "cultural differences." For one thing, I believe such normative commitments imagine too strong and unmediated a link between "experience" and "analysis." In such academic and pedagogical situations, what mainstream Westerners encounter are not "experiences" but "analyses" put forward by individuals whose cul-tural contexts differ from their own. While such analyses may draw upon life experiences, they are accounts that are also inevitably suffused with normative assessments, political appraisals, and causal claims. In any cultural context, the "weight of experience" does not *guarantee* that the account or analysis of the "experience" will reflect an accurate understanding of the historical origins of particular local practices, the sociopolitical or causal implications of local institutions, or the normative pros and cons of different strategies that aim to endorse or challenge the local status quo. Furthermore, in any cultural context, similar "experiences" result in very different accounts, analyses, and evaluations of local institutions and practices. There are few, if any, contexts or communities where all individuals or all women agree about what it is like to "live as women in their cultures." When there are extensive disagreements about what it is likc to "livc as womcn" in particular Third-World cultural con texts, and where these disagreements reflect differences in normative understandings and political agendas, it is not clear to me that mainstream Westerners, especially feminists, either can or ought to cultivate a stance of avoiding critical engagement with these analyses.

In academic contexts committed to fostering multiculturalism, mainstream Westerners' avoidance of critical engagement with analyses put forward by members of Third-World communities seem at odds with an important goal of multicultural education. Marilyn Friedman describes this goal when she argues that a multicultural curriculum can "help open up public cultural space for dialogue between Westerners and members of non-Western groups as well as between privileged Westerners and those Westerners who have traditionally been marginalized and silenced within Western culture." [37] While I endorse Friedman's goal, I believe that this goal is not facilitated by mainstream Westerners avoiding critical engagement with views expressed by Third-World subjects, since that forecloses the sorts of exchanges that genuine "dialogue" requires.

Such foreclosures can leave Third-World individuals unsure about whether their failures to make sense will be pointed out, or whether their failures to convince will be subject to interrogation. Being in such situations feels like participating in some sort of "ritual of diversity," where the "Insider" has the instrumental role of "speaking difference" but is not seen to have her own stakes in hearing a rich range of responses and criticisms that would enable her to refine, rearticulate, or defend her account. In short, to be an "Authentic Insider" sometimes results in not being treated as an "authentic scholar" who has the abilities and the training to respond constructively to criticism and to defend her views. The choice to express one's views or present one's analyses in public fora is, for any subject, a choice to receive and react to a variety of responses to one's ideas and positions, positive as well as critical. I find it unsettling to think that when I present my views in public or academic contexts, I need to specifically signify that critical responses to my views from mainstream members of the audience are permissible or welcome.[38] I would argue that, in public discursive encounters, refraining from criticism as a form of "deference" to "Authentic Insiders" functions to defer a rich and genuine engagement with their views and work.

Beyond the "Anthropological Perspective": Strategic "Occupations," and Excesses of "Identity" /

Mainstream Westerners, including feminists, need to consider the fact that just because Third-World contexts have been subject to stereotypic misrepresentation does not imply that misrepresentation is *all* that they suffer from, or that they have no genuinely morally objectionable features of their own. "Refusing to judge" issues affecting Third-World communities, or the representations of these issues by "Insider" subjects, is often a facile and problematic attempt to compensate for a history of misjudgment. Such refusals can become simply one more "Western" gesture that confirms the moral inequality of Third-World cultures by shielding them from the moral and political evaluations that "Western" contexts and practices are subject to. The commitment to refrain from any critical engagement with issues affecting "Third-World cultures" is no more conducive to an adequate representation of these cultures than is misrepresentation. Granting Third-World cultures, or the views of Third-World subjects, a blanket immunity from criticism might function to assuage mainstream Westerners' guilt over misrepresentation and hegemony, but it does very little to politically engage with the problems of individuals and groups who suffer injustice and mistreatment within these contexts. While there are "arrogant" forms of criticisms of one's Others, not all such criticism is necessarily arrogant; and there is potential for serious arrogance in refusing to share one's critical responses in situations that are meant to be "dialogues."

There seems to be a serious tension, if not an outright contradiction, between the commitment to learning about Other cultures and the commitment to refrain from moral or political judgments about them. It is not clear to me that one can really learn about another culture while not subjecting it to *any* critical or normative evaluation, any more than one can really learn about another person without subjecting her to a variety of appraisals and evaluations, both positive and negative. Most often, the commitment "not to judge" Other cultures seems in effect to be a commitment "not to *express* one's judgments"—which only serves to insulate these unexpressed judgments from challenges, corrections, or interrogations they might profit from. In some cases, this "refusal to judge" extends from "Third-World issues" to scholarship on Third-World issues by "insiders." In instances that some friends have witnessed, highly problematic views and claims about Third-World contexts and issues by "Authentic Insiders" have passed without challenge from mainstream Western scholars who would certainly have challenged identical claims made by "outsiders." These "refusals to judge" in turn put an inordinate amount of pressure on other Third-World individuals present, who are left in the position of being the only people in the audience with "legitimacy" to raise critical questions about the views presented. In addition, when one "Insider" criticizes another, there is a concomitant risk of having the disagreements evaluated in terms of the "relative authenticity" of the two individuals, rather than in terms of critical substance.

I would argue that what mainstream Westerners who seek to come to terms with a history of misrepresentation of Other cultures need to cultivate is not a "refusal to judge." Rather, they need to be willing to engage in the considerably more difficult tasks of trying to distinguish misrepresentation and "cultural imperialism" from normatively justifiable criticisms of Third-World institutions and practices. They need to be willing to take on the risks and effort of sharing their critical responses, and subjecting their views and evaluations to refinement and revision in the light of different (and often multiple) analyses of these institutions and practices by "Insiders."

"Refusals to criticize" that stem from the "anthropological perspective" cause particular difficulties for valuable discursive exchanges between mainstream Western feminists and Third-World feminists, precisely because feminist perspectives and politics must go "beyond anthropology" in important ways. All feminist perspectives and politics in some ways share the "anthropological" concern of understanding the perspectives and points of view of those who are "inside" and affected by the institutions and practices that are the objects of feminist inquiry. But while such understandings are important to feminist analyses, such understanding does not usually constitute the "terminus" of feminist inquiry. The goal of a feminist politics is seldom merely to come to a refined and sensitive understanding of various points of view held by those immediately affected by an issue. In the broadest sense, feminist political projects involve commitments to normative and political inquiry, which calls for questioning, assessing, analyzing, and criticizing various points of view. Feminist political perspectives suggest alternatives that seem more normatively adequate and politically salient and attempts redescriptions that confront and challenge some existing points of view in the process of working for social change.

Mainstream Western feminists might have a less "anthropological" relationship to Third-World feminist views and analyses if they recognized that our relationships to our "home" contexts are often in some significant ways similar to their own. There is an important respect in which we all, as feminists, are not outsiders and "Anthropologists" within our own cultures, nor "Native Informants" whose task is to provide raw materials for the reflections of our "Others," nor necessarily those most grievously affected by the institutions and practices we criticize. We are *political subjects* engaged in critical political analyses about things we consider crucial, and care about, in the variety of contexts that constitute our "locations." If Western and Third-World feminists are, in crucial ways political subjects, we need to see relationships between us as political relationships that always involve struggle and contestation, as well as prospects for political solidarity and cooperation.

Seeing the relationship between mainstream Western feminists and Third-World feminists as political would be facilitated by a number of recognitions that call aspects of the "anthropological stance" into question. One such recognition is that there are substantial normative disagreements among those who are "insiders" to *any* context about the meanings and values of particular cultural practices and institutions, about their centrality or place within a culture, and about whether these practices and institutions in fact comport with what are the core values of the culture. When the Civil Rights movement challenged the practice of racial segregation, it was clear that different groups of Americans substantially disagreed upon the meanings and material implications of racial segregation. While segregation was clearly an "American institution," it was also the subject of serious moral and political disagreement among American citizens. Many institutions and practices within Third-World contexts and communities are equally subject to moral and political dispute among their members.[39]

Third-World *feminist* perspectives, as I argued previously, are often integral parts of this ongoing social dialogue and political conversation within their communities, and are themselves often multiple and heterogeneous. Feminists within a particular national context do not necessarily agree in their "take" on particular institutions and practices or on what should be done about them. Just as U.S. feminists have had substantial disagreements about how to understand pornography and what, if anything, to do about it, Indian feminists have their disagreements about pornography as well as about more "Indian" issues such as sex-selective abortions. Insofar as Western feminist interest in "Third-World issues" is political, Indian feminists no choice but to judge and choose between a variety of perspectives on these issues, despite the genuine difficulties of this sort of project.

Besides, a great many issues that politically engage feminists cannot be neatly classified as "Western" or "Third-World" issues. Many of the issues that concern feminists from communities of color in the West also affect women in mainstream white communities, but they have different dimensions and raise specific questions for feminists of color where these issues intersect with specific race and class structures within their communities. When Kimberle Crenshaw critiques the understandings, rhetoric, and institutional structures of U.S. agendas for addressing domestic violence, on the grounds that they do not adequately represent the predicaments and interests of working-class women of color, immigrant women, and women who are not English speakers, she is both addressing issues particularly pertinent to women of color and issues that require the attention and engagement of white feminists if significant changes are to occur.[40] A range of issues of concern to feminists have this sort of structure. They require Third-World feminists to think these issues within the configurations of their own specific communities, and to counter perspectives that are inattentive to these configurations. However, they also require all of us to attend to the various configurations these issues have within and across communities. Without such conjoint attention, feminist policies and remedies will fail to serve the interests of a wide range of differently situated women.

Many "Third-World women's issues" are no longer geographically confined to communities in Third-World nations, as immigration transfuses many of these issues across national boundaries. Female genital mutilation can no longer be seen as an issue pertaining only to "Third-World nations." It is now not only an international issue debated in international human rights forums, but also a Canadian, French, and English issue, as Western nations and legal systems confront questions of law and public policy on this matter.[41] Many "Third-World issues" are, at another level of description, issues that ought to be of concern to mainstream Westerners *qua* citizens of their states. Regimes that violate the human rights of many marginalized groups, including women, receive the economic and political backing of Western nations. Western nations sell arms to fundamentalist regimes in the Third World, even as fundamentalists within Western nations rally support for policies inimical to the interests of Third-World communities within and outside their nation states. A host of issues pertaining to development, technology, and ecological preservation are increasingly transnational. A great many of these issues urgently require feminist collaboration across borders of nation, culture, and community.

I would argue that both for Westerners in general and for Western feminists, "attending to Third-World difference" is less a matter of seeing our "difference" in contrast to Western "sameness" than it is a complicated process of attending to, and trying to understand, a variety of similarities and differences that occur both within and across Western and Third-

World contexts. It involves all of us learning to see and articulate both the different "levels" of analysis and generalizations that are involved in the process of positing certain features as "similarities" or "differences" within and across these contexts, and the political functions that any articulations of "sameness" or "difference" might play within and across these contexts. It involves the difficult process of working toward shared understandings on a variety of issues while engaging in the dangerous but necessary crossing of regional, communal, and national borders, without losing sight of the different meanings that these borders and these crossings might have for different individuals and groups.

I wish to end with some considerations on how I think Third-World individuals, especially feminists, ought to deal with the three roles I have discussed. I would also like to consider the implications of my recommendations for the agendas of multiculturalism within U.S. academia. Let me start by saying that I do not think that Third-World individuals can or should entirely "escape" these roles. If these roles arise out of "Preoccupations," they structure the very entry of many Third-World subjects into the spaces of academic discourse. And though they might not always be comfortable places to inhabit, these roles have helped foster the entry of Third-World voices into Western academic discourse under the aegis of multiculturalism, an entry that is still new and often minimal.[42] These roles have played a part in the realization that inquiries and issues pertaining to Third-World contexts are pertinent and important components of intellectual and academic concern, and that individuals from Third-World backgrounds have vital contributions to make in these areas.

Previously, I made the point that each of these roles does have a significant use. Well-intentioned Westerners whose uncritical understandings of multiculturalism lead them to "impose" these roles are hardly, I believe, the worst dangers to the shaping of contemporary Western academic life. There are many more dangerous and conservative voices who combine Western cultural chauvinism with a distaste for multiculturalist agendas in their entirety, and with a virulent dislike for Third-World cultures and communities. They are not enamored of the Third-World individuals they have now begun to encounter in their academic midst.[43] In confrontations with such conservative Western voices, insisting on the cultural richness of Other cultures or on the blotted record of the West's historical and ongoing machinations in Third-World contexts are very useful moves to make.

My sense of these three roles is that they are all locations that Third-World individuals should "occupy strategically." Preoccupations can be resisted and negotiated by "strategic occupation." That is, these roles should be "occupied" with attention to the specific discursive functions they might serve in particular conversations. These roles become dangerous for many Third-World subjects precisely when they are not "strategically occupied" but rather lived as reified and all-absorbing discursive "identities." They are dangerous in the way that any role can be dangerous when it fixes and consumes all of a person's identity, leaving her no room for other varieties of meaningful connection to her communities, and to the world. These roles, like roles in general, are best lived "in perspective," with the claims and tensions of one's other callings in mind.

I have previously given examples of the ways in which these roles can restrict the discursive spaces that individuals from Third-World backgrounds can occupy. It is one thing for a feminist academic from a Third-World background to sometimes accept or even insist upon "addressing Third-World issues." It is another to come to see "doing Third-World issues" as one's only appointed task or to constantly yield to situations where such address is insisted upon as "the" job one is there to do. Strategically "occupying a position" requires the ability to see, and the skills to evade, such "Im-position." For instance, a Third-World subject might have good reason, in particular contexts, to insist on addressing issues she is interested in that may not be "Third-World issues." As academics, there are usually many things that are matters of one's "background" that are not matters of one's "home."

The roles of Emissary, Mirror, and Authentic Insider are dangerous for both Third-World individuals and for mainstream Westerners precisely when they fail to be seen as roles that Third-World subjects might see fit to play within limits, and come to be seen instead as "identities" that limit and fix the "script" for the discursive contributions of Third-World subjects. Having the sort of "room of one's own" provided by these roles is certainly preferable to having no room at all. But when imposed as the only quarters Third-World individuals can inhabit, they function more like a child's experience of being "sent to one's room," and they are cramped quarters at that. The "room of one's own" model, of multiculturalism or of feminist politics, does not enable us to deal with important political questions that have to do with the complexities of national and global cohabitation.

For Third-World feminists confronted by these roles, I would advocate a strategy of both acceding to these roles and exceeding them. One might find it useful in some instances to "strategically occupy" these roles while also calling attention to one's strategy of occupation. One may find it useful to occupy these roles even as one mocks them, laughs at some of their absurdities, and complains about their limitations. While there is an element of "play" in such play-acting, it is hardly "free play." Having to think about these roles and one's strategies of occupation is always difficult and burdensome, and often irritating. It does leave one, however, with a useful sense of the ways in which what passes for a "free exchange of ideas" is not free, and of the factors that may cause it not to be an "exchange."

To think that one can manage entirely to escape these roles is, I think, a mistake, since one is often "looped back" into some aspects of these roles even as one tries to avoid others. Consider the very project I am caught up in as I write this paper. On the one hand, I am engaged in explicating and criticizing these roles. On the other, even as I write this, I am aware that among other things I have done, I have not entirely escaped functioning as a Mirror to some Westerners. I have relied upon my experiences and my standing as a Third-World feminist "Insider" with respect to these roles, even as I have raised questions about "authenticity" and "insiderhood." To occupy these roles strategically is not to escape them, but rather to be aware of the ways in which one is occupying them and the purposes they may serve in any specific situation.

I believe that individuals from Third-World backgrounds have vitally important roles to play in shaping the agendas and understandings of multiculturalism, and that their critical interventions could serve a variety of useful purposes. Such voices could insist, contra prominent anti-multiculturalists, that the tendency to "grant Other cultures immunity from criticism" may have less to do with a predilection for "relativism" and more to do with well-intentioned attempts to "counter" a history of Western misrepresentation of its "Others." They could help articulate a position that I believe needs articulation—that many of us from Third-World backgrounds have reasons of our own for rejecting such offers of "immunity from criticism." They could help to forcefully make the point that while " Looking Up To" one's Others may *seem* a good strategy to counter a history of "Looking Down Upon" one's Others, it does not satisfy those of us who have reasons to prefer that such encounters with our Others occur Eye-to-Eye and Face-to-Face.

I believe Third-World individuals are crucial partners for many mainstream Western voices engaged in criticism of the agendas and understandings of those who are virulently opposed to all forms of "multiculturalism" even as we serve as critical interlocutors of some of the understandings and strategies at work in versions of academic multiculturalism espoused by mainstream Westerners. Not all visions or versions of multiculturalism are moral or political equals, and both mainstream Western and Third-World subjects need to engage with the question of what sort of multicultural perspectives we wish to support or endorse.

Improving the range of texts we attend to and of issues we take seriously, and encouraging the inclusion of a range of marginalized voices into academic institutions and public debates, remain important social and political tasks. But the stakes involved in this project are, I believe, often overly defined from the point of view of mainstream Western individuals, whereby a diverse and multicultural education is often seen simply as existing to reduce the parochialism and enlarge the understandings of mainstream Western subjects. This perspective effaces the stakes that Third-World individuals have in this project, stakes that go far beyond a simple "inclusion." These broader stakes include critical interventions not only in mainstream Western culture's perspectives on itself but also in many Third-World discourses about their own contexts and communities. These stakes include people of Third-World background having greater access to knowledge about Third-World contexts and communities different from their own, thus expanding their own vision in useful ways. These stakes include critical interventions with respect to different versions of multiculturalism. These stakes also include attending to the shifting, complex, and often problematic ways in which the boundaries between "Western" and "Third-World" cultures and communities, as well as the boundaries between different Third-World cultures and communities themselves, are drawn and maintained.

I am arguing that the stakes that Third-World subjects have in multiculturalism are much larger than simply adding the leaven of "difference" to the academic loaf, or seeking our own little "turfs of difference." As Himani Bannerji puts it:

> Our struggle is for a fundamental change in social relationships rather than for a per community quota of representations in the parliament of "races" and "ethnicities." We are engaged in politics, linking theories with practices, examining ideologies through our lives, and our lives through revolutionary ideas. We are not going shopping in the market of cultural differences.[44]

If education is importantly something that trains us to be intelligent and critical citizens of our nations as well as informed participants in a world where many issues increasingly cross, and cut across, national boundaries, what we need are institutional structures, pedagogical perspectives, and political visions that will help to develop and sustain robust, credible, and genuinely enriching forms of multiculturalism, both within and without academic institutions.

Five /
Eating Cultures

Incorporation, Identity,
and Indian Food[1]

If we no longer think of the relationship between cultures and their adherents as perfectly contiguous, totally synchronous, wholly correspondent, and if we think of cultures as permeable, and on the whole, defensive boundaries between polities, a more promising situation appears. Thus to see Others not as ontologically given but as historically constituted would be to erode the exclusivist biases we so often ascribe to cultures, our own not least. Cultures may then be represented as zones of control or of abandonment, of recollection and of forgetting, of force or of dependence, of exclusiveness or of sharing, all taking place in the global history that is our element. Exile, immigration, and the crossing of boundaries are experiences that can therefore provide us with new narrative forms or, in John Berger's phrase, with other ways of telling.

—Edward W. Said[2]

Introduction /

This essay consists of ruminations on a variety of relationships between food and cultural identity in colonial and postcolonial contexts. Although I focus on the relationships between Indian food and Indian identity, the analysis offered has, I believe, broader implications for the ways we ought to understand the complex relationships between food and identity in a variety of settings, as well as for the ways in which we understand and engage with colonialism and its legacies.

I am interested in the ways in which food is located within cultural and across cultural boundaries, and the ways in which food is linked to issues of identity, prestige, social place, and symbolic meanings. Thinking about food has much to reveal about how we understand our personal and collective identities. Seemingly simple acts of eating are flavored with complicated, and sometimes contradictory, cultural meanings. Thinking about food can help to reveal the rich and messy textures of our attempts at self-understanding, as well as our interesting and problematic understandings of our relationship to social Others.

I will be using food to think about the relationships between colonizers and colonized, about the constitution of different visions of the colonizing project, and about the construction of anticolonialist visions of national culture. I will also use food to talk about the political relationships within the heterogeneous components of contemporary nation states, and about the negotiations of political and cultural identity by members of "ethnic" minorities in contemporary Western societies. Using food to think about colonial and postcolonial history and political realities permits the complexities and paradoxes involved to be thought about vividly and concretely. Such a level of concreteness might, I hope, safeguard against the dangers of sacrificing nuance and detail to totalizing pictures of colonialism and contemporary political landscapes.

Questions of how people connect what they eat to their personal, social, and political identities, of how they use what they eat to distinguish themselves from others within and outside specific social groups, and of the role "cuisine" plays in the scripts of "Nation" and "National identity" have not typically provided "food for thought" for social and political philosophers.[3] The seeming mundaneness of food, its connections to the body, and its gendered linkage to the women's work in the domestic realm, have probably each contributed to the lack of attention these topics have received from philosophers. The two issues concerning food that seem to have received the most attention from social philosophers are questions concerning ethical and social obligations posed by famine and hunger,[4] and questions of vegetarianism and animal rights.[5] In addition, feminist philosophers in particular have begun to explore questions of the connections between eating disorders, body image, and various cultural scripts of gender.[6] I am aware of venturing in this essay into unfamiliar territory, with respect to disciplinary configurations and to my own disciplinary training.

This chapter consists of three sections. In the first section, I link the colonial British "fabrication" of curry powder to their "fabrication" of India, explore the connections between colonial attitudes to Indian food and colonial attitudes to India, and discuss the Indian nationalist response to colonization. I then examine the links between food norms and political and religious animosities in contemporary India. In the second section, I move to curry as an "ethnic food" in Western contexts, discussing the role of "Indian food" in the place of the diasporic Indian community in contemporary England. I address the problematic roles assigned to women in immigrant Indian communities as these communities struggle with the task of balancing forms of assimilation with attempts to preserve cultural identity, and argue that these roles have their roots in the place assigned to women in the Indian nationalist movement. In the third section, I focus on some general implications of the proliferation of "ethnic cuisines" in contemporary Western contexts, and examine the notion that mainstream Westerners' attitudes to "ethnic foods" involve forms of "food colonialism" and "culinary imperialism." I proceed to think about the social meaning of "ethnic food" from the perspective of immigrants to Western contexts, arguing that discussions of multiculturalism and respect for Others must focus not only on relationships between "mainstream citizens" and "ethnic Others" but also on the complex relationships between various minority "ethnic" groups.

There is a geographical shift in the locus of my discussion in each of the three sections. The first section focuses on colonial and postcolonial India; the second section shifts to the immigrant Indian community in England; and the third section focuses in a general way on immigrants within contemporary Western societies in the context of issues of multiculturalism. These shifts follow the migration of curry from India to England and to its contemporary incarnation as an aspect of "ethnic food," providing a vehicle for discussing various facets of colonial and postcolonial India, as well as of contemporary diasporic Indian communities. My discussion also shifts in another way, from food as metaphor and symbol to food as a material practice. I move from metaphoric and symbolic meanings of food in discussing the "imagined Indias" of the colonial encounter and its aftermath to a more concrete discussion of the production and consumption of "ethnic food" in contemporary Western contexts.

As I move into my discussion of curry and colonialism, let me say that the connections between food, identity, and the colonial enterprise are far wider than anything this paper addresses. The search for "spices from the East" played a significant role in early colonial adventures, contributing among other things to the search for sea routes to India, a search that led to Columbus's accidental "discovery of America," and to an early instance of ethnic confusion that resulted in the native peoples of the American continents being dubbed "Indians." Colonialism contributed to the development of the plantation economies of sugar, tea, rubber, and the like, a development connected to the slave trade and to the conversion of numerous colonized populations into indentured plantation labor. John Stuart Mill has no doubts about colonialism's connection to both capitalism and to the "convenient production of tropical commodities" when he writes:

> These [outlying possessions of ours] are hardly to be looked upon as countries, but more properly as outlying agricultural or manufacturing estastes. . . . Our West Indian colonies, for example, cannot be regarded as countries with a productive capital of their own, . . . [but are rather] the place where England finds it convenient to carry on the production of sugar, coffee, and a few other tropical commodities. All the capital employed is English capital.[7]

This paper does not claim to address any of this complex general history of food and colonialism. What follows in the next section is not so much the colonial history of "curry" as an attempt to use "curry" to talk about identities engendered by the colonial experience.

Eating Curry, Eating India /

I shall begin with some observations about the links between curry, colonialism, and Indian identity, inspired by Susan Zlotnick's paper, "Domesticating Imperialism: Curry and Cookbooks in Victorian England,"[8] where Zlotnick analyzes how the Victorian British naturalized and nationalized curry. Not only were curry dishes regularly served to guests in Victorian homes,[9] but also recipes for curry were found in sections of cookbooks devoted to "British cooking," and not in the sections on "Foreign Recipes."[10] Zlotnick connects the incorporation of curry into Victorian English cuisine to the role that the ideology of domesticity played as "a distinguishing feature of Englishness when the English . . . regularly begin to abandon their firesides for colonial destinations" and to the connections between the Victorian ideology of domesticity and the project of colonization.[11] Zlotnick argues that colonialism's

> desire for the Other, and the fear of hybridity it unleashes, could be deactivated through the metaphors of domestication. Middle-class women, as morally regenerative and utterly domestic figures, could take into their homes a hybrid like curry, the mongrelized offspring of England's union with India, and through the ideological effect of domesticating it, erase its foreign origins and represent it as purely English.[12]

While Zlotnick's paper reads the incorporation of curry into Victorian British life, I shall attempt to address this incorporation from the perspective of a postcolonial Indian. A good place to start is with the perplexing nature of the existence of curry. Curry exists of course in one fairly simple sense, on the menus of Indian restaurants and in bottles of curry powder to be found even in unpretentious U.S. grocery stores. But search through the shelves in an Indian kitchen, or grocery store, and you will find no bottles labeled "curry powder." What Indians buy or make are often called "masalas" (as in *Mississippi Masala*),[13] different mixtures of ground spices used to season a variety of dishes. What we called curry in my vegetarian South Indian home were some dishes of spiced mixed vegetables eaten with rice, the spices bearing little resemblance to curry powder.

Trying to decipher what relationship this "curry of home" had with British curry powder and the British term "curry," I looked in the *Oxford English Dictionary* and had the perfect postcolonial moment when I discovered the English term was derived from the Tamil word *kari*. Tamil happens to be my mother-tongue, and "curry" now joins "catamaran" and "mulligatawny" on my list of Tamil words in the English language. The OED defines curry thus: "A preparation of meat, fish, fruit or vegetables, cooked with bruised spices and turmeric, and used as a relish with rice."[14] This is fairly accurate, except that many of the spicy vegetable dishes my mother makes to eat with rice are called not "curry" but other specific Tamil terms.

So British curry powder is really a "fabricated" entity, the logic of colonial commerce imposing a term that signified a particular type of dish onto a specific mixture of spices, which then became a fixed and familiar product, as Indian if you like as Major Grey's mango chutney, which is found in the more pretentious U.S. grocery stores and bears only a family resemblance to the chutneys of home. So, when the British incorporated curry into British cuisine, as Zlotnick vividly describes, they were incorporating the Other into the self,[15] but on the self's terms. They were incorporating not Indian food, but their own "invention" of curry powder, a pattern not too different from the way in which India itself was ingested into the Empire—for India as a modern political entity was "fabricated" through the intervention of British rule, which replaced the masala of the Moghul empire and various kingdoms and princely states with the unitary signifier "India," much as British curry powder replaced local masalas.[16]

So, for the British, eating curry was in a sense eating India—at least the "tasty" India of spices and muslins, silks and shawls, that transformed British tastes;[17] the imaginary India whose allure was necessary to provoke an imperial interest in incorporating this Jewel into the British Crown. But there was another India too in the imperial imagination, one less appetizing, but serving its own purpose in evoking the colonial enterprise—the India of ignorant natives, indolent and incompetent rulers, of vile practices and ungrateful mutinies, of snakes and scorpions, of the heat and the dust and the hard-to-convert heathens—an India that vividly signified the need for the civilizing mission of British rule.

Of these two Indias, the alluring version of India seems to have been more at home in England itself than in the homes of Englishmen in charge of running the Empire in India. The incorporation of curry into "British" cuisine in England, and of Indian artifacts into English homes, was in striking contrast to the attitudes of British colonialists resident in India. Nupur Chaudhuri points out:

> To protect their status as rulers and defend British culture in India, the Anglo-Indians during the nineteenth century chose racial exclusiveness and rejected Indian goods and dishes. . . . Thus, even when the Victorians at home decorated their homes with Indian decorative objects and started to eat curry, nineteenth century memsahibs, to create a British lifestyle in the sub-continent, seem to have collectively rejected Indian objects in their colonial homes, and refused Indian dishes in their diet.[18]

Thus, my point that the British incorporation of curry involved a "fabricated" entity that was incorporated on the self's terms needs to be further complicated. There was no single "British Colonial Subject" or a unified set of terms discernible in the British response to curry. The culinary products of the colonies had different symbolic meaning at dinner tables in England than they did at English dinner tables in the colonies. Making curry part of native British cuisine in England did not expose British curry eaters to the risk of "going native." Incorporating things Indian was an easier task for those resident in England, who did not have to work at distinguishing themselves from their colonial subjects. Their counterparts in India, however, confronted with the proximity of Indians, had to keep their distance, one that was necessary to maintain their belief in their "civilizing" mission.

Interestingly, even as curry became part of English cuisine in England, the market strategy for selling British "curry powder" to the English seems to have involved numerous depictions of Indians testifying to its "authenticity" and excellence, and presumably its superiority to "Indian" curry powder! Zlotnick describes advertisements where figures as disparate as the Maharajah of Kuch Behar and the Viceroy of India's chef, testify to the excellence and superiority of J. Edmund's "The Empress" brand curry powders. As Zlotnick shrewdly notes:

> In all of these testimonials, England emerges as a beneficent nation, dispensing curry powder and pastes to grateful Indians. Moreover, these Indian subjects are not merely testifying to the superior qualities of Mr. Edmund's products, but they are thanking Mr. Edmunds—and by extension the British public—for bestowing "The Empress" upon them, both the curry and the Queen.[19]

Thus, British curry powder proclaims its excellence in England, even as the English in India work at resisting the incorporation of curry into their domestic diets! Just as there was not a unitary British response to curry, there was no unitary British colonial response to India and no single script that captured the British sense of their "civilizing mission." One view of the "civilizing colonial project" is remarkably well set out in Thomas Babbington Macaulay's "Minute on Indian Education," which favors giving Indians a solid British education that would make "natives of this country thoroughly good English scholars,"[20] and would create "a class of persons, Indian in blood and color, but English in taste, in opinions, in morals and in intellect."[21] Macaulay's desire to transform Indians into good Englishmen is neither a disinterested desire to benefit Indians nor a project designed to "anglicize" *all* Indians. It is explicitly designed to facilitate the colonial enterprise by forming "a class who may be interpreters between us and the millions whom we govern."[22]

However, all colonizers did not share Macaulay's vision of the pedagogical or cultural agenda of the colonizing project. Quite different versions of the colonial enterprise are visible in early imperialist debates between British "Anglicists" and "Orientalists" with regard to India and Indians. The research of nineteenth-century Orientalists like William Jones and H. T. Colebrook into Sanskrit literature, philosophy, and history contributed to "the notion of a 'golden age' which had existed in a remote and unchartered period of Indian history."[23] Uma Chakravarti argues that the early Orientalists saw themselves as engaged in reintroducing the Hindu elite to the "impenetrable mystery" of its ancient lore. The Sanskritic tradition, "locked up" till then in the hands of a closed priesthood, was being thrown open and its treasures made available to the people in its "pristine" form; the truths of indigenous traditions were being recuperated. In sum, the Europeans who had successfully constituted their own "true" history were now engaged in giving to Indians the greatest gift of all—a history.[24]

Where Anglicists like Macaulay saw the colonial project as devoted to making Indians into "Englishmen," the Orientalists saw themselves as engaged in recalling Indians to an authentic "Indianness" through the retrieval of their "lost" history and civilization. The Orientalist invocation of an ancient Indian "golden age" was, however, more than an attempt to bestow the gift of history on Indians; it was, not surprisingly, also implicated in narratives that gifted Europeans with a new and flattering view of European history. Research in comparative philology by Orientalists such as Max Muller concluded that Sanskrit was the closest language to an original "Aryan" Indo-European language, and that Europeans and Indians were of the same "racial stock." Max Muller's breathless praise for the ancient Indians as

> the framers of the most wonderful language, the fellow workers in the constitution of the most wonderful concepts, the fathers of the most natural religions, the makers of the most transparent mythologies, the inventors of the most subtle philosophy and the givers of the most elaborate laws.[25]

simultaneously incorporated these same "ancient Indians" into proto-European history as "our nearest intellectual relatives, the Aryans of India."[26] Such representations of this "Aryan connection" served to extend and lengthen the historical pedigree of "European civilization," even as the "degeneration" of this "ancient civilization" in modern times served to underwrite Western cultural superiority and the mandate for colonization. The Orientalist rewriting of Indian history was, at another level, clearly a rewriting of European history. Perhaps stories about "Others" are inevitably stories about oneself.

Just as the British "incorporation" of curry powder made the products of Empire into the familiar fare of "home," the Orientalist incorporation of this "historic Indian golden age" made it part of the history of "home," and translated its glories into yet more historical evidence for European historical and cultural superiority. In another odd twist in the colonial tale, this Orientalist incorporation of India's "golden age" was also part of an invention of a "world history" that was linked to European anti-

Semitism. Max Muller distinguished between two major "races," the superior Aryan and the inferior Semitic, and concluded that the Aryans were "the prominent actors in the great drama of history" and that "it seems to be their mission to link all parts of the world together by the chains of civilization and religion."[27] In a bizarre sleight of historical hand, the incorporation of "ancient Indians" into "European" history also serves as a means to eject "the Semitic race" from European history, a nineteenth-century prefiguring of more strenuous twentieth-century attempts at "ethnic cleansing."[28]

Despite their differences, both Anglicists and Orientalists were engaged in a project of "remaking Indians" in a colonial context that was simultaneously "remaking India." The indigenous Indian intelligentsia were, however, not passive subjects who simply absorbed either vision of themselves, but were active agents who constituted both themselves and their own nationalist versions of India in a manner that borrowed from and subverted both the Anglicist and Orientalist visions. Many of them used their "anglicized" education to deploy the discourses of rights, autonomy, and self-determination for nationalist ends, and called attention to the material exploitation and expropriation involved in a colonial project that was allegedly being undertaken to "civilize" and "protect" the colonized. Many nationalists also used the Orientalist invocation of an historic "golden age" of India to call for reforms of practices such as child-marriage, pointing to the greater rights and status believed to have been accorded women in the "golden age," in order to create pride in an "Indian culture" that would ground an anticolonialist Indian nationalism.

The colonial "Westernization" of India hence paradoxically resulted in the formation of nationalist-minded Indian "subjects," whose imagined India was a different place from that of their colonizers, and who proved to be a much more troublesome "fabrication" than curry powder. The passage to "India" was clearly an extremely complicated journey for both the colonized and the colonizers. Such nationalist "reworkings" of aspects of colonial rhetoric, as well as the harsh material realities of colonial rule, led in various colonies to the insurgencies, mutinies, rebellions, and struggles that eventually resulted in the demise of colonial rule.

I have tried to suggest that the influence of the colonies on colonizing powers is as complicated a matter as the impact of the colonizers on their colonies. While colonialism was clearly causally implicated in the development of national identities in the colonies, the colonies also shaped the nationalist narratives of the colonizing powers. However, I would resist using any facet of my previous discussion of British colonialism in India to draw an unnuanced "Big Picture" of colonialism in general. I think it is important to recognize that the process of colonization was hardly a *uniform* one—there were probably as many differently inflected versions of colonization as there were colonizing nation-states, each with its own vision of its colonizing mandate. And, as the debate on India between the Anglicists and Orientalists suggests, a particular colonizing power did not necessarily have a single unified picture of its colonial agenda. Furthermore, particular colonial powers did not relate in exactly the same ways to each of their colonies. The British "romance" with India and things "Indian," although tainted by coercion, violence, and power, as many romances are, did not have its exact counterpart with respect to other British colonies, say in Africa. Not all colonies were drafted into European proto-history, nor were their peoples discovered to be relatives in the "Aryan Nation."

India, with its huge array of linguistic, religious, and cultural differences, its intricate local hierarchies and political arrangements, the results of many "local" kingdoms negotiating their existence with a series of previous Empires, was arguably less destructively affected by colonialism than were many other colonized peoples. Consider, for instance, the impact of "internal" colonization on those "other Indians"—communities of Native Americans—for whom the colonial "encounter" amounted in many cases to virtual genocide (carried out in part through an extermination of their food supply), vast territorial expropriation, and coercive encounters with cultural and religious "conversion." Although many colonial encounters may have "moments" where the colonizers respond to the colonized both as "incorporated or internalized Other" and as "demonic Other,"[29] the relative impacts of these two "moments" vary from encounter to encounter, changing with shifts in the economic and political agendas of the colonizing powers. Metaphoric pictures of the colonial project, though suggestive and sometimes useful, also run the risk of creating totalizing images of "Colonialism," which can only be resisted by an insistence on an attentive and detailed understanding of particular colonial encounters.

One must also be careful in generalizing about the effects of colonialism on postcolonial nation-states. The traces of British influence on postcolonial India are visible in many ways—from Victorian Gothic railway stations, to the penal code, to the educational system, to our national mania for cricket, and to the retention of English as a national "link language." In striking contrast, I realize how little discernible influence British cuisine has had on everyday Indian *food*. This is not, however, to say that there has been no "Western" influence on what contemporary Indians consume. "Luxury" commodities such as chocolates, cookies, and ice cream are now routinely consumed by middle-class Indians. The recent "liberalization" of the Indian economy has resulted in the entry of Western soft drinks and fast-food chains, albeit predominantly American rather than British, into the Indian market. In sharp contrast to its plebeian place in Western contexts, such fast food is marketed as "trendy" and "fashionable" in India, and is predominantly consumed by better-off urban Indians, who alone can afford the relatively high prices charged for these foods. Western impact on Third-World food consumption has also included strenuous attempts, involving misleading advertising, to market baby formulas to Third-World women, with detrimental impacts on the health of infants no longer breast-fed.

There is a complex dynamic in the ways in which certain aspects of "Western culture" are assimilated into postcolonial contexts, while other aspects are confronted with resistance, a dynamic that goes back to colonial times. It is interesting to note that the dual response of the British bourgeoisie to the colonies, both as an "incorporated Other" and as a "demonic Other," was mirrored by the dual response of the colonized bourgeoisie to its colonizers. Items like cricket or the English language have now been indigenized to an extent where they are experienced as entirely Indian.[30] But I, as a post-Independence child, in a context where actual Englishmen had largely returned home, remember my grandmother's contemptuous remarks about the dirty, meat-eating British, who did not bathe often enough, and her referring to them with a Tamil slur that translates as "white crows"—crows being scavengers and carrion-eaters, as well as birds of ill-omen. I suspect colonial privilege often obstructed the British from recognizing that their prejudiced contempt for the "natives" was entirely reciprocated by sensibilities such as those of my grandmother, for whom their position outside the caste system and their predilection for beef translated them into "untouchables" in her eyes. While I find my grandmother's caste biases entirely repugnant, I have to admit an odd and irrational satisfaction in the knowledge that, in the colonial encounter, the British too were translated by a framework of contempt that matched their own in virulence, though not in force.

The relationship between food and animosity has a complex history in India. My grandmother's visceral repugnance for "beef eaters" extended not only to the British but also to fellow Indians—to the "untouchables," to Muslims,[31] to Christians—in short to all those who did not share her belief in the symbolic sacredness of the cow and the "pollution" involved in the eating of beef. Even today, some of the conflagrations of communal con-flict,[32] mostly instigated by right-wing Hindu fundamentalist parties, are provoked by rumored acts of symbolic desecration involving animal parts—reports of pork thrown into Muslim neighborhoods and places of worship, beef into their Hindu counterparts. Insulated by the distance of exile, I reflect with anguish on how the cow that is not eaten by caste-Hindus because it is considered sacred, and the pig that is not eaten by Muslims because it is considered unclean, both become vehicles for the expression of communal hostility, hatred, and intolerance, their dismemberment and blood evoking all the dismemberment and blood of Partition.[33]

Of course "cultures" are full of contradictions, even about their hatreds. My grandmother, despite her attitudes about "beef-eaters," was capable of delivering sincere homilies about how other people's religions, traditions, and gods were worthy of respect. It has occurred to me that this is an easier logic for polytheists, who are quite prepared to embrace the gods of others, as long as they are not required to surrender their own. So in the same India wracked by communal and religious violence, my mother's family shrine has long included statues of the Virgin Mary and of the Buddha, and pictures of Sikh saints. I'm fairly certain my mother would happily have added Muslim icons, if she hadn't been foiled by Islam's prohibition about representing God in idol form. I recognize with a certain irony that my mother's incorporation of the gods of Others is, like the British incorporation of curry, an example of assimilating Others on the Self's terms, a "cultural habit" that does not seem unique to colonialism.

I recognize that I am a product of the odd inconsistencies of my family's version of Hinduism, where my grandmother's contempt for "beef-eaters" could coexist with injunctions to respect the gods of Others, and with equanimity about sending all three of her children to Catholic schools in Bombay. Her son, my father, is thus a product of a Catholic school education, as am I, her granddaughter.[34] This was an experience that left me with the intriguing picture of myself as a pagan condemned to eternity in Limbo, and with an amused sense of the inconsistencies of a Catholicism that insisted on the Otherness of Hindu "idol worshipers," where I was struck instead by the similarities of incense, holy water, and holy ash, the polytheistic overtones of intercessions to a multiplicity of saints, and by the images of Christ and the Virgin Mary, whose difference from "idols" I was unable to discern. To return to the matter of beef, I have to admit that it occurred to even my childish sensibilities that the killing of the fatted calf for the prodigal's return was not a parable that translated well into my own cultural context, not to mention other queasy matters like consuming the body and blood of Christ.

At the risk of belaboring the obvious, I wish to point out the complexities of my grandmother's attitudes toward eaters of beef.[35] It links her contempt for our British colonizers to her problematic caste-linked Hindu attitudes towards Others who are Indian, attitudes that are themselves full of culturally mediated paradoxes and contradictions. Her ability to be oblivious to these contradictions, and to take herself and her attitudes as unquestionably normative, seem to me to confer upon her an odd kinship to the British she despised. Her attitudes remind me too that the complex moral and political tasks of respecting one's Others is clearly not only a task that haunts and confronts postcolonial Western societies, but also many of their postcolonial Third-World counterparts, where the useful unitary fiction of "nationhood" that was welded in anticolonial struggles now confronts the abiding and often divisive heterogeneity of national populations.

I wish to move away from a picture of colonization as a sudden "interruption" of previously existing, self-governing nation-states, which were then "restored" to national self-determination when the colonizers returned home. Thinking back to the "sense of India" I had as a young child, it is clear to me that I grew up with a picture of an "India that the British had taken over," that Indians then fought to "regain," a struggle that unfortunately resulted in "cracking India"[36] into India and Pakistan, a result of ill-intentioned British machinations. It was much later that I recognized how much this picture was the result of the version of the nationalist struggle I had been taught. As I acquired a more detailed sense of history, I recognized both that the terrain that is now contemporary India, Pakistan, and Bangladesh did not evenly constitute a precolonial "India as a unified political unit," and that the "cracking India" that took place at Partition and resulted in the twin births of India and Pakistan was only one of a series of "crackings" and "rejoinings" that had historically traversed that territory.[37] The "India" I knew was the political "effect" of colonization and of the ensuing nationalist struggle that allowed us definitively to constitute ourselves as "Indians." It was later, too, that I realized the degree to which the political agency of "Indians" was implicated in the realities of Partition. These realizations about the historical construction of modern postcolonial nation-states enabled me to make sense of something that had puzzled me as a child—of why so many national borders on the map of Africa consisted of straight lines.

I am reminded of the "cracked" and "fabricated" nature of contemporary India when I consider the odd nature of "Indian food." For one thing, "Pakistani food" has arguably more in common with certain North Indian cuisines than either has in common with a variety of South Indian cuisines, all of which have their regional variations. For instance, many of the wheat-based unleavened breads served in Indian restaurants—*chapatis*, *rotis*, *puris*, *parathas*, and the like—while common to Pakistani and North Indian cuisines, were not often eaten in South Indian homes. Many South Indian dishes are rice based, such as the steamed dumplings called "idlis," and pancakes called "dosas," both made from fermented rice-and-lentil paste, and are seldom prepared in North Indian homes or served in "Indian" restaurants in the West. I have often accompanied North Indian friends to South Indian eateries, known as "Udipi restaurants" around Bombay, so that they could indulge in these South Indian specialties.[38] Thus, "Indian food" lacks the clear referent in India that it has in Western contexts. While I can intelligibly say "Let's eat Indian food" in Western contexts, this would make little semantic sense in India.[39] And it was in the United States, eating curried goat in a Jamaican restaurant, that I vividly recognized the dispersed culinary effects of colonialism and the difficulty of "tasting India" with distinctiveness.

Incorporating Indians, Feeding England /

While colonialism resulted in the migration of curry to England as well as to its far-flung colonies, postcolonial times have resulted in the migration of Indians to England, where food plays an interesting role in the place of the Indian community. Many contemporary Indian immigrants came to England not directly from India but from former British East African colonies, where Indians were initially imported to build British railroads and where they had settled for several generations before leaving as a result of postcolonial political upheavals. Many were British passport-holders, the results of a colonial largesse that did not anticipate the return of the native, demanding to settle in England and exercise the power of British citizenship.

While curry may have been incorporated with ease into British cuisine, "the desire to assimilate and possess what is external to the self"[40] did not extend to actual people of Indian origin, whose arrival into English society resulted in a national dyspepsia, whose most pronounced symptoms were Enoch Powell and the National Front, and the development of the pastime of "Paki-bashing," a sport now as English as cricket.[41] Apparently, Macaulay's Anglicist hopes for the pedagogical production of brown Englishmen in the colonies failed to prevent a national blanching in the face of contemporary Indian immigration.[42]

Even today, British nationals of Indian origin are "Pakis" for the purposes of insult,[43] more matter-of-factly referred to as "Asians," and call themselves "Black" as a political category.[44] However, there seems to be no British equivalent of the terms Asian American, or Mexican American—a term that would symbolize the incorporation of Indians into the body of British citizens. This lack persists despite the existence of many an "Indian translated into English medium,"[45] to use Salman Rushdie's phrase—people who can identify with Hanif Kureishi's protagonist who says in the opening line of *The Buddha of Suburbia*, "My name is Karim Amir, and I am an Englishman born and bred, almost."[46]

The inability to see members of Third-World immigrant communities as full-fledged participants in Western political contexts goes beyond semantic gaps in acknowledging their presence among the body of Western citizens. Third-World immigrants to Western countries face the expectation that they should feel grateful for having been granted entry. Complaints they might voice about the problematic attitudes and policies they confront in these contexts are often heard merely as symptoms of their ingratitude. The response they encounter is similar to the colonial "Why don't they appreciate us after what we did for them?" attitude that Edward Said describes, an attitude he sees as rooted in "an imagined history of Western endowments and free hand-outs, followed by a reprehensible sequence of ungrateful bitings of that grandly giving 'Western' hand."[47]

The persistence of such attitudes in contemporary Western contexts serves to efface the contributions made by immigrant communities to the life of contemporary Western nations. Food seems to play an important role in the places people of Indian origin have made for themselves in contemporary England. Unlike Bram Stoker's Dracula, who Zlotnick reads as an alien feeding off the British,[48] many people of Indian origin in England derive their livelihood from feeding the British, an example perhaps of feeding the hand that bites you! One of the major contributions made by people of Indian origin to British national life are grocery stores, such as Paradise Stores, owned by Karim's Uncle Anwar, which "opened at eight in the morning and closed at ten at night. They didn't even have Sundays off now."[49] These stores provide the amenities to shop at times not otherwise possible, in a context that, unlike the United States, is not widely blessed with twenty-four-hour supermarkets. The English landscape is also dotted with Indian restaurants that not only serve the curry that the British have so naturalized but also a variety of vegetarian dishes that offer respite to British vegans and vegetarians, where pub-food and fish-and-chips offer few opportunities for finding anything they can eat. At the other end of the food chain, if you like, there are the women of Indian origin who clean the toilets in virtually every rest room I've ever been to in Gatwick and Heathrow.

"Indian food" as it is represented by "Indian restaurants" in Western contexts has, like most immigrants, undergone a series of adaptations and assimilations to the dominant context. The levels of "spiciness" and "hotness" of the dishes served are often evidently toned down to suit the less-seasoned palates of many Western consumers. While some items served in such "restaurant cuisine" approximate some of the everyday fare eaten in Indian homes, a good deal do not. The food in Indian restaurants in the West usually approximates a particular genre of North Indian cuisine, bearing only limited resemblance to the food I ate at home, or to the food served in many of the regional restaurants around India. One of the most noticeable features of contrast between the "Indian food" served in Indian restaurants in the West and the food served in restaurants across India is the much larger degree of regional variation in the latter. In effect, a narrow and standardized subsection of the wide range of dishes and cuisines present in Indian communities becomes reified in the menus of these restaurants, becoming emblematic and representative "authentic Indian food" for Western consumers. Eating in these restaurants, I taste India only faintly via a complex nostalgia of associations, something hard to explain to Western friends who seem oddly disappointed to learn that my acquaintance with, say, *tandoori* chicken is as shallow as theirs, being limited to such restaurant-related contexts.

In much the same way as specific dishes get singled out as "Indian cuisine," certain practices and norms get singled out as emblematic of "our culture and way of life," both in Indian communities in India, and in Indian diasporic communities. These norms and practices are seen as vital to "cultural authenticity and preservation," even as other norms and practices yield to adaptation and change. Not surprisingly, many of the norms and practices that acquire this emblematic status have to do with women and women's sexuality. Both colonial and postcolonial immigrations have resulted in the assigning of problematic roles to women. Just as Zlotnick argues that British women were considered to have a significant role in preserving Englishmen and English culture in the colonies, I would argue that women of Indian origin are assigned a significant and peculiar role in maintaining Indian identity in England and in other immigrant Indian communities. While Indian immigrants have "assimilated" into British culture in various ways, the retention of "Indian cultural identity" has often been grounded in an insistence upon arranged marriages to other Indians, especially on the part of daughters.

In the *Buddha of Suburbia*, Anwar, the owner of Paradise Stores, who has managed for years to ignore the odd dress, politics, and sexual habits of his daughter Jamila, engages in a "Gandhian" hunger strike to blackmail her into marrying the man of his choice, an Indian from India, starving himself to bend her to his will in this ultimate issue of patriarchal "honor."[50] Anwar makes his sense of the "Gandhian" connection explicit when he declares, "If Gandhi could shove out the British from India by not eating, I can get my family to obey me by exactly the same."[51] Women become, once again, especially around issues of marriage and procreation, the imaginary site of resistance to incorporation into an "alien" culture, and to the dreadful prospect of "mixed-race" grandchildren, whom Anwar undoubtedly dreads as much as William Thackeray's Victorian Mr. Sedley dreaded the prospect of "mahogany grandchildren" in *Vanity Fair*.[52]

The demand for cultural conformity that confronts Jamila around the issue of marriage reveals that gender plays a powerful role in immigrant communities, in distinguishing between behavior that constitutes acceptable forms of "assimilation" into the dominant culture, and that which constitutes a "failure to preserve one's cultural identity." When Karim pleads on Jamila's behalf that today people "just marry the person they are into, if they bothered to get married at all," Anwar replies, "That is not our way, boy. Our way is firm."[53] Anwar feels no contradiction between his culturally righteous attitude to Jamila's marriage and his own sneaky indulgence in pork pies when his wife, Jeeta, isn't looking—an indulgence counter to the food rules of his Muslim background that prohibit the eating of pork.[54] Neither Anwar nor Jamila are aware of the degree to which their conflict over the issue of her marriage has nineteenth-century roots in the role assigned to Indian women in the attempts to construct an anti-colonial nationalist identity.

Partha Chatterjee points out that the Indian nationalist project involved "an ideological justification for the selective appropriation of western modernity" that continues to this day. Chatterjee argues that the twin moves involved in the nationalist project were "to cultivate the material techniques of modern western civilization" while "retaining and strengthening the distinctive spiritual essence of the national culture."[55] Learning from the colonizers "the modern sciences and arts of the material world" was necessary to match the colonizers in strength to overthrow them. However, as Chatterjee points out:

> In the entire phase of the nationalist struggle, the crucial need was to protect, preserve and strengthen the inner core of the national culture, its spiritual essence. No encroachments by the colonizer must be allowed in that inner sanctum. In the world, imitation of and adaptation to western norms was a necessity; at home, they were tantamount to annihilation of one's very identity. . . . Adjustments would have to be made in the external world of material activity, and men would bear the brunt of this task. . . . The home was the principal site for expressing the spiritual quality of the national culture, and women must take the main responsibility of protecting and nurturing this quality. No matter what the changes in the external condition of life for women, they must not lose their essentially spiritual (i.e., feminine) virtues; they must not, in other words, become *essentially* westernized.[56]

Feminists in contemporary Third-World nations such as India, or who are members of immigrant communities in the West, whose entire politics often risks dismissal as a symptom of "Westernization," need to pay particular attention to how gender roles continue to be implicated in the scripts of their respective nationalisms and "cultural identities."[57] Without an awareness of the selective and gendered ways in which "cultural identity" is constructed by respective communities, it is difficult to counter allegations that feminist agendas constitute an "aping" of "Western values," and to resist views that present a binary opposition between "feminism" and the "preservation of cultural identity."

The fictional conflict over Jamila's marriage depicted in the *Buddha of Suburbia* is replicated by real life conflicts over Indian women's marriage and sexuality in a number of diasporic Indian communities. Talking of the Indian immigrant community in the United States, Lata Mani argues:

> Questions of tradition and modernity have, since the nineteenth century, been debated on the literal and figurative bodies of women. It thus comes as no surprise that the burden of negotiating the new world is borne disproportionately by women, whose behaviors and desires, real or imagined, become the litmus test for the South Asian community's anxieties or sense of well-being. For instance, the fear of dating that consumes many South Asian families is primarily a fear of women dating . . . it is women who are called on to preserve the ways of the old country.[58]

Just as nineteenth-century English memsahibs in India avoided Indian goods and dishes to maintain their "cultural distinctiveness," twentieth-century Indian women in Indian diasporic communities are expected to safeguard the "cultural distinctiveness" of their communities by refraining from dating, from marriages that are self-arranged, and, most stringently of all, from same-sex relationships. The crucial role assigned to arranged marriages in these scripts of "cultural distinctiveness" confronts many diasporic Indian lesbians with the difficult choice of either submitting to a heterosexual marriage or to losing the support of the family and community that provides some bulwark against the racism they confront from the dominant culture.[59]

Mani succinctly summarizes the adverse effects of these scripts of "cultural preservation" on South Asian women as follows:

> It leads to a naturalization of Indian "tradition" and to the assumption of its generalized, uncritical acceptance in the subcontinent. Critical questioning thus becomes aligned with a negation of Indianness. As a strategy for managing dissent it is especially chilling, since challenging parental authority and aspirations leads to a troubling sense of inauthenticity. Women, made responsible within this discourse for upholding tradition, are particularly vulnerable. Caught between parental desire for conformity with cultural norms that are at odds with their peers' and their own often uneasy integration into U.S. society, many second generation women find themselves literally struggling to know their place and identity.[60]

Feminists from diasporic communities in the West are often confronted with a dual struggle, against the patriarchal and heterosexist constructions of "our culture and values" by their communities, and against the often racist attitudes and agendas of the state. A major source of conflict between the British state and immigrants of Indian origin has been immigration laws that problematize Indian arranged marriages involving the import of marriage partners from India—a conflict whose low point had British immigration officials subjecting prospective Indian brides to the indignity of "virginity tests" upon their arrival.[61] The British state "manipulates women's 'oppression' in Indian and Pakistani 'culture' to legitimate virginity tests, immigration controls, and policing of Asian marriages and family life."[62] In such contexts, feminists have to insist *both* on women's rights to deviate from community-defined "cultural scripts" and on the rights of women and all members of their communities to be free from racist regulations by the state. As Mani describes the "complex strategy" of these feminist struggles:

> On the one hand, they have challenged the self-serving appropriation of "women's issues" by a racist British state. Simultaneously, they have resisted both the "protection" of men in the black community when it has come with a defense of practices oppressive to women, and white feminist attempts to rescue them from patriarchy. In short, black feminists in Britain have refused "salvation," whether by the state in the name of civilized modernity, by black men on behalf of tradition and community integrity, or by white feminists in the interest of ethnocentric versions of women's liberation.[63]

Eating Ethnic, Thinking Postcolonial Realities /

Given the significant role food plays in the economic lives of several immigrant communities in Western countries, I shall proceed to reflect on some of the meanings of "ethnic" foods in contemporary Western contexts, and their implications for current concerns about multiculturalism. I shall begin by discussing Lisa Heldke's ideas of "food colonialism" and "anticolonialist eating" from a postcolonial Indian perspective, hoping to illuminate some differences such a shift reveals.[64] Heldke criticizes a "colonialist stance" among some Americans who eat ethnic foods, in that they display a shallow interest in "exotic" foods, exploit the food of Others to enhance their own prestige and sophistication, and "eat ethnic" without any real interest in, or concern for, the cultural contexts of the ethnic foods eaten.[65] Heldke urges that Westerners think about eating ethnic in an "anticolonialist mode," and suggests a variety of practices to acquire knowledge about the cultural contexts of ethnic foods—from cooking these foods, to reading about the history and culture of their countries of origin, to learning about the cultural contexts of ethnic foods from members of ethnic food cultures.[66]

Heldke is not alone in criticizing activities and attitudes that qualify for the label, "culinary imperialism." In a discussion of M.F.K. Fisher's culinary autobiography, *The Gastronomical Me*, Anne Goldman writes:

> By writing about the food, and by implication the culture of people distinct from herself acquisitively–desirable to sample because "exotic"– Fisher represents such "foreign" traditions as commodities to be (literally) assimilated for her own use. Despite occasional acknowledgments of the material advantages that underwrite the independent self she is at pains to construct in this reminiscence, Fisher pays scant attention to the fact that her self-reliant, feminine Anglo-American "I", who can savor a four-hour, five-course dinner alone, is in large part defined against, and thus contingent upon, the hurried digestions of others.[67]

I am not unsympathetic to Goldman's critique of "culinary imperialism" or to Heldke's critique of "food colonialism." However, I hope to complicate this discussion of "food colonialism" by thinking about ethnic foods from the point of view of immigrants to Western contexts, rather than from that of mainstream Western citizens. I intend to then return to the issues raised by Heldke and Goldman, issues pertaining to appropriate stances toward the cultural objects, artifacts, and practices of one's Others. I will begin by explaining why I start in a different place, with positive attitudes to eating the food of "Others."

The caste-based dietary rules of my specific community in their strictest form required vegetarianism and prohibited the consumption of food cooked by non-Brahmins. In the household I lived in as a child, my grandmother insisted on these rules, but in an oddly selective manner. These rules no longer applied strictly to the men of the family when they were at work or in their social life outside the household. The rules, however, applied quite strictly within the home. How-ever, my grandmother would eat North Indian junk food on her walks to the beach, a violation of caste-food rules in which I was a childish coconspirator, sworn not to reveal these indulgences to others at home. I do not really know how my grandmother squared her violation of these rules at the beach with her insistence upon them at home. My grandmother's scrupulousness about these rules within the home might be connected to the construction of the home as a site of cultural purity where women were responsible for the preservation of Indian culture. Her status as an older woman, however, freed her to an extent from surveillance and accountability, permitting her to leave home for walks that were not permitted my mother, allowing her the opportunity, like Anwar, to eat in violation of community food-rules when "no one was looking."

Despite the complications beneath my grandmother's violation of caste food-rules, her dietary transgressions seem symptomatic of a growing tendency of Indians to eat food outside their own parochial food-traditions, and to care less about various breaches of caste food-norms, even within the home. Growing up in a context where food was intimately connected to caste status and various regimes of "purity," it is "food parochialism" that tends to strike me as dangerous, while a willingness to eat the food of Others seems to indicate at least a growing democracy of the palate. While eating "ethnic foods" in restaurants might result only in shallow, commodified, and consumerist interaction with an "Other" culinary culture, it seems preferable at least to the complete lack of acquaintance that permits the different foods of "Others" to appear simply as marks of their "strangeness" and "Otherness."

Eating in these restaurants, I also register how "ethnic restaurants" are an important form of economic enterprise for many immigrants to the West, and how Westerners' taste for "ethnic cuisines" contributes to the economic survival of immigrants, the desire for culinary novelty making a positive difference to profit margins. Many immigrants would, I suspect, describe the proliferation of interest in ethnic cuisines *positively*, as an aspect of formerly colonized outsiders infiltrating and transforming Western life—where, for instance, England would no longer be England without its Indian restaurants and grocery stores. While the proliferation of Western interest in "ethnic" cuisines might run the danger of reinforcing the attitudes Heldke describes as "food colonialism," the creation of such interest also involves the agency of shrewd ethnic immigrants helping to create, and making a living out of, the "Western" desire for culinary novelty.

The conditions under which such immigrant purveyors of ethnic cuisines exercise their agency should not, however, be romanticized. I am sympathetic to Heldke's critique when she argues that the low prices such "ethnic" foods command, as well as the low tips that are often regarded as justified by those who eat these foods, are connected to a devaluing of what such "ethnic food" is worth, in contrast say to the high prices and tips consumers pay for "culturally elevated" food such as French cuisine. Heldke argues:

> Restaurant owners and workers from these countries often come to the U.S. to escape repressive, exploitative conditions in their own country—conditions often created or exacerbated by U.S. government policies and corporate policies. They open restaurants where all members of the family work long hours, seven days a week. Yet we who eat in these restaurants often remain deliberately ignorant of these conditions. . . . We happily pay the low bills—and leave poor tips besides. That is, our cultural colonialist behavior has material consequences as well.[68]

While I believe it is useful to urge "Western eaters" to reflect on their participation in "food colonialist" attitudes, there are genuine difficulties that are likely to confront "Western eaters" who wish to mitigate their "food colonialism" by acquiring deeper knowledge of the cultural contexts of the ethnic foods they eat. Trying to acquire such knowledge from members of a particular "ethnic food culture" is not an easy task. Members of "ethnic" food cultures are often no more knowledgeable about the cultural contexts of their food than people in general are about their own food cultures.[69] Attempts to give or receive such "cultural information" about "ethnic foods" in the context of eating in "ethnic restaurants" is complicated by the complex and sometimes tenuous relationship between the food served in these restaurants and the food more routinely eaten by members of the particular "ethnic" group, complexities I have previously referred to. As a veteran of many such attempts at "cultural exchange" in Indian restaurants, I must admit that my attempts to address the complicated relationships between the food we were eating and "Indian food" probably left my friends feeling as confused as informed, and me feeling more than a little pedantic!

Apart from the difficulties involved in trying to provide "cultural information" about hybrid entities such as "ethnic food" in restaurants, there are also questions about what such knowledge means to different subjects, and what uses they might put it to. At least at times, the desire to be "eating ethnic Culture" in addition to one's ethnic food can be problematic. For instance, a mainstream Western eater's cultural knowledge about "ethnic foods" could be used to constitute herself as a "colonial savant," adding to her worldliness and prestige in much the same manner as "knowledge" of faraway places she has visited as a tourist might add to her perceived sophistication. My point is that a superficial sort of intellectual curiosity about the cultural contexts of ethnic foods could, paradoxically, serve to add another element to "food colonialism"—where eating ethnic foods would further contribute to Westerners' prestige and sophistication because their eating was enhanced by a few sprinkles of spicy information about the "cultural context" of the ethnic food eaten.

The relationship between "knowledge" of Others and respect for their cultural differences is a complicated and contingent matter. Lack of respect for Others is not always a mere function of ignorance about their cultures, but is often rooted in misinterpretations and inadequate conceptualizations of what one does know about those cultures. Furthermore, an interest in "Other cultures" has been tied to complex imperialist agendas. Anthropology, for instance, is still in the process of coming to terms with its colonialist history and entanglements in imperialist projects, and with power relationships that continue to mark encounters between those who study and those studied.[70]

How mainstream Westerners might eat "ethnic foods" without lapsing into "food colonialism" is a difficult question. I would argue that Western eaters of ethnic foods need to cultivate more reflective attention to complexities involved in the production and consumption of the "ethnic foods" they eat. They might, for instance, reflect on the race and class structures that affect the lives of the workers who prepare and serve that food, and on the implications of class differences between immigrants who own these restaurants and the immigrants who work for them. They might think about the fact that while low-cost "mainstream" eating places, such as diners and fast-food chains, employ a predominantly *female* labor-force,[71] many "ethnic" restaurants employ mostly *male* immigrants. They might consider the roles that factors such as class, race, and gender play in the economic exploitation involved in the food industry in general. They might register the fact that while the "ethnic foods" they consume involve the commodification of race and ethnicity, other foods they consume that are not "ethnically marked," such as the bananas,[72] grapes, and lettuce in supermarkets, might well be the products of the exploited labor of Third-World or migrant workers. They might reflect on the fact that some of the same restaurants that provide them with cheap and "exotic" ethnic food often serve as regular eating-places for "ethnic" male immigrants away from their families, and as social meeting-places for them.

In short, attention to and reflectiveness about the material and political realities of food production and consumption would help counter the passive and unthinking eating of "ethnic foods" that partially constitutes "food colonialism."[73] However, no amount of concerned reflection alone can undo the fact that mainstream eaters would remain privileged consumers, benefiting from the structural inequalities and unpleasant material realities that often form the contexts in which "ethnic food" is produced and consumed. "Colonialist" and "imperialist" encounters involve more than problematic "attitudes" or "stances" toward Others. They involve relationships between groups that are embedded in historically constituted relationships of power between different groups and different "cultures," relationships that will change in fundamental ways only with large-scale changes in these power relationships. If mainstream individuals believe that concern and reflection alone can completely free them from "colonialist eating," they mistakenly conflate changes in their individual stances and attitudes with concrete changes in social relationships of power.

On the other hand, reflection on the conditions under which "ethnic food" is produced and consumed is certainly preferable to its passive consumption by mainstream eaters. Ideally, such reflection might play a part in motivating political support for concrete changes in economic and social relationships, in both national and international contexts. I would insist that what mainstream Western eaters who are concerned about "food colonialism" need to think about most are not the original cultural contexts of these "ethnic foods" but rather the complex social and political implications of who produces and who eats such "ethnic foods" within Western contexts. Much as they may, at times willingly, signify a "somewhere else," ethnic foods as well as members of ethnic communities in the West also need to be seen as integral parts of the Western contexts they inhabit.

This recognition is particularly important because members of ethnic immigrant communities, though they may wish to retain some aspects of their "ethnic roots," also often wish to be seen as legitimate members of the cultural context they inhabit in the West, and not as a mere "representative of a foreign culture somewhere else." As Amy Ling declares, "I may not be able to persuade anyone to like tofu or Asian American writers, but I can tell them . . . we're here."[74] Or, as Mitsuye Yamada's poem "Mirror, Mirror" puts it:

People keep asking me where I come from
says my son
Trouble is I'm american on the inside
and oriental on the outside.

No Doug
Turn that outside in
THIS is what American looks like.[75]

If "ethnic" restaurants are perceived as an integral part of contemporary Western landscapes, lack of knowledge about particular ethnic cuisines can be seen as a result of the complex cultural landscape, where ethnic and mainstream eaters alike eat more than they understand. A white American eating in an Indian restaurant becomes part of the fraternity of ignorance generated by complex multicultural and multiracial contexts, just as I do when I eat in an Ethiopian restaurant in New York, or at my local diner. It is important to remember that "ethnic foods" in Western contexts are not only eaten by "mainstream Western eaters" and by members of that particular ethnic food culture, but also by members of *other* "ethnic groups" as well.

I have been struck by the degree to which discussions about colonialism and postcolonialism focus on the relationship between "Western colonizers" and "colonized Third-World peoples," and seldom on the impact of colonialism on the relationships between different colonized Third-World people. This tendency is mirrored in general discussions of multiculturalism in ethnically diverse contemporary Western societies, which tend to focus on the relationships between "mainstream whites" and their "ethnic Others." I worry that this tendency leads to "the West" and to "mainstream whites" retaining an overwhelming centrality in these discussions, a centrality that appears both problematic and anachronistic at a time when conflicts between members of different minority "ethnic groups" appear with increasing frequency.[76] One legacy of colonial history is that members of "dominant" or "mainstream" groups are encouraged to have contemptuous or "culturally imperialist" attitudes to their Others. However, forms of cultural insularity, parochialism, and contempt for one's Others are not the unique purview of white Westerners. I would argue that serious attempts to think through the task of fostering respect for one's Others must focus not only on relationships between "mainstream citizens" and "ethnic Others" but also on the complex and often politically charged relationships between members of various ethnic groups.[77]

Where prejudiced attitudes, as well as large-scale social structures such as *de facto* occupational and residential segregation, still conspire to restrict the contacts many of us have with members of other ethnic groups, as friends, as neighbors, as fellow students and workers, and as fellow citizens, the recognition that these separations diminish the collective possibilities of all our lives is imperative. In such situations, gustatory relish for the food of "Others" may help contribute to an appreciation of their presence in the national community, despite ignorance about the cultural contexts of their foods. We risk privileging the *mind* too much if we ignore the ways in which a more carnal relish may sometimes contribute to appreciation in ways as powerful as intellectual "understanding."

I need to clarify my position at this point. Criticizing the fact that "food, as we know, has long been the acceptable face of multi-culturalism,"[78] Sneja Gunew goes on to say, "In Australia, one of the few unthreatening ways to speak of multi-culturalism is in relation to food, in other words, to say that all these migrants have improved the diversity of the national cuisine. The usual way in which this diversity is acceptably celebrated is through a multi-cultural food festival."[79] While I do appreciate the critical point Gunew is making, I am also inclined to be less negative about the role of food in multiculturalism. One reason for my more positive view of the place of food in "multicultural contexts" is that there are far too many "unacceptable faces" of multiculturalism in many countries that portray immigrants as draining national resources, as taking away jobs from nationals, as straining the welfare system, as contributing to crime, poverty, and the pollution of the national cultural fabric. In such contexts, "acceptable faces" of multiculturalism, however limited, are not without purpose.

I must admit too that my responses are colored by my own experiences of summer "multicultural food festivals" in downtown Poughkeepsie,

New York, events that are one of the few vibrant uses of urban public space in the community. The multiethnic composition not only of the food and its vendors, but also of the members of the community who participate in its consumption, make these food festivals one of the rare public events where one is visually, viscerally, and positively conscious of the range of diverse ethnicities and identities that in fact constitute us as a community. I am influenced too by rich and provocative accounts of various lessons people seem to learn from "eating the food of Others." Talking of a Middle Eastern friend in whose house she often ate, Louise DeSalvo says, "I learned in her house, too, that dinner could consistently be a delicious occasion. Her father also cooked—extremely rare in the fifties. And I saw the special pleasure a woman takes from eating a meal at her own table that she hasn't had to prepare."[80]

While I wish to focus attention on populations from former colonies entering and transforming Western societies, I do not wish to suggest that the presence and impact of colonizers in former colonies is *identical* to the impact that people from former colonies have had on the West, something unfortunately suggested by Gordon Lewis's description of this process as "a colonialism in reverse."[81] The presence of many people of Third-World origins in Western societies is rooted in the injustices of colonialism and racism, such as the forced transfer of enslaved African peoples and the harsh treatment of indentured labor "imported" from the Third World. Many immigrants of Third-World background continue to confront the realities of racism, unequal treatment, and unequal citizenship in Western societies. The effects that people from former colonies have had on Western societies have rarely been mediated by the ease of power.

On the other hand, I am sympathetic to Lewis's recognition that immigration to the West has led to a new sense of what it means to be "English."[82] Lewis is echoed by Salman Rushdie, who points out that English, "no longer an English language, now grows from many roots; and those whom it once colonized are carving out large territories in the language for themselves."[83] Sneja Gunew reminds us that "the monuments of British literature these days include works by such writers as Salman Rushdie, Ben Okri, and Kazuo Ishiguro . . . there is now a general awareness that literatures in English are quite a different matter from English literature."[84] The transformative effects of people of Third-World background upon the economic, political, and cultural fabric of postcolonial Western societies cannot be denied. I would, however, like to complement Lewis's insight by pointing out that the presence of people of Third-World background in Western societies redefines not only what it means to be English or French or American, but also what it means to be Indian or Chinese or West Indian, and creates different ways in which such identities can be claimed or negotiated.[85] Cuisines too, as I have pointed out, change in these shifts and encounters, with "mainstream" and "ethnic" cuisines incorporating and borrowing from each other even as they maintain their distinctiveness.

Colonialisms and their aftermath have not only involved the movement of Third-World people to Western countries, but also the movement of colonized people from one former colony to another. Having grown up partly in Uganda, I am aware of how the presence of people from the Indian subcontinent in countries like Uganda and Kenya was linked to the larger history of Empire. As an ethnic Tamil, I am aware of how the British "export" of Tamil laborers to work in plantations is partly responsible for the presence of Tamil populations in countries such as Sri Lanka and Malaysia, a presence that is implicated in current political struggles over national identity in these countries. Colonialism and its aftermath are also deeply implicated in the formation of contemporary "ethnic identities," identities that Appadurai argues are "direct products of and responses to the policies of various nation states over the last century or more."[86] Appadurai says:

> Much of the intensity of communal terror between Hindus and Muslims in India can be traced to the special ways in which religious communities were put into separate electorates by the British in the early part of the twentieth century. The divide between Sinhalas and Tamils in Sri Lanka owes at least as much to decisions about the Sinhala language as the exclusive medium of instruction in the postcolonial university system in Sri Lanka and to the exploitation of religious hatreds in the context of electoral politics there.[87]

Colonial and postcolonial history have not only redefined for many of us the idea of "home" but also complicated the meanings of exile. Referring to the "landscape of persons who constitute the shifting world in which we live," Appadurai points out that we live in a world where increasingly "more persons and groups deal with the realities of having to move, or the fantasies of wanting to move," and that today,

> men and women from villages in India think not just of moving to Poona or Madras, but of moving to Dubai or Houston, and refugees from Sri Lanka find themselves in South India as well as in Canada, just as the Hmong are driven to London as well as to Philadelphia.[88]

These various global migrations pose some interesting and difficult questions with regard to thinking about the "cultural flows" that occur in their wake. It has struck me that there are often interesting asymmetries between representations of mainstream Western culture's relationships to the artifacts and products of "Other cultures," and representations of the relationships of "Other cultures" to the artifacts and products of "Western culture." Representations of the former relationship are often marked by worries about Western culture's rapacious and imperialist appetite for "exotica" and "Otherness." Representations of the latter sort of relationship are often marked by a different set of worries—about Western culture's homogenizing and corrupting impact on "Other cultures," spotting once pristine landscapes with McDonald's and Coca-Cola, and corrupting "Others" with the habits of consumerism and the desire for "Western" gadgets and commodities. While I do not wish to suggest that such representations are entirely unwarranted, I also find myself troubled by some of their possible implications.

Part of what worries me about these representations is their overly uniform representations of "Other cultures" as the "victims of Western culture"—victims either of "Western consumerism" or of other rapacious and corruptive inroads by "Western culture." The agency of "Others" often gets completely effaced in these representations. They convey little sense of shrewdness and enterprise involved in the activities of Others who "market Otherness" to Western consumers, little sense of the ways in which "Western commodities" are adapted and hybridized in Other places, and little sense of the fact that "commodity consumerism" in non-Western contexts might well be a result of growing middle classes and market economies *within* these contexts, rather than an effect of something purely nameable as "Western culture." Part of what worries me too is an underlying tendency to see both "Western culture" and a great many "Other cultures" as simpler and less hybrid than they already are. I would urge paying more attention to the selective processes that lead to marking certain products and commodities as "exotic" and "ethnic" and other products as "Western" in a variety of contexts, attending to why and how certain commodities come to be thus marked, while other aspects of this multidirectional transnational flow and its "cross-cultural" effects remain unmarked and unnoticed.

Postcolonial global reality is a history of multiple migrations, rooted in a number of different historical processes. War, ethnic conflicts within and between postcolonial nation-states, the creation of refugee populations, and the lure of economic opportunities play different roles in these migrations, adding new layers of political complexity and cultural negotiation to often already heterogeneous national communities. Many nations across the world confront the complex political tasks of maintaining the allegiances of heterogeneous communities to the fragile notion of a unified "nationhood." For citizens of Western and Third-World countries alike, the political task of coming to terms with complex heterogeneous and pluralistic societies remains urgent. The common tendency to talk about multiculturalism as a peculiarly "Western" problem is, therefore, "parochial because it insistently refuses to recognize that the challenge of diasporic pluralism is now global."[89]

There are few ready-made recipes for how to combine the various ingredients of contemporary nation-states into political and cultural arrangements that are nourishing to all their members. Thinking about food might offer some lessons about how to think about the cultural identities and commodities that enter into our heterogeneous societies. To return to the curry with which I began, I believe its complicated history reveals the ways in which "cultural products" are often constructed and the varying ways in which they are deployed over time in the construction of national and ethnic identities. It has lessons to teach us, I believe, about the political processes that lead to certain products and commodities emerging as "exotic" and "ethnic" even as others are naturalized, nationalized, and indigenized, and about how these markings change and shift across contexts and over time. It forces us to think about the vocabularies we use and the complexities that confront us as we try to analyze such multidirectional transnational flows and their "cross-cultural" effects. Food might also offer some useful metaphors for our complex political realities. For instance, there have been suggestions that the American picture of the nation as a "melting pot" be replaced by the concept of a "stir fry," where the ingredients, though combined, retain their distinctiveness. I shall end by adding to this hoard the metaphoric usefulness of "masalas," those various combinations of assorted spices, each with its own subtle contribution to seasoning the curry of national life.

Notes /
One / Contesting Cultures

1. A shorter version of this paper, entitled "A Culture of One's Own: Situating Feminist Perspectives Inside Third World Cultures," was presented at the American Political Science Association Meeting, Washington, D.C., September 1993.

2. Original quote from Mikhail M. Bakhtin, *The Dialogic Imagination: Four Essays*, ed. Michael Holquist, trans. Caryl Emerson and Michael Holquist, (Austin: University of Texas Press, 1981). Quoted, with changes of the "he's" in Bakhtin's text to "she's" by Norma Alarcon, "Traddutora, Traditora: A Paradigmatic Figure of Chicana Feminism" in *Scattered Hegemonies: Postmodernity and Transnational Feminist Practices*, Inderpal Grewal and Caren Kaplan, eds. (Minneapolis: University of Minnesota Press, 1994), p. 119.

3. Fred Pfeil, "No Basta Teorizar: In-Difference to Solidarity in Contemporary Fiction, Theory and Practice," in *Scattered Hegemonies: Postmodernity and Transnational Feminist Practices*, Inderpal Grewal and Caren Kaplan, eds. (Minneapolis: University of Minnesota Press, 1994), pp. 222–223.

4. See, for instance, Barbara Smith, *Home Girls: A Black Feminist Anthology* (New York: Kitchen Table/Women of Color Press, 1983).

5. Christina Crosby further criticizes this assumption for being an assumption that "ontology is the ground of epistemology." "Dealing with Differences," in *Feminists Theorize the Political*, Judith Butler and Joan W. Scott, eds. (New York: Routledge, 1992), p. 137.

6. I have no desire to reify the category of "Third-World feminist" by implying that all feminists from Third-World backgrounds confront these dismissals. Nor do I wish to suggest that all Third-World women who engage in women-centered politics embrace the term "feminist." The term "feminism" has sometimes been questioned and sometimes rejected by Third-World women because of its perceived limitations. See for instance, Madhu Kishwar, "Why I Do Not Call Myself a Feminist," *Manushi* 61 (Nov.–Dec., 1990). Others refuse to surrender the term. See Cheryl Johnson-Odim's reasons for this position in "Common Themes, Different Contexts: Third World Women and Feminism," in C. Mohanty, A. Russo, and L. Torres, eds., *Third World Women and the Politics of Feminism* (Bloomington: Indiana University Press, 1991).

7. bell hooks, "Choosing the Margin as Space of Radical Openness," *Framework* 36 (1989), p. 16.

8. See the essays in *Identity Politics and Women: Cultural Reassertions and Feminisms in International Perspective*, Valentine M. Moghadam, ed. (Boulder, Colo.: Westview Press, 1994).

9. Mary Fainsod Katzenstein, "Organizing Against Violence: Strategies of the Indian Feminist Movement," *Pacific Affairs* 62, 1 (1989), p. 69.

10. I have no desire to portray my mother as a perennially passive "victim." I was born within a year of my parents' marriage, so the mother I knew when I was young was a relatively "new" wife. A few years into her marriage, my mother did in fact both implicitly and explicitly contest her mother-in-law's treatment of her, a fairly common pattern. It is interesting to me, however, that the articulate and formidable woman my mother became continued to be "proud" of her earlier "innocence."

11. Pointing to the problematic implications of the use of the figure of the Mother to symbolize the Nation, Nalini Natarajan asks, "How does the figure of Mother cement nation?" Natarajan answers, "She suggests common mythic origins. Like the land (which gives shelter and 'bears'), she is eternal, patient, essential. During moments of 'national' resurgence, the land is figured as a woman and a mother. . . . Thus, 'Mother India' is an enormously powerful cultural signifier, gaining strength not only from atavistic memories from Hindu epics, Sita, Sati, Savitri, Draupadi, but also its use in moments of national (typically conflated with Hindu) cultural resurgence." See Nalini Natarajan, "Woman, Nation, and Narration in Midnight's Children" in *Scattered Hegemonies: Postmodernity and Transnational Feminist Practices*, Inderpal Grewal and Caren Kaplan, eds. (Minneapolis: University of Minnesota Press, 1994). As a result of such conflations of Mother and Nation, there is some risk in my use of the term "mother-cultures." But I think there is an interesting difference in comparing the cultural contexts in which one was raised to a *particular mother*, rather than to an *idealized Mother*. Particular mothers not only differ from other mothers, but also deviate in many interesting ways from the idealized Mother.

12. This is a cultural awareness that seems to carry over into communities of the Indian diaspora. I found it interesting that a number of the selections in *Our Feet Walk the Sky: Women of the South Asian Diaspora*, edited by The Women of South Asian Descent Collective (San Francisco: Aunt Lute Books, 1993), address women's problems in the context of marriage.

13. For accounts of problems faced by women of color and women in immigrant communities in the United States who are victims of domestic violence, see Kimberle Crenshaw, "Mapping the Margins: Intersectionality, Identity Politics and Violence against Women of Color," *Stanford Law Review* 43, 6 (July 1991); and Uma Narayan, "'Male-Order' Brides: Immigrant Women, Domestic Violence and Immigration Law," *Hypatia* 10, 1 (Winter 1995).

14. Ibid.

15. In some cases, coming together in feminist groups or participating in consciousness-raising sessions have been crucial to bringing about the *recognition* that some problems faced by women, such as domestic violence or job discrimination, were not rare and random, but more frequent and systematic than previously assumed. I am suggesting that, in other cases, the widespread nature of some particular problems affecting women is well known and acknowledged in a particular cultural context. In these cases, what feminist political participation contributes is not so much a recognition of the frequency of the problem but the political terms in which to understand these problems and to challenge the structures that contribute to their frequency.

16. See Madhu Kishwar and Ruth Vanita, eds., *In Search of Answers: Indian Voices from Manushi* (London: Zed Press, 1984). Also see Mary Fainsod Katzen-

stein, "Organizing Against Violence: Strategies of the Indian Feminist Movement," *Pacific Affairs* 62, 1 (1989).

17. As Charlotte Bunch puts it, "Feminism has been ridiculed and stereotyped worldwide, and the issues we have raised have usually not been taken seriously by the media. But, remarkably, despite this bad press, feminism has continued to grow. Women's groups all over the world, but especially in the Third World, are taking up issues ranging from housing, nutrition, and poverty to militarism, sexual and reproductive freedom, and violence against women." See her "Global Feminisms: Going Beyond the Boundaries," speech given in 1985, reprinted in *Frontline Feminism 1975–1995: Essays from Sojourner's First 20 Years* (San Francisco: Aunt Lute Books, 1995), p. 456.

18. Inderpal Grewal, "Autobiographic Subjects and Diasporic Locations: Meatless Days and Borderlands" in *Scattered Hegemonies: Postmodernity, and Transnational Feminist Practices*, Inderpal Grewal and Caren Kaplan, eds. (Minneapolis: University of Minnesota Press, 1994), p. 244.

19. This was usually in fact a partial rejection, as I make clear later in the essay.

20. Partha Chatterjee quotes Bhudev Mukhopadhyay's "Essay on the Family," published in Bengali in 1882, as saying, "In the Arya system, the wife is a goddess. In the European system, she is a partner and companion." See his "Colonialism, Nationalism and Colonized Women: The Contest in India," *American Ethnologist*, (1989), p. 626.

21. Sucheta Mazumdar, "Women on the March: Right-Wing Mobilization in Contemporary India," *Feminist Review* 49 (Spring 1995), p. 4.

22. Ibid.

23. For instance, see Lata Mani, "Contentious Traditions: The Debate on SATI in Colonial India," *Cultural Critique* 7 (1987), pp. 119–156.

24. Richard Shannon, *The Crisis of Imperialism, 1865–1915* (St. Albans: Paladin, 1976), p. 13.

25. G.W.F. Hegel, *The Philosophy of History*, trans. J. Sibree (New York: Dover, 1956), p. 99.

26. Karl Marx, "On Imperialism in India" in *The Marx-Engels Reader*, ed. Robert Tucker (New York: Norton, 1972), p. 578–79.

27. See the chapter on "Eating Cultures: Incorporation, Identity, and Indian Food" in this volume.

28. Andre Beteille, "Some Observations on the Comparative Method," *Economic and Political Weekly*, October 6, 1990.

29. The line between "traditionalists" and "modernists" is a blurred rather than a sharp line, and one that often shifted over time.

30. Partha Chatterjee, "Colonialism, Nationalism and Colonized Women: The Contest in India," *American Ethnologist* (1989), p. 623

31. Antoinette Burton, *Burdens of History: British Feminists, Indian Women and Imperial Culture, 1865–1915* (Chapel Hill: University of North Carolina Press, 1994), p. 35.

32. Ibid., p. 45.

33. Ibid., p. 211. Burton's book deals with British feminists in England. For a complex account of how various Western women "in the colonies" related to political issues of local women's status and empowerment, see Kumari Jayawardena, *The White Women's Other Burden* (New York: Routledge, 1995).

34. Burton, *Burdens of History*, p. 20.

35. Ibid., p. 31.

36. Indian women made significant contributions to the Independence movement. Of their nationalist activities, Suruchi Thapar says, "Within the home, they spun and wove khadi, held classes to educate other women and contributed significantly to nationalist literature. . . . Shelter and nursing care were also provided to nationalist leaders who were in hiding from British authorities. . . . In addition, they held meetings and demonstrations, took part in satyagraha, picketed toddy and foreign-cloth shops, went to prison and also suffered brutalities at the hands of the British police." Suruchi Thapar, "Women as Activists; Women as Symbols: A Study of the Indian Nationalist Movement," *Feminist Review* 44 (Summer 1993), p. 81.

37. Sucheta Mazumdar, "Moving Away From A Secular Vision? Women, Nation and the Cultural Construction of Hindu India," in *Identity Politics and Women: Cultural Reassertions and Feminisms in International Perspective*, Valentine M. Moghadam, ed. (Boulder, Colo.: Westview Press, 1994), p. 257.

38. Partha Chatterjee, "Colonialism, Nationalism and Colonized Women: The Contest in India," *American Ethnologist* (1989), p. 625.

39. Himani Bannerji, "Fashioning a Self: Educational Proposals for and by Women in Popular Magazines in Colonial Bengal," *Economic and Political Weekly* (Oct. 26, 1991), p. 58.

40. Arguing that "the social order connecting home and the world in which nationalists paced the new woman was contrasted not only with that of modern Western society; it was explicitly distinguished from the patriarchy of indigenous tradition," Chatterjee adds, "The new patriarchy was also sharply distinguished from the immediate social and cultural condition in which the majority of the people lived, for the 'new' woman was quite the reverse of the 'common' woman, who was coarse, vulgar, loud, quarrelsome, devoid of superior moral sense, sexually promiscuous, subjected to brutal physical oppression by males." Partha Chatterjee, "Colonialism, Nationalism and Colonized Women: The Contest in India," *American Ethnologist* (1989), p. 627.

41. Antonio Gramsci, *Selections from the Prison Notebooks*, trans. Quintin Hoare, (London: Lawrence and Wishart, 1971), p. 324.

42. Kumari Jayawardena makes a similar point when she argues that terms like "Western" when deployed against South Asian feminists are "red herrings—crude attempts to denounce the women's struggle . . . used today by right-wing and authoritarian regimes to deny women their rights. See the Introduction to her *The White Women's Other Burden* (New York: Routledge, 1995), p. 15. For related critiques of appeals to "tradition and culture" to justify denials of human rights to Third-World women, see Arati Rao, "The Politics of Gender and Culture in International Human Rights Discourse," and Ann Elizabeth Mayer, "Cultural Particularism as a Bar to Women's Rights: Reflections on the Middle Eastern Experience," both in *Women's Rights, Human Rights*, Julie Peters and Andrea Wolper, eds. (New York: Routledge, 1995).

43. Hindu fundamentalists, for instance, had no problem using "the language of rights, asserting that they should have the right, as Hindus and as women" to commit and propagate *sati*. Sucheta Mazumdar, "Moving Away From A Secular Vision? Women, Nation and the Cultural Construction of Hindu India," in *Identity Politics and Women: Cultural Reassertions and Feminisms in International*

Perspective, Valentine M. Moghadam, ed. (Boulder, Colo.: Westview Press, 1994), p. 284.

44. I do not succeed, of course. I will never know, but find it difficult not to imagine some of what this meant. The same paternal grandmother who tormented my mother came to Bombay from South India as a very young wife, cut off from her kinfolk as well as from her linguistic community, subject to her own mother-in-law and the harsh exigencies of lower-middle class urban life. She had thirteen children, of whom only three survived infancy.

45. For a discussion of the complex nature of the nineteenth-century Indian reformers' and the colonial government's discourses on India, see the essays in *Recasting Women: Essays in Indian Colonial History*, Kumkum Sangari and Suresh Vaid, eds. (New Brunswick, N.J.: Rutgers University Press, 1990).

46. See Kumari Jayawardena's discussion of nineteenth-century missionary girls' schools in India and Sri Lanka in her chapter, "Christianity and the 'Westernized Oriental Gentlewomen'," in her *The White Women's Other Burden* (New York: Routledge, 1995).

47. Partha Chatterjee, "Colonialism, Nationalism and Colonized Women: The Contest in India," *American Ethnologist* (1989), p. 628.

48. Ibid.

49. Ibid.

50. In discussing Western women's struggles for higher education, Kumari Jayawardena points out "women's university colleges were first started in London (Bedford College, 1849) and Cambridge (Girton 1869 and Newnham 1873). The most bitter struggle, however, was that of medical women beginning in 1865 when Elizabeth Garrett Anderson, having passed the examinations held by the Society of Apothecaries, was refused admission to medical colleges in England. In 1870, seven women were admitted as medical students to the University of Edinburgh, but after opposition from a section of the faculty and students (and a court case) they were expelled." *The White Woman's Other Burden: Western Women and South Asia During British Rule* (New York: Routledge, 1995), p. 76.

51. This case received a lot of attention in the Indian press, and was also the subject of a segment on *60 Minutes* that aired on January 3rd, 1993.

52. The nature and rapidity of these changes are clearly connected to the privileged class and caste context of the women in my family. While I do not wish to represent these changes as representative of changes that have affected *all* Indian women, I also wish to point out that these sorts of changes have affected the lives of millions of Indian women even as they have by-passed millions of others. The lives of many groups of poor and lower-caste women who have migrated to urban areas have also been marked by significant changes in gender roles, different in degree and kind, but changes nevertheless.

53. I remember my maternal grandfather in "traditional" South Indian dress. The explanation of this difference might have to do with my paternal grandfather working in Bombay while my maternal grandfather worked in a smaller South Indian town.

54. Inderpal Grewal and Çaren Kaplan point out the interesting fact that the Indian Mattel affiliate chose to market Barbie dressed in a sari while Ken remains dressed in "American" clothes! See their "Introduction: Transnational Feminist Practices and Questions of Postmodernity," in *Scattered Hegemonies* (Minneapolis: University of Minnesota Press, 1996), p. 13.

55. As Partha Chatterjee explains, "The dress of the *bhadramahila*, for instance, went through a whole phase of experimentation before what was known as the *brahmika* sari (a form of wearing the sari in combination with blouse, petticoat and shoes made fashionable in Brahmo households) became accepted as standard for middle-class women." Partha Chatterjee, "Colonialism, Nationalism and Colonized Women: The Contest in India," *American Ethnologist* (1989), p. 629. It is also interesting to note that in recent years, the *salwar kameez*, which consists of "pants" with a long top, often worn with a long scarf-like *dupatta* over the shoulders, seems to be replacing the sari as the preferred mode of "Indian" dress for many younger women, especially in urban areas. In this process, a type of dress that was initially only worn by women in *some* Indian communities, and completely not worn in others, is rapidly being converted into a "national" garment.

56. In some countries, "Western" dress for women seems more of an issue than it appears. Chung-Hee Soh indicates that despite Korean men as well as the majority of urban professional women having given up the traditional *hanbok*, some female politicians still wear it, and the President's wife always wears it for occasions of state. She also provides an interesting analysis of the reasons some female politicians wear the *hanbok* while others do not. See "Skirts, Trousers, or Hanbok? The Politics of Image Making Among Korean Women Legislators," *Women's Studies International Forum* 15, 3 (May–June 1992).

57. These skirts and dresses "acceptable" in Bombay were at least mid-calf length. Considerably shorter items of apparel I "acceptably" wore in the context of the Indian community in Uganda were left behind by a previous maternal veto!

58. Partha Chatterjee, "Colonialism, Nationalism and Colonized Women: The Contest in India," *American Ethnologist* (1989), p. 624. Also see his *Nationalist Thought and the Colonial World: A Derivative Discourse?* (London: Zed Books, 1986.)

59. For example, Aijaz Ahmed points out that "there is a powerful political movement in India which says . . . that Indian socialists are not true Indians because Marxism *originated* in Europe; that the Indian state should not be a secular state because secularism is a western construct." Aijaz Ahmad, "The Politics of Literary Postcoloniality," *Race and Class* 36 (January–March 1995), p. 5.

60. Cherrie Moraga, "From a Long Line of Vendidas: Chicanas and Feminism," in *Theorizing Feminism: Parallel Trends in the Humanities and Social Sciences*, Anne C. Herman and Abigail J. Stewart, eds. (Boulder, Colo.: Westview Press, 1994), p. 38. Moraga goes on to point out how this strategy is used to equate "lesbians" with "feminists," reinforcing the idea that lesbianism is "a white thing," a strategy that is used to depict Chicana lesbian feminists as doubly "alien"; p. 42. For a discussion of the dismissal of feminism as "white" in the context of the African American community, see Barbara Smith's "Introduction" to *Home Girls* (New York: Kitchen Table/Women of Color Press, 1983).

61. Marie-Aimee Helie-Lucas, quoted by Gayatri Chakravarti Spivak in "French Feminism Revisited." In *Feminists Theorize the Political*, Judith Butler and Joan W. Scott, eds. (New York: Routledge, 1992), p. 71.

62. Rosi Braidotti, "The Exile, the Nomad and the Migrant: Reflections on International Feminism," *Women's Studies International Forum* 15, 1 (1992), pp. 7–8.

63. See Luke Charles Harris and Uma Narayan, "Affirmative Action and the Myth of Preferential Treatment: A Transformative Critique of the Terms of the

Affirmative Action Debate," *Harvard BlackLetter Law Journal* II (Spring 1994).

64. See Linda Gordon and Nancy Fraser, "The Genealogy of Dependency: Tracing A Keyword of the U.S. Welfare State," *Signs* 19, 2 (Winter 1993).

65. Benedict Anderson, *Imagined Communities: Reflections on the Origin and Spread of Nationalism*, rev. ed. (London: Verso 1991).

66. Gayatri Chakravarti Spivak, "French Feminism Revisited," in *Feminists Theorize the Political*, Judith Butler and Joan W. Scott, eds. (New York: Routledge, 1992), p. 71.

67. Virginia Woolf, *Three Guineas* (New York: Harcourt, Brace and Company, 1938).

68. Inderpal Grewal and Caren Kaplan, "Introduction: Transnational Feminist Practices and Questions of Postmodernity," in *Scattered Hegemonies*, p. 17.

69. For more information about the different constellations of interests that foster Islamization in different countries, leading to varied strategies for controlling women, see Deniz Kandiyoti, ed., *Women, Islam and the State* (Philadelphia: Temple University Press, 1991.)

70. See Sara Diamond, *Spiritual Warfare* (Boston: South End Press, 1989).

Two / Restoring History and Politics to "Third-World Traditions"

1. Kumkum Sangari and Suresh Vaid, "Recasting Women: An Introduction," in *Recasting Women: Essays in Colonial History*, K. Sangari and S. Vaid, eds. (New Brunswick, N.J.: Rutgers University Press, 1990), p. 18.

2. Mary Daly, "Indian Suttee: The Ultimate Consummation of Marriage," in *Gyn/Ecology: The MetaEthics of Radical Feminism* (Boston: Beacon Press, 1978), pp. 113–133.

3. As a matter of fairness, I prefer not to cite examples without explaining what I find objectionable about particular representations and analyses. In any case, since Daly's chapter provides me with good examples of the problems I wish to discuss, I prefer not to criticize specifically other works, but leave it to my readers to spot other instances when they come across them.

4. The term "Third World" was initially developed during the Cold War era as a political term to broadly designate nations that had formerly been Western colonies and that sought to construct an identity that differentiated them both from Western nations and from the nations of the former "Soviet bloc." Political movements have also applied the term "Third World" to designate communities of color in Western contexts because of the similarities between their relationships to Western nations and mainstream Western cultures and those of peoples in former Western colonies. Thus, in its broadest sense, the term "Third World" applies both to the inhabitants of former Western colonies and to communities of color within Western nations. However, since this paper focuses on an Indian practice, my use of the term "Third World" in this paper tends to be slanted toward non-Western national contexts. However, the general facets of the "colonialist stance" that I analyze might well illuminate problems in Western feminist representations of problems affecting women of color in their own national contexts.

5. For examples of such critiques see bell hooks, *Ain't I A Woman* (Boston: South End Press, 1981), and *From Margin to Center* (Boston: South End Press, 1984); Cherrie Moraga and Gloria Anzaldúa, eds., *This Bridge Called My Back:*

Writings by Radical Women of Color (New York: Kitchen Table/Women of Color Press, 1981); and Valerie Amos and Pratibha Parmar, "Challenging Imperial Feminism" in *Feminist Review* 17 (Autumn 1984).

6. For a discussion of several varieties of problematic "inclusion" and "exclusion" of the perspectives of women of color in mainstream feminist theorizing, see Maria C. Lugones, "On the Logic of Pluralist Feminism," in *Feminist Ethics*, Claudia Card, ed. (Lawrence, Kans.: University Press of Kansas, 1991).

7. The term "communities of resistance" originates from and "refers to the broad-based opposition of refugee, migrant and black groups in Britain to the idea of a common nation—Europe 1992." Chandra Talpade Mohanty, "Cartographies of Struggle: Third World Women and the Politics of Feminism," in *Third World Women and the Politics of Feminism*, Chandra Talpade Mohanty, Ann Russo, and Lourdes Torres, eds. (Bloomington: Indiana University Press, 1991), p. 5.

8. I also invite readers to read Daly's chapters on "African Genital Mutilation" and "Chinese Footbinding" in the same book, after they read this essay, to see how the "colonialist stance" plays a role in Daly's discussion of these topics. I also invite readers to look at Audre Lorde's critical response to *Gyn/Ecology* in her "Open Letter to Mary Daly," in *Sister/Outsider: Essays and Speeches* (Trumansburg, N.Y.: Crossing Press, 1984), pp. 66–71.

9. These lines read, "The Indian rite of suttee, or widow-burning, might at first appear totally alien to contemporary Western society, where widows are not ceremoniously burned alive on the funeral pyres of their husbands. Closer examination unveils its connectedness to 'our' rituals." Mary Daly, *Gyn/Ecology*, p. 114.

10. Mary Daly, *Gyn/Ecology*, pp. 114–115.

11. Even in the Bengal Presidency, which has one of the highest recorded rates of *sati* in the nineteenth-century, estimates indicate that widow-immolations affected roughly 0.2 percent of all widows. For a considerable amount of data regarding nineteenth-century incidence of *sati*, see Anand Yang, "Whose *Sati*? Widow-burning in Early Nineteenth Century India," in *Expanding the Boundaries of Women's History: Essays on Women in the Third World*, Cheryl Johnson-Odim and Margaret Strobel, eds. (Bloomington: Indiana University Press, 1992), pp. 74–100.

12. "European Witchburnings: Purifying the Body of Christ," in *Gyn/Ecology*, pp. 178–122.

13. Mary Daly, *Gyn/Ecology*, p. 179.

14. See Veena Talwar Oldenburg, "Dowry Murders in India: A Preliminary Examination of the Historical Evidence," in Meredeth Turshen and Briavel Holcomb, eds. *Women's Lives and Public Policy: The International Experience*, (Westport, Conn.: Greenwood Press, 1993).

15. See the chapter "Contesting Cultures" in this volume, especially the section entitled "Burdens of History."

16. Mary Daly, *Gyn/Ecology*, p. 117. Since *sati* was practiced by some Brahmin communities, it would have had to also spread to others of "higher caste" if Daly's view of its "origins" is correct!

17. While Veena Talwar Oldenburg suggests something similar to Daly when she ventures that *sati* developed out of the practice of *jauhar*, a practice that was confined to the wives of "princes and warriors," she is talking about *sati* in *one* region of India, Rajasthan (see note 55). However, there is little reason to assume the *same* "origins" for this practice in all the areas in which it occurred, especially

since *jauhar* was practiced in even fewer areas than was *sati*. Daly is assuming that *sati* had unitary origins and causes in all areas in which it occurred, which might well not be the case.

18. Daly's representation of *sati* as a "Hindu" practice is rendered additionally problematic because of the complexities involved in finding a basis for *sati* in "Hinduism," a problem I will address in the next section.

19. It seems important to feminist scholarship to understand the variety of factors that led to widow-immolations occurring in some communities and geographical areas and not in others, despite the widespread stigmatization of widows in Hindu society and the more uniform prevalence of other forms of mistreatment of widows. Feminist analysis arguably has a stake in understanding why specific atrocities against women committed in the name of "Tradition" were more widely perpetrated by some groups and not by others, and the factors that affected these variations. For a considerable amount of data regarding nineteenth-century incidence of *sati*, see Anand Yang, "Whose *Sati*?" in *Expanding the Boundaries of Women's History*, Cheryl Johnson-Odimand and Margaret Strobel, eds. (Bloomington: Indiana University Press, 1992), pp. 74–100.

20. Chandra Talpade Mohanty, "Under Western Eyes: Feminist Scholarship and Colonial Discourses" in *Third World Women and the Politics of Feminism*, p. 59.

21. Radhika Parameswaran, "'Coverage of Bride Burning' in the Dallas Observer: A Cultural Analysis of the 'Other'," *Frontiers*, 16, 2/3, pp. 69–100.

22. Ibid., p. 87.

23. See "Cross-Cultural Connections, Border-Crossings, and 'Death By Culture': Thinking About Dowry-Murders in India and Domestic-Violence Murders in the United States," also in this volume.

24. Gustav Niebuhr, "Unholy Fires on Hallowed Ground," *New York Times*, Sunday, June 23, 1996, E-5. Not only does the article not represent these church burnings as "American," but it also refers to the "horror and outrage of many Americans" and cites a number of moves being made by Jewish groups, the Christian Coalition, and U.S. politicians to actively respond to these burnings.

25. Marnia Lazreg, "Feminism and Difference: The Perils of Writing as a Woman on Women in Algeria," *Feminist Issues* 14, 1 (Spring 1988), p. 87.

26. Romila Thapar, "Perspective in History," *Seminar* 342, February 1988, reprinted in *Sati*, Mulk Raj Anand, ed. (Delhi: B.R. Publishing Corporation, 1989), p. 84.

27. Romila Thapar, "Perspective in History." Ashis Nandy suggests a similar historical picture when he argues that there were only three historical periods when *sati* was a large-scale problem—when the southern Vijayanagaram kingdom was collapsing in the sixteenth century, when the Rajput principalities were under attack in the Middle Ages, and when the British were establishing domination in Bengal in the late eighteenth and early nineteenth centuries. Ashis Nandy, "The Sociology of *Sati*," in *Sati*, Mulk Raj Anand, ed. (Delhi: B.R. Publishing Corporation, 1989), p. 158. These "epidemics" of *sati* that Nandy discusses not only occurred at different historical periods but also were located in geographically distinct parts of contemporary India. In addition, Thapar disagrees with Nandy about whether the historical evidence supports his view that there was an "epidemic of *sati*" at the time of Vijayanagaram's collapse.

28. The functions served range from consolidation of caste-status to the exclud-

ing of women from claims to the husband's property. For instance, Thapar points out that the time when Brahmin widows were first "permitted" to become *satis* in the second century A.D. was a time when Brahmin property holders increased in number, owing to land grants they received from royalty. The Bengali communities, which had the highest numbers of *satis* in colonial times, followed the Dayabhag system of inheritance that gave the wife inheritance claims to her husband's property, unlike the inheritance system in most Hindu communities, which only entitled her to food, clothing, and shelter. See Thapar, "Perspective in History," *Seminar* 342 (February 1988).

29. As Lazreg goes on to note, "Because women are subsumed under religion in fundamental terms, they are inevitably seen as evolving in nonhistorical time. They virtually have no history. Any analysis of change is therefore foreclosed." Marnia Lazreg, "Feminism and Difference: The Perils of Writing as a Woman on Women in Algeria," *Feminist Issues* 14, 1 (Spring 1988), p. 87.

30. Ibid.

31. Mary Daly, *Gyn/Ecology*, p. 127.

32. Antoinette Burton argues that the "oppressed woman of the colonies" was a figure central to the claims for political rights and agency for Western women generated by what she describes as "imperial feminism" in her *Burdens of History: British Feminists, Indian Women and Imperial Culture, 1865–1915* (Chapel Hill: University of North Carolina Press, 1994), pp. 30–31.

33. Mary Daly, *Gyn/Ecology*, p. 119.

34. Katherine Mayo, *Mother India* (New York: Blue Ribbon Books, 1927).

35. Daly also fails to mention that Mayo's "earlier book, *Isles of Fear*, made the case against granting independence to the Philippines." Joanna Liddle and Rama Joshi, *Daughters of Independence: Gender, Caste and Class in India* (New Brunswick, N.J.: Rutgers University Press, 1986), p. 31.

36. Elizabeth Bumiller, *May You Be the Mother of a Hundred Sons: A Journey Among the Women of India* (New York: Fawcett Columbine, 1990), p. 21.

37. It is also clear that Mayo's book was widely read by the British as having successfully made the case. Liddle and Joshi cite a 1927 report in the *London New Statesman and Nation*, whose bizarre rhetoric speaks for itself. The report stated that Mayo's book revealed "the filthy personal habits of even the most highly educated classes in India—which, like the degradation of Hindu women, are unequaled even among the most primitive African or Australian savages. . . . Katherine Mayo makes the claim for Swaraj {self-rule} seem nonsense and the will to grant it almost a crime." See *Daughters of Independence: Gender, Caste and Class in India* (New Brunswick, N.J.: Rutgers University Press, 1986), p. 31.

38. Sharon Sievers, "Six (or More) Feminists in Search of a Historian," in *Expanding the Boundaries of Women's History: Essays on Women in the Third World*, Cheryl Johnson-Odim and Margaret Strobel, eds. (Bloomington: Indiana University Press, 1992), p. 322.

39. For the views of one nineteenth-century Indian nationalist reformer, see *The English Works of Rammohun Roy*, Kalidas Nag and Debyajyoti Burman, eds. (Calcutta: Sadharan Brahmosamaj, 1945–1948), part 3.

40. Mary Daly, *Gyn/Ecology*, p. 129.

41. Sievers, "Six or More Feminists," p. 322.

42. In this respect, my perspective seems close to that of Chandra Mohanty, who selects particular examples of Western feminist discourse on Third-World

women out for critical analysis rather than objecting to them in totality. See her "Under Western Eyes: Feminist Scholarship and Colonial Discourses," in *Third World Women and the Politics of Feminism.*

43. Lata Mani, "Contentious Traditions: The Debate on *SATI* in Colonial India," *Cultural Critique* (Fall 1987).

44. Views of *sati* as a widespread "Hindu" or "Indian" practice seem at odds with official historical data, which shows only 8,134 *satis* occurring between 1815 and 1828, with 63 percent of the cases being concentrated in the area around Calcutta. Ashis Nandy has suggested that rates of *sati* rose sharply in this period, and argues that the surge can be traced to the upper-class Bengali gentry resorting to *sati* as "an important proof of their conformity to older norms at a time when these norms had become shaky within" as a result of British colonial rule. Ashis Nandy, "*Sati*: A Nineteenth Century Tale of Women, Violence and Protest," in *Rammohun Roy and the Process of Modernization in India*, V. C. Joshi, ed. (Delhi: Vikas, 1975), p. 175.

45. Mani, "Contentious Traditions: The Debate on *SATI* in Colonial India," in *Cultural Critique* (Fall 1987), p. 124.

46. I must point out the odd nature of the assumption that "natives" were likely to be driven to outrage by interference in religious matters in ways that they would not be outraged by other sorts of interference in the status quo, which was after all what the whole process of colonial rule amounted to! The imaginary figure of the morally outraged interventionist colonial seems almost noble in comparison with actual colonial officials absorbed in worries about the *realpolitik* implications of intervention!

47. Mani herself characterizes part of her project with colonial *sati* as trying to show "what is occluded in the following statement which represents a dominant story about colonialism and the question of woman: we came, we saw, we were horrified, we intervened." Lata Mani, "Multiple Mediations: Feminist Scholarship in the Age of Multinational Reception," *Feminist Review*, 35 (Summer 1990), p. 35. *Sati*, however, continues to be used as a paradigmatic example for thinking about the pros and cons of colonial intervention in "native" practices, without attention to relevant historical details. Talking about the possibility of arrogant forms of struggle against practices affecting Third-World women by Western middle-class feminists, Marilyn Friedman says, "It is tempting to work against such forms of oppression from the outside, even without consulting the women who endure them, much as the British did when they used their imperial power to criminalize the Hindu practice of suttee . . . in India during the nineteenth century." See her "Multicultural Education and Feminist Ethics" *Hypatia* 10, 2 (Spring 1995), p. 64. Part of the problem I have with Friedman's point is that the British initially *did* attempt to "consult" the women who were about to undergo *sati*, to ensure they were doing so "voluntarily." (See note 61 below.) Further, while it is true that the British "consulted" Indian pundits rather than Indian women on the issue of criminally abolishing *sati*, it is difficult to see quite *how* they might have gone about specifically consulting the women who were going to "endure" *sati*, since there would be no way to predict which women would be widowed, and which among them would commit *sati*.

48. From *The Correspondence of Lord William Cavendish Bentinck, Vol. 1: 1828–1831*, C. H. Phillips, ed. (Oxford: Oxford University Press, 1977). Quoted in Yang, "Whose Sati?" in *Expanding the Boundaries of Women's History*, p. 75.

49. These disagreements over scriptural interpretation are hardly surprising, given that Hinduism, unlike Christianity, does not have a core scriptural text. Thus, the question of where to look for such scriptural evidence was hardly self-evident. The interpretative task was not made any easier by the fact that there seemed to be few, if any, clear and unambiguous textual endorsements of *sati*. I would encourage readers to consult Mani's text of a host of interesting details about this interpretative process. It not only raised questions about what certain passages meant, but also questions about which texts were to be accorded greater importance, about the legitimacy of "customary" rather than "scripturally sanctioned" practices, about the authority granted to varying interpretations, and so on.

50. See Romila Thapar, "Perspective In History," *Seminar* 342 (February 1988), reprinted in *Sati*, Mulk Raj Anand, ed. (Delhi: B.R. Publishing Corporation, 1989).

51. Lata Mani, "Contentious Traditions: The Debate on *SATI* in Colonial India," *Cultural Critique*, (Fall, 1987), p. 135.

52. I suspect that the British view that "if *sati* was an authentic Hindu tradition it must be grounded in Hindu scripture" was grounded in their assumption that all religions are as scripturally grounded as Christianity, which is simply not the case with Hinduism. I suspect that the Indian pundits they consulted went along with this "scripturally grounded" view of Hinduism both because it gave them power and because it approximated their own particular priestly Brahmin "take" on Hinduism.

53. Thapar also accounts for the fact that a large number of Brahmin widows were immolated as *satis* by pointing to the practice among elderly Kulin Brahmins in Bengal of marrying a number of wives, leading to a greater number of Brahmin widows. Thapar, "Perspective in History," in *Sati*, p. 91.

54. Ashis Nandy, *At the Edge of Psychology: Essays in Politics and Culture* (New Delhi: Oxford University Press, 1980). There seems to be considerable debate about Nandy's claims. For an account of Nandy's later views on *sati*, see his "*Sati* as Profit Versus *Sati* as a Spectacle: The Public Debate on Roop Kanwar's Death," in *Sati, The Blessing and the Curse: The Burning of Wives in India*, John Stratton Hawley, ed. (Oxford: Oxford University Press, 1994). See also the interesting critiques of Nandy in the two "Comments" by Ainslie T. Embree and Veena Talwar Oldenburg in the same volume.

55. Veena Talwar Oldenburg suggests that *sati* in Rajasthan might be connected to the practice of *jauhar*, whereby wives of Rajput kings and noblemen defeated in war participated in collective cremations to avoid capture and "dishonor." Oldenburg proposes that "the Brahmins of the northwest . . . borrowed the practice of jauhar from the Rajputs, and modified the concept over time to suit their own Sanskritic gender ideology of the good rather than the brave woman." See her "Comment: The Continuing Invention of the *Sati* Tradition," in *Sati, The Blessing and the Curse: The Burning of Wives in India*, John Stratton Hawley, ed. (Oxford: Oxford University Press, 1994), pp. 164–165.

56. Gayatri Spivak, "Can the Subaltern Speak? Speculations on Widow Sacrifice," *Wedge* (Winter/Spring 1985) (p. 103 of version I have). Reprinted in *Marxism and the Interpretation of Culture*, Cary Nelson and Lawrence Grossberg, eds. (Chicago: University of Illinois Press, 1988), p. 307.

57. Although the figure of Sati is well known, I suspect that the details of the mythological story are not as well known, and not carefully attended to, promoting the sense that the mythological Sati committed *sati*. Veena Talwar Oldenburg

provides yet another example of the oddly ubiquitous phenomenon I mention, when she writes: "Padmini, the queen of Chitor who has been immortalized by the balladeers of Rajasthan, is sometimes thought to be the best-commemorated example of *sati*; but actually her death was by jauhar, and that is quite a different thing." See her "Comment," in *Sati, The Blessing and the Curse*, p. 165.

58. Gayatri Spivak makes this point that there was "no debate on the nonexceptional fate of widows," in her "Can the Subaltern Speak? Speculations on Widow Sacrifice," *Wedge* (Winter/Spring 1985) (p. 98 of version I have). Reprinted in *Marxism and the Interpretation of Culture*, Cary Nelson and Lawrence Grossberg, eds. (Chicago: University of Illinois Press, 1988), p. 302.

59. C. A. Bayly, "From Ritual to Ceremony: Death Ritual and Society in Hindu North India since 1600," in *Mirrors of Mortality: Studies in the Social History of Death*, Joachim Whaley, ed. (New York: St. Martin's Press, 1981), p. 174.

60. Thanks to Susan Zlotnick for pointing out that the "hiddenness" of women in seclusion might have been too close for comfort for the Victorians, whose ideology of domesticity also immured women in the house, if somewhat less thoroughly.

61. There is also something both "spectacular" and "hidden" about the very debate on *sati*. The sustained public debate on *sati* made it a monumental "Indian spectacle." On the other hand, the "basis" for its "validity" was perceived to be "hidden" in arcane and esoteric texts requiring scholarly interpretation.

62. Initially, the British decided that *sati* should be allowed when it was "countenanced by religion" and prevented where it was forbidden. They defined *sati* as illegal when the woman was under compulsion, intoxicated, pregnant, or had a child under three, and directed British officials to be present to prevent "illegal *satis*" from taking place. Part of the task of these officials was to talk to the widows to ensure they were not being "coerced." See Vasudha Dhagamwar, "Saint, Victim or Criminal," *Seminar* 342, February 1988, reprinted in *Sati*, Mulk Raj Anand, ed. (Delhi: B.R. Publishing Corporation, 1989), p. 120. As Mani points out, the "legislative prohibition of *sati* was preceded by its legalization, a procedure that involved British officials in determining and enforcing a colonial version of the practice deemed traditional and authentic." Lata Mani, "Multiple Mediations: Feminist Scholarship in the Age of Multinational Reception," *Feminist Review* 35 (Summer 1990), p. 35. This suggests that the criterion for the "authenticity" of colonial *sati* fluctuated in focus from its legitimation by scriptural texts to being an issue of its voluntary nature, grounded in the women's will.

63. Lata Mani, "Multiple Mediations: Feminist Scholarship in the Age of Multinational Reception," *Feminist Review* 35 (Summer 1990), p. 33.

64. Veena Talwar Oldenburg, "The Roop Kanwar Case: Feminist Responses," in *Sati, The Blessing and the Curse*, p. 102.

65. Ibid.

66. Kumkum Sangari and Suresh Vaid, "Institutions, Beliefs, Ideologies: Widow Immolation in Contemporary Rajasthan," *Economic and Political Weekly* 26, 17 (April 27, 1991), p. WS-3.

67. There are many interesting similarities between these cases. Both involved very young wives—Om Kunwar was sixteen and Roop Kanwar was nineteen. Both women were very recently married, and both their husbands died not suddenly but after prolonged illnesses. Their youth and recent entry into the conjugal home are both factors that increased their vulnerability to coercion compared to an

older wife of longer standing who might have had time to acquire greater status, ties, and allies in her conjugal context.

68. The husband's father was a school teacher. The husband was hoping to go to medical school—having failed the entrance exam for the second time shortly before his death. His potential status and affluence as a doctor undoubtedly accounts at least in part for why Roop Kanwar's parents may have decided to marry their daughter into a poorer family.

69. Veena Talwar Oldenburg, "The Roop Kanwar Case: Feminist Responses," in *Sati, The Blessing and the Curse*, p. 116.

70. I should point out that the linkage I am suggesting is different from Daly's representations of these connections that I criticized earlier.

71. John Stratton Hawley, "Introduction," in *Sati, The Blessing and the Curse: The Burning of Wives in India*, John Hawley, ed. (Oxford: Oxford University Press, 1994), p. 8.

72. Kumkum Sangari and Suresh Vaid, "Institutions, Beliefs, Ideologies: Widow Immolation in Contemporary Rajasthan," *Economic and Political Weekly* 26, 17 (April 27, 1991), p. WS–5.

73. Both their husbands died after prolonged health problems, providing time for these economic calculations to take hold and be "planned" for.

74. Oldenburg points out that while "Rajput martial values are a product of their historical circumstances," they were "molded into a supposed racial identity by colonial bureaucrats," "The Roop Kanwar Case: Feminist Responses," in *Sati, The Blessing and the Curse*, p. 165.

75. Kumkum Sangari and Suresh Vaid, "Institutions, Beliefs, Ideologies: Widow Immolation in Contemporary Rajasthan," *Economic and Political Weekly* 26: 17 (April 27, 1991), p.WS–8.

76. Veena Talwar Oldenburg, "The Roop Kanwar Case: Feminist Responses," in *Sati, The Blessing and the Curse*, p. 110.

77. I have no desire to suggest that these pilgrims and worshippers act merely out of religious beliefs, with no sense of the political implications of their "worship" of *sati*. Very few of those who attended the mass rallies held to "glorify" Roop Kanwar's *sati* could have failed to realize that they were *also* participating in an event meant to garner support for and testify to the strength of Hindu fundamentalist parties.

78. For more details, see Lindsey Harlan, "Perfection and Devotion: *Sati* Tradition in Rajasthan," in *Sati, The Blessing and the Curse*. Also see Kumkum Sangari and Suresh Vaid, "Institutions, Beliefs, Ideologies: Widow Immolation in Contemporary Rajasthan," *Economic and Political Weekly* 26: 17 (April 27, 1991).

79. Lindsey Harlan, "Perfection and Devotion," in *Sati, The Blessing and the Curse*, p. 81.

80. Veena Talwar Oldenburg, "The Roop Kanwar Case: Feminist Responses," p. 114.

81. Ibid., p. 116.

82. Kumkum Sangari and Suresh Vaid, "Institutions, Beliefs, Ideologies: Widow Immolation in Contemporary Rajasthan," *Economic and Political Weekly* 26, 17 (April 27, 1991), p. WS– 15.

83. Ibid., p. WS–16.

84. It is important to clarify the logic of feminist contestation here. The fundamentalist defense of *sati* rests on portraying it both as: (1) an ancient Indian cul-

tural tradition; and (2) an admirable practice that should inspire respect and reverence from Indians. While feminists attacked both of the fundamentalist premises, as it was politically vital that they do, they did *not* imply that if it had been an Indian tradition it would have been morally acceptable.

85. Madhu Kishwar and Ruth Vanita, "The Burning of Roop Kanwar," *Manushi*, No. 42.

86. Veena Talwar Oldenburg, "The Roop Kanwar Case: Feminist Responses," p. 116.

87. Ibid., p. 118.

88. This might be part of the point Gayatri Spivak makes when she expresses skepticism about the subaltern's speech in "Can the Subaltern Speak? Speculations on Widow Sacrifice," *Wedge* (Winter/Spring 1985), pp. 120–130.

89. Veena Talwar Oldenburg, "The Roop Kanwar Case: Feminist Responses," p. 125.

90. Lata Mani, "Multiple Mediations," *Feminist Review* (1990), p. 37.

91. Indira Jaising, "Women, Religion and the Law," *The Lawyers Collective* 2, 11.

92. Of course both *sati* and the "ideal of femininity" embodied in *sati* also deserve to be challenged apart from their status as "traditions." The focus of recent contestation on *sati's* status as tradition should not be taken as a sign that Indian feminists would find it any less objectionable if it had in fact been less problematically a "longstanding Indian tradition."

93. Kumkum Sangari, "Perpetuating the Myth," *Seminar* 342, February 1988, reprinted in *Sati*, Mulk Raj Anand, ed. (Delhi: B.R. Publishing Corporation, 1989), pp. 104–105.

94. Inderpal Grewal and Caren Kaplan make an important point when they argue that "we need to examine fundamentalisms around the world and seek to understand why Muslim fundamentalism appears in the media today as the primary progenitor of oppressive conditions for women when Christian, Jewish, Hindu, Confucian, and other forms of extreme fundamentalisms exert profound controls over women's lives." See their "Introduction: Transnational Feminist Practices and Questions of Postmodernity," in *Scattered Hegemonies: Postmodernity and Transnational Feminist Practices* (Minneapolis: University of Minnesota Press, 1994), p. 19.

95. This is a term used by Benedict Anderson in *Imagined Communities: Reflections on the Origin and Spread of Nationalism* (New York: Verso Books, 1983), p. 15.

Three / Cross-Cultural Connections, Border-Crossings, and "Death by Culture"

1. Quite contingently, most of the Americans with whom I have discussed this topic are not of Indian background. I do not know whether the misconceptions about *sati* and dowry-murders that I discuss are widely shared by members of the diasporic Indian community in the United States. It would not necessarily surprise me if that were the case, but I have little to go on. As a result, when I discuss "American" responses and understandings, I refer to the responses of Americans who are not of Indian background.

2. I have reasons for preferring not to cite either of them.

3. "Restoring History and Politics to 'Third World Traditions': Contrasting the Colonialist Stance and Contemporary Contestations of *Sati*" in this volume. Also

see Radhika Parameswaran, "Coverage of 'Bride-Burning' in the Dallas Observer: A Cultural Analysis of the 'Other,'" *Frontiers* 16, 2/3 (1996).

4. They lie outside the borders of this essay in part because I believe each of these questions warrants exploration in its own right, and because they are not questions I have done work on. I chose a more limited focus for this essay to enable me to begin thinking about these sorts of questions.

5. One of the best known examples is to be found in Daniel Patrick Moynihan, *The Politics of Guaranteed Income: The Nixon Administration and the Family Assistance Plan* (New York: Random House, 1973). As Linda Gordon and Nancy Fraser put it:

> The 1960's and 1970's discourse about poverty recapitulated traditions of misogyny towards African-American women; in Daniel Moynihan's diagnosis, for instance, "matriarchal" families had "emasculated" Black men and created a "culture of poverty" based on a "tangle of family pathology." This discourse placed Black AFDC claimants in a double-bind; they were pathologically independent with respect to men and pathologically dependent with respect to government. By the 1980's the racial imagery of dependency had shifted. . . . Now the pre-eminent stereotype is the unmarried teenage mother caught in the "welfare trap" and rendered drone-like and passive.

See their "Decoding Dependency: Inscriptions of Power in a Keyword of the U.S. Welfare State," in *Reconstructing Political Theory: Feminist Perspectives*, Mary Lyndon Shanley and Uma Narayan, eds., forthcoming from Polity Press.

6. The paper in whose title Mani uses these terms reflects on the different values and significance her work on *sati* had to audiences in the United States, Britain, and India. I would like to borrow her useful terms to call attention to the general need to think about how feminist issues get differently shaped and "mediated" in particular national contexts, and the further "mediations" that occur when they cross national boundaries. See Lata Mani, "Multiple Mediations: Feminist Scholarship in the Age of Multinational Reception," *Feminist Review* 35 (Summer 1990).

7. I invite my readers who have academic books and articles on the subject of domestic violence in U.S. contexts to go through them and see how often they find mention of this statistic.

8. For a discussion of some of the problems inherent in the focus on the O.J. Simpson case, see the dialogue between Tammy Bruce and Julianne Malveaux in the article "Can We Talk?" in *On The Issues, The Progressive Women's Quarterly* (Summer 1996).

9. Mary Fainsod Katzenstein, "Organizing Against Violence: Strategies of the Indian Women's Movement," *Pacific Affairs* 62, 1 (Spring 1989), p. 61.

10. Ibid.

11. From "Discussion Forum: From the Commission on the Status of Women in India to the End of the Women's Decade: Some Personal Reflections," *Samya Shakti* 2, 1 (1985), p. 80.

12. Katzenstein, "Organizing Against Violence: Strategies of the Indian Women's Movement," p. 54.

13. Katzenstein points out that the Delhi-based group, Saheli, "concerned itself particularly with issues of dowry and domestic violence" and that the Bombay-based Forum against Oppression of Women took up issues of police rape and

dowry-murders. See "Organizing Against Violence," *Pacific Affairs* (1989)pp. 56–57.

14. For details, see Mary Fainsod Katzenstein, "Organizing Against Violence," pp. 57–58.

15. From "Discussion Forum" in *Samya Shakti* 2, 1 (1985), p. 98.

16. The other was the issue of the "deficit of women" in the Indian population. Although cause for concern, there are several features that make this issue difficult to organize around. Unlike dowry-murders, this was not a phenomenon whose "causes" were readily clear. It was also less clear how groups might "organize" around this issue.

17. Madhu Kishwar, "Why I Do Not Call Myself a Feminist," *Manushi* 61 (Nov./Dec. 1990).

18. Madhu Kishwar, "Why I Do Not Call Myself a Feminist," p. 5.

19. Ibid., p. 6.

20. It is interesting to note that feminist groups in many diasporic South Asian communities in Western national contexts have organized shelters for battered women in their communities. For instance, there are shelters organized and operated by South Asian women in New Jersey and in Chicago.

21. Statistics were for 1994 and found in a *Crime Index* based on reports to the Federal Bureau of Investigation's Uniform Crime Reporting Program. The data appear in the FBI's annual publication, *Crime in the United States*. The data I obtained were on the Internet, dated November 19, 1995, and reported some "highlights of the 1994 edition" of the FBI publication.

22. Here are a few examples of the variations I found. The FBI data says, "Forty seven percent of murder victims were related to (12 percent) or acquainted with (35 percent) their assailants" (a statement that neither specifies the gender of the victims, nor the precise nature of their relationship to or acquaintance with their assailants) and that "among all female murder victims in 1994, 28 percent were slain by husbands or boyfriends." On the other hand, I found the information that, "In the U.S., 9 out of 10 women murdered are murdered by men, half at the hands of a male partner," in Lori Heise, *Gender Violence as Health Issue*, fact sheet, Violence, Health and Development Project, Center for Women's Global Leadership, Rutgers University, 1992. While the first part of the above information corresponds to FBI statistics, the second half gives a figure almost twice that of the FBI statistics.

A second example: I found, "In the U.S. 4 women are killed every day by their husbands or boyfriends," in "Facts on Domestic Violence," courtesy Lynne Synder, Y Care, Chicago, reprinted in *WAC Stats* ("The Facts About Women" put out by the Women's Action Coalition, The New Press, New York, 1993). This corresponds to the 1,400 number I worked out from FBI data. However, I also found in *WAC Stats* the information that "every 11 days in the U.S. a woman is murdered by her husband, boyfriend or live-in lover," attributed to "Statistics 1988, 1989" by National Clearinghouse for the Defense of Battered Women, Philadelphia. This latter information suggests a *much* lower number of women annually killed by their partners (under forty) than the FBI statistics.

23. The number of women killed by *intimates* (defined as spouses, ex-spouses or boyfriends) rose from 1,396 in 1977 to 1,510 in 1992, according to "Violence between Intimates," *Bureau of Justice Statistics*, U.S. Department of Justice, November 1994. These figures seemed close enough to the 1,400 figure I am using, at least for my purposes.

24. Quoted in a resolution on Dowry-Deaths in India by the Committee on Human Rights that I found on the Internet. It attributes the definition to the Indian Penal Code.

25. I was not at all sure what the FBI's 28 percent statistic did reflect. I wondered whether it reflected criminal convictions, or cases where there had been sufficient evidence for criminal prosecution, or cases where the partner was simply suspected of the murder. My hunch that the FBI statistics reflected criminal convictions was reinforced by the fact that another source cited figures similar to the FBI's and said "28 percent of women murdered were *known* to be murdered by their partners." I am grateful to my sociologist colleague Marque Miringoff confirming that the FBI statistics reflected criminal convictions.

26. While the Indian journal *Manushi* does cover general issues of domestic violence in India, I do not think it makes much difference at the level of popular U.S. public understanding.

27. Veena Talwar Oldenburg, "Dowry Murders in India: A Preliminary Examination of the Historical Evidence," in *Women's Lives and Public Policy: The International Experience*, Meredeth Turshen and Briavel Holcomb, eds. (Westport, Conn.: Greenwood Press, 1993), p. 146.

28. Elizabeth Bumiller, *May You Be the Mother of a Hundred Sons: A Journey Among the Women of India* (New York: Fawcett Columbine, 1990), p. 44.

29. Bumiller, *May You Be the Mother of a Hundred Sons*, p. 45.

30. Ibid.

31. Some of these works are "general discussions of women in Indian culture" that situate "Hindu religious doctrines" at the center of their "analysis of Indian culture" and mention dowry and dowry-murders "in passing," more or less as "examples of the effects of Hindu religious views on women's well-being." Others center their discussions on dowry and dowry-murder, and then deploy very many of the same elements of "Hindu religious doctrine" in ways that suggest they are "explanations" for dowry-murders.

32. Sushila Mehta, *Revolution and the Status of Women in India* (New Delhi: Metropolitan Book Co., 1982), p. 208.

33. Arguing that "there has been an overemphasis on the mystical and religious aspects of Indian society," Martha Nussbaum and Amartya Sen go on to add: "The image of the 'mystical East,' and specifically India, is not a matter only of popular conception but has a good deal of following in the typical Indologist's summary view of Indian intellectual history. In this respect there is also no real gulf between the things that the Western scholars have typically tended to emphasize in Indian culture and what Indian Indologists have themselves most often highlighted. This close correspondence may not, however, be particularly remarkable, since approaches to 'cultural summarizing' are generally quite 'infectious,' and, no less importantly, modern Indian scholarship is greatly derivative from the West." Martha C. Nussbaum and Amartya Sen, "Internal Criticism and Indian Rationalist Traditions," in *Relativism: Interpretation and Confrontation*, Michael Krauz, ed. (Notre Dame, Ind.: University of Notre Dame Press, 1989), pp. 301–303. I argue that the "general picture" of "Indian culture" they point to seems to have problematic effects on social science explanations of Indian phenomena. I would also add that writings by Indians on "Indian culture" tend, in turn, to be assimilated into "Western scholarship" on India—whereby, for instance, Sushila Mehta's views

on dowry and dowry-murder "reappear" in works by Western feminists on "Indian women's issues."

34. See Louis Dumont, "Dowry in Hindu Marriage: As a Social Scientist Sees It," *Economic Weekly*, April 11, 1959.

35. See Indira Rajaraman, "Economics of Bride Price and Dowry," *Economic And Political Weekly*, February 19, 1983.

36. Sushila Mehta, *Revolution and the Status of Women in India*, p. 208.

37. I admit that I tend to be wary about "general explanations for dowry" since I suspect that the understandings of dowry as well as its functions have differed across specific communities at various periods of historical time. In the case of dowry, as in the case of *sati*, I think that a number of "social explanations" tend to treat these phenomena as more "unitary" than they actually are, constructing them as "unified phenomenon" in that very process.

38. Veena Talwar Oldenburg, "Dowry Murders in India: A Preliminary Examination of the Historical Evidence," in *Women's Lives and Public Policy: The International Experience*, by Meredeth Turshen and Briavel Holcomb, eds. (Westport, Conn.: Greenwood Press, 1993), p. 148.

39. Contemporary dowry also seems to be becoming a "postnuptial" rather than a "prenuptial" exchange. A recent study of 150 women victimized and harassed over dowry found that in *60 percent* of the cases, dowry was only demanded *after* the marriage had taken place, a point at which the bride's parents are vulnerable to pressures to "save the marriage at any cost" and where the husband's family can exert the threat of "desertion." In roughly two-thirds of the cases where dowry was in fact demanded before marriage, it was demanded very shortly before the marriage was solemnized, at a time when arrangements for the marriage had been finalized, and when the women's family feared social stigma in calling off the wedding. See Ranjana Kumari, *Brides Are Not For Burning*, pp. 44–45.

40. Consumer goods and cash seem to be the two most common components of dowry demands. In about 15 percent of the cases studied by Kumari, there were also demands that the daughter be given a share of her parents' estate, forms of property that women were not traditionally expected to inherit and for which dowry was regarded as a "substitute." Kumari notes that these families are willing to "flout this tradition when it comes to their wives and daughters in-law" while insisting on tradition when it comes to their own daughters' and sisters' claims to family property! See *Brides Are Not For Burning*, p. 48.

41. Bumiller, *May You Be the Mother of a Hundred Sons* (New York: Fawcett Columbine, 1990), p. 47.

42. It is interesting to consider the "authenticating" or "authorizing" function that "personal encounters" clearly tend to have in the production of "knowledge about Other cultures," a function underlined by the fact that *A Journey Among the Women of India* is a subtitle of Bumiller's book. One of the lessons I learned from reading this book was how complicated this matter of "authorization" was. To be fair to Bumiller, she does not position herself as an "authority" on India or on Indian women, but as a "foreigner" encountering a context she knows little about. But the fact of her "having been there" and the fact that all the "Indian women's issues" she addresses are mediated by narratives of her encounters with an assortment of "real Indian women" work to convey a sense of verisimilitude, that in turn

works to deflect attention from the "issues of framing" I have tried to call attention to.

43. I also have problems with a different kind of "cultural explanation," quite common in Indian discussions of these issues, that sees the institution of dowry as the "central culprit" in dowry-murders. Let me try to explain my problem. Dowry has been illegal since the Dowry Prohibition Act of 1961. The Act outlaws dowry, defined as "the property a woman brings to her husband at marriage," and coercive demands for dowry. It does not prohibit either "gifts to the groom's family" that are of a "customary nature," or the giving of property to the daughter herself, thereby providing two clear loopholes that make the Act virtually impossible to apply. I am increasingly unsure whether the inefficacy of this law in prohibiting dowry is entirely a bad thing. If successful, it might prevent a great many women from receiving their "traditional" share of parental property, without necessarily ensuring that they get any share at all. Even if dowry prohibition was combined with a law that gave women rights to a full postmortem share of parental property, there is little guarantee that many women might not be cheated out of it by brothers and male kin. Besides, while a successful prohibition of dowry would certainly prevent some women being killed, it may also leave many others without the margin of economic security dowry provides during their marriage. Dowryless women may be safe from dowry-murder but may be less empowered in having no assets of their own until their parents' death, leaving them more vulnerable when they confront other forms of harassment during those years.

44. Radhika Parameswaran, "Coverage of 'Bride-Burning' in the Dallas Observer," *Frontiers* (1996).

45. Yes, this roughly approximates the range of topics on "Indian women" found in Bumiller's book.

46. I leave these questions unanswered in part because I think the answers are complicated and would require a great deal more thought and reflection than I can give them at this time.

47. Yes, Bumiller's book *did* receive reviews corresponding to these quotes!

48. Kimberle Crenshaw, "Intersectionality and Identity Politics: Learning from Violence Against Women of Color," in *Reconstructing Political Theory: Feminist Perspectives*, Mary L. Shanley and Uma Narayan, eds., forthcoming from Polity Press.

49. She may also find mention of a different problem, whereby greater incidence of wife assault among blue-collar workers, the unemployed, and the partially employed, as well as among African Americans and Hispanic Americans, results in "the popular explanation that these subcultures have proviolence norms." Daniel G. Saunders, "Husbands Who Assault: Multiple Profiles Requiring Multiple Responses," in *Legal Responses to Wife Assault: Current Trends and Evaluation*, edited by N. Zoe Hilton (Newbury Park, Cal.: Sage Publications, 1993), p. 12. Saunders goes on to argue against this view. However, it does point out the degree to which problems within minority racial or ethnic communities in the United States are more likely to receive explanations in terms of specific "*cultural* pathologies" that differ from the kinds of "general explanations" given for domestic violence.

50. Crenshaw, "Intersectionality and Identity Politics."

51. See both Crenshaw and Nancy Hirschman's "The Theory and Practice of

Freedom: The Case of Battered Women," in *Reconstructing Political Theory: Feminist Perspectives*.

52. Initially, discourses about "self-esteem" and "low self-esteem" struck me as quite American and less likely to be deployed in the Indian context. But considering how rapidly ideas from Western contexts are "exported" to Third-World countries, I now do not feel sure about this.

53. I am not claiming that these statistics are *unavailable*—just that they have proved very *difficult* for myself, and even for others more skilled at locating empirical data, to find.

54. Thanks to my colleague Marque Miringoff, I eventually did find data that indicates that 69 percent of wives and ex-wives and 60 percent of girlfriends killed by intimates were killed by firearms in "Violence between Intimates," *Bureau of Justice Statistics, Selected Findings*, U.S. Department of Justice, November 1994. I also found data that indicated that 42 percent of all family murder victims were killed by firearms, and that 53 percent of spousal murder victims died from gun shots in "Murder in Families," *Bureau of Justice Statistics, Special Report*, Washington, D.C., July 1994.

Four / Through the Looking-Glass Darkly

1. One may be regarded as (or regard oneself as) marginal to "mainstream Western culture" on the basis of race, ethnicity, or religion. As a result, the range of subjects that I refer to by the term "Third-World subject" in this essay does not perfectly overlap with either the term "non-Western subject" nor with the term "person of color." While the term "Third-World subject" or "Third-World community" has been used to refer both to populations of color within Western nation states and to the nationals of many Third-World countries, "non-Western" is not a term usually applied to the former. There is a different problem of scope with reference to the term "person of color." If understood strictly as picking out those who are "nonwhite," the term has the potential to exclude some groups of persons who are often "officially classified" as "white"—for instance some individuals of Middle Eastern background, such as Lebanese, Turks, or Iranians—but whose "cultural background" is regarded as marginal to "mainstream Western culture." For information on the standards used to officially define racial and ethnic categories in the U.S., see *Statistical Policy Directive No. 15*, issued by the U.S. Office of Management and Budget.

2. I by no means wish to suggest that curricular diversity and inclusion are only the concerns of mainstream Westerners, or to efface the numerous struggles of faculty and students of color who have often contributed vitally to generating such institutional concern and effort. My point is just that the understandings of mainstream Westerners often *strongly shape* the ways in which these projects take institutional form.

3. Thus, Allan Bloom suggests that the only lesson one could learn from a study of non-Western cultures is that "each and every one of them is ethnocentric" and Arthur M. Schlesinger is convinced that the "liberating ideas of individual liberty, political democracy, the rule of law, human rights, and cultural freedom . . . are *European* ideas." See Arthur M. Schlesinger Jr., "The Disuniting of America: Reflections on a Multicultural Society," and Allan Bloom, "The Closing of the

American Mind," both in *Campus Wars: Multi-culturalism and the Politics of Difference*, John Arthur and Amy Shapiro, eds., (Boulder, Colo.: Westview Press, 1995).

4. With respect to certain "Third-World cultures" such as those of India and China, the tendency is to focus not only on "High Culture" but also on "Ancient High Culture." Naheed Islam reports that her review of South Asia departments in the U.S. "shows an emphasis on Ancient Indian Studies." See Naheed Islam, "In the Belly of the Multicultural Beast I am Named South Asian," in *Our Feet Walk the Sky: Women of the South Asian Diaspora*, edited by the Women of South Asian Descent Collective (San Francisco: Aunt Lute Books, 1993), p. 243. Such cases raise additional questions. What sort of multiculturalism is being promoted when certain "cultures" are represented mostly in terms of an "historic past"? What sorts of understandings of these "cultures" foster such a focus and what are its implications? To what extent does such a focus suggest that modern Indian or Chinese culture are not "different enough," having lost the "authentic difference" they once had?

5. To cite just one example, consider the examples in *Beyond the Western Tradition*, Daniel Bonevac, William Boon and Stephen Phillips, eds., (Mountain View, Cal.: Mayfield Publishing Co., 1992) The bulk of the readings designed to represent the "traditions" of South Asia and East Asia are selections from either explicitly scriptural texts or from ethico-religious texts. There is very little sociopolitical background provided to situate the views in these texts. The selections from more "modern" figures such as Rammohun Roy and Aurobindo also focus on their writing about *religion* rather than on their more political or nationalist writings. I find such representations of what is "beyond" the "Western tradition" one of the deeply problematic approaches to "multiculturalism."

6. For examples of such critiques, see the essays in *Feminist Interpretations and Political Theory*, Mary Lyndon Shanley and Carole Pateman, ed. (State College: Pennsylvania State University Press, 1991). Also see Carole Pateman, *The Sexual Contract* (Stanford, Cal,: Stanford University Press and Polity Press, 1988) and *The Disorder of Women: Democracy, Feminism and Political Theory* (Stanford University Press and Polity Press, 1990); and Susan Muller Okin, *Justice, Gender and the Family* (New York: Basic Books, 1989).

7. Marilyn Friedman makes a related point about some forms of multiculturalism when she notes, "The non-Western works that Western canon promoters tolerate are often limited simply to non-Western classics: the Koran, the *Analects* of Confucius, the Bhagavad Gita and so on. The nonclassical multicultural works that focus on oppressive global practices remain just as controversial as ever." "Multicultural Education and Feminist Ethics," *Hypatia* 10, 2 (Spring 1995), p. 62.

8. Ananda Coomaraswamy, *The Dance of Shiva* (New York: The Noonday Press, 1957). Coomaraswamy was research fellow in Oriental Art at the Boston Museum of Fine Arts from 1917 to 1947.

9. An example of such oppositions is to be found on the book cover which asserts that Coomaraswamy "suggests that the vigor of European action must be united with the serenity of Asiatic thought if civilization is not to destroy itself."

10. Ananda Coomaraswamy, *The Dance of Shiva* (New York: Noonday Press, 1957), see pp. 6–7.

11. See the chapter entitled "Status of Indian Women," in *The Dance of Shiva: Fourteen Indian Essays* (New York: Noonday Press, 1957), pp. 98–123. Among

other things, this chapter justifies and celebrates *sati*, and contains gems such as: "Western critics have often asserted that the Oriental women is a slave. . . . We can only reply that we do not identify freedom with self-assertion, and that the Oriental woman is what she is, only because our social and religious culture has permitted her to be, and to remain, essentially feminine" (p. 113).

12. For a discussion of "Orientalism," see Edward Said, *Orientalism* (London: Routledge and Kegan Paul, 1978).

13. I have forgotten the conversational background that led to this point, though I do know we were not specifically talking about India—we could have been talking about the ideological functions of religion or the growth of religious fundamentalisms across the world.

14. It is important to point out that not *all* Western feminists share these reservations. A great deal of work on "Third-World women" is currently being done by Western scholars, feminists as well as others. For an account of the problematic ways in which the category of "Third-World women" is constructed in some of these works, see Chandra Talpade Mohanty, "Under Western Eyes: Feminist Scholarship and Colonial Discourses," in *Third World Women and the Politics of Feminism*, Chandra Talpade Mohanty, Ann Russo and Lourdes Torres, eds. (Bloomington: Indiana University Press).

15. See "Contesting Cultures: 'Westernization,' Respect for Cultures, and Third-World Feminists" in this volume.

16. Antoinette Burton, *Burden's of History: British Feminists, Indian Women and Imperial Culture 1865–1915* (Chapel Hill: University of North Carolina Press, 1994). The quote is from a review of Burton's book by Saloni Mathur, *Women's Review of Books* 13, 8 (May 1996.)

17. This concern that Third-World subjects act as "emissaries" to counter Western cultural arrogance puts the concerns of Western subjects rather than those of Third-World subjects at the center of the agenda. At these moments, the understandings that shape the "Emissary position" are also marked by the "focus on the Big Bad West" that I discuss in the next section.

18. Leila Ahmed, "Western Ethnocentrism and Perceptions of the Harem," *Feminist Studies* 8, 3 (Fall 1982).

19. Nawal el Saadawi, "Dissidence and Creativity," in *Women, A Cultural Review* 6, 1 (Summer 1995).

20. I borrow the term "arrogant perception" from Maria Lugones. See her "Playfulness, World-Travelling, and Loving Perception," *Hypatia* 2, 2 (Summer, 1987).

21. I choose to omit both a reference and specific details of location, since I do not wish to single this work by a young scholar out for criticism. It is in many ways an extremely interesting, thoughtful, and well-written paper that I learned a great deal from, and not at all the sort of scholarship I wish to discourage or disparage. But it is also one that clearly embodied the type of limitations I want to talk about with respect to work on Third-World contexts that focus on the world views and agendas of the West.

22. Part of the problem in trying to do this might be that there is not much "record" of "native" accounts of magic, except as filtered and distorted through the colonial gaze and voice. This problem might be similar to the problem that Gayatri Spivak raises in her paper, "Can the Subaltern Speak?" where she points out that there is no historical documentation or even "trace" of the actual subjec-

tivities of the women who were *satis* in colonial India, only "representations" of their subjectivities by English colonials and Indian male elites. Even if so, it is a lack that I would prefer were named, addressed, and explained.

23. Ann Laura Stoler, "Carnal Knowledge and Imperial Power: Gender, Race and Morality in Colonial Asia," in *Gender at the Crossroads of Knowledge: Feminist Anthropology in the Postmodern Era*, Miceala di Leonardo, ed. (Berkeley and Los Angeles: University of California Press, 1991), p. 51.

24. Jane Haggis, "Gendering Colonialism of Colonizing Gender?: Recent Women's Studies Approaches to White Women and the History of British Colonialism," in *Women's Studies International Forum* 13, 1/2 (1990), p. III.

25. Ibid., p. 113.

26. Ibid., p. 114.

27. I refer to the title of her essay, "Returning the Gaze: An Introduction," in *Returning the Gaze: Essays on Racism, Feminism and Politics*, Himani Bannerji, ed. (Toronto: Sister Vision, 1993).

28. Leila Ahmed, "Western Ethnocentrism and Perceptions of the Harem," *Feminist Studies* 8, 3 (Fall 1982), p. 522.

29. Schlesinger explicitly asserts "it was the British, not the Indians, who ended (or did their best to end) the horrible custom of *sati*—widows burning themselves alive on their husband's funeral pyres." Bloom displays the same assumptions when he describes a "routine question" he poses to his students to "make them think": "If you had been a British administrator in India, would you have let the natives under your governance burn the widow at the funeral of a man who had died?" See Arthur M. Schlesinger Jr., "The Disuniting of America: Reflections on a Multicultural Society," and Allan Bloom, "The Closing of the American Mind", both in *Campus Wars: Multi-culturalism and the Politics of Difference*, John Arthur and Amy Shapiro, eds. (Boulder, Colo.: Westview Press, 1995).

30. For a list of such work see the references to works by Lata Mani, Romila Thapar, and Veena Talwar Oldenburg in "Restoring History and Politics to 'Third World Traditions': Contrasting the Colonialist Stance and Contemporary Contestations of *Sati*" in this volume. Such works redescribe the ways in which *sati* was a problem without denying that it was a problem, and attend to the political agendas both of Indians who supported the practice and of Indians who were in favor of its abolition.

31. Issues of class, caste, gender, and religious bigotry are clearly matters of political debate and contestation in Third-World contexts, as are state policies and specific "issues."

32. See Kamala Visweswaran, "Predicaments of the Hyphen," in *Our Feet Walk the Sky: Women of the South Asian Diaspora*, Women of South Asian Descent Collective, eds. (San Francisco: Aunt Lute Books, 1993).

33. Lata Mani, "Multiple Mediations: Feminist Scholarship in an Age of Multinational Reception," *Feminist Review* 35 (Summer 1990), p. 25.

34. Indira Karamcheti, "The Graves of Academe," in *Our Feet Walk the Sky*, p. 277.

35. See for instance, Haleh Afshar, "Why Fundamentalism? Iranian Women and their Support for Islam," and Ildiko Beller-Hann, "Women and Fundamentalism in Northeast Turkey," both in *Women, A Cultural Review* 6, 1 (Summer 1995).

36. Marilyn Friedman, "Multi-cultural Education and Feminist Ethics," *Hypatia* 10, 2, (Spring 1995), p. 65.

37. Marilyn Friedman, "Multi-cultural Education and Feminist Ethics," *Hypatia* 10, 2, (Spring 1995).

38. My response to Marilyn Friedman's position that mainstream Westerners refrain from challenging the views of women from Other cultural backgrounds unless invited or welcomed to do so (see the preceding note) was resistance to the seeming implication that members of Third-World communities have the responsibility for "bestowing permission to criticize" on mainstream individuals who encounter their views. Part of my resistance stems from my normative sense that expressing one's views publicly requires a willingness to respond to challenges to one's views. Another part of my resistance resulted from imagining how uncomfortable I would feel having to explicitly communicate that I was "giving permission" to mainstream members of my audience to express criticisms of my views.

39. Remembering the complexity and heterogeneity within Third-World contexts would also help mainstream Westerners to refrain from generalizations about "Other cultures." For instance, I was disturbed by Marilyn Friedman's well-intentioned view that mainstream Westerners "must remember that self-determination, and its near relations of individuality, independence, and autonomy are not the sorts of preeminent values for nonwestern cultures that they are in Western traditions." Marilyn Friedman, "Multi-cultural Education and Feminist Ethics," *Hypatia* 10, 2, (Spring 1995), p. 65. I was unclear about just what sort of "cultural difference" was being suggested by Friedman and anxious about its political implications. This is not only a very large generalization about an internally heterogeneous category of "non-Western cultures" and about complex values such as individuality, independence, and autonomy, but also a description that suggests a sharp contrast between "Western" and "non-Western" cultures without attending to serious divergences over the meaning and importance accorded to these values *within* various cultural contexts. I would argue that all our ideas about the differences in the value commitments of different cultural contexts, and our accounts of how these are to be explicated and assessed, need to themselves be topics of "multicultural dialogue" and not something to be "assumed" and "remembered" beforehand.

40. Kimberle Crenshaw, "Intersectionality and Identity Politics: Learning from Violence Against Women of Color," in *Reconstructing Political Theory: Feminist Perspectives*, Mary L. Shanley and Uma Narayan, eds., forthcoming from Polity Press.

41. See Bronwyn Winter, "Women, the Law and Cultural Relativism in France: The Case of Excision," in *Signs* 19, 4 (Summer 1994); Judith Seddon, "Possible or Impossible? A Tale of Two Worlds in One Country," *Yale Journal of Law and Feminism* 5, 265 (1993); and Valerie Oosterveld, "Refugee Statues for Female Circumcision Fugitives: Building a Canadian Precedent, *University of Toronto Faculty of Law Review* 5 (Spring 1993).

42. For a Canadian discussion of how minimal such entry continues to be, see "Returning the Gaze: An Introduction," in *Returning the Gaze: Essays on Racism, Feminism and Politics*, Himani Bannerji, ed. (Toronto: Sister Vision, 1993).

43. There are always exceptions, of course. There is the phenomenon of "token" Third-World subjects being deployed in the ongoing attacks on multiculturalism, affirmative action, and the like, where their identities are paradoxically deployed to give a "multicultural face" to attacks on multiculturalism! There are also other facets to the deployment of such subjects. Kamala Visweswaran won-

ders "if the unwarranted attention given to Dinesh D'Souza's book *Illiberal Education* isn't related to the politics of the hyphenated Indian, many of whom are members of a large and increasingly powerful business community anxious to prove to the conservative interests who run this country that it too stands for the same liberal values of 'competition' and the 'free market.'" See her "Predicaments of the Hyphen," in *Our Feet Walk the Sky*, p. 305.

44. Himani Bannerji, "Returning the Gaze: An Introduction," in *Returning the Gaze* (Toronto: Sister Vision, 1993), p. xxix.

Five / Eating Cultures

1. Versions of this paper were presented at the Interdisciplinary Conference on Food and Culture sponsored by the University of New Hampshire, March 1994, and at the American Political Science Association meeting, New York, September 1994. I am deeply indebted to Lisa Heldke, Elizabeth Kelly, and Susan Zlotnick for inspiring me to think about food, culture, and politics, and for their helpful comments. I am also grateful to Jennifer Church, Guy Colvin, Kristie Foelle, Donna Heiland, Karen Robertson, and John Stouter for their helpful comments on various drafts of this paper. A somewhat shorter version of this paper was initially published in *Social Identities* 1, 1 (January 1995). David Theo Goldberg's editorial comments helped to improve this paper in very many ways.

2. Edward W. Said, "Representing the Colonized: Anthropology's Interlocutors," *Critical Inquiry* 15, 2 (Winter 1989), p. 225.

3. *Cooking, Eating, Thinking: Transformative Philosophies of Food*, Deane W. Curtin and Lisa M. Heldke, eds. (Bloomington: Indiana University Press, 1992) is the one volume I know that has several essays by philosophers on aspects of food and eating.

4. See for instance the essays in *World Hunger and Moral Obligation*, William Aiken and Hugh La Follette, eds. (Englewood Cliffs, N.J.: Prentice-Hall, 1977).

5. See for instance, Tom Reagon, *The Case for Animal Rights* (Berkeley, Cal.: University of California Press, 1983); Tom Reagon and Peter Singer, eds., *Animal Rights and Human Obligations* (Englewood Cliffs, N.J.: Prentice-Hall, 1989); and Peter Singer, *Animal Liberation* (New York: New York Review, 1990).

6. See Susan Bordo, "Anorexia Nervosa: Psychopathology as the Crystallization of Culture," in *Cooking, Eating, Thinking,* Deane W. Curtin and Lisa M. Heldke, eds. (Bloomington: Indian University Press, 1992).

7. John Stuart Mill, *Principles of Political Economy*, vol. 3., J.M. Robinson, ed. (Toronto: University of Toronto Press, 1965).

8. Susan Zlotnick, "Domesticating Imperialism: Curry and Cookbooks in Victorian England," *Frontiers: A Journal of Women's Studies*, 16, 2/3, p. 54.

9. Zlotnick quotes the anonymous female author of *Modern Domestic Cookery* (1851, p. 311) as saying, "Curry, which was formerly a dish almost exclusively for the table of those who had made a long residence in India, is now so completely naturalized, that few dinners are thought complete unless one is on the table." See Zlotnick, "Domesticating Imperialism," p. 60.

10. Zlotnick points out that Eliza Acton's *Modern Cookery in All Its Branches* includes recipes for curry, not in its chapter entitled "Foreign and Jewish Cookery," but intermingled with traditional English fare in a chapter entitled, "Curries, Potted Meats, etc." in "Domesticating Imperialism," p. 60.

11. Zlotnick, "Domesticating Imperialism," p. 54.

12. Ibid.

13. The film *Mississippi Masala,* made by Mira Nair, was released in 1992. For an interesting discussion of the film, see Dharini Rasiah, *"Mississippi Masala* and *Khush*: Redefining Community," in *Our Feet Walk The Sky: Women of the South Asian Diaspora,* Women of South Asian Descent Collective, eds. (San Francisco: Aunt Lute Books, 1993).

14. *The Shorter Oxford English Dictionary,* Guild Publishing, 1983, p. 475.

15. Pointing out that "Othering, or projecting negative attributes onto the colonized subject is a basic tenet of postcolonial studies, and one that has been criticized for its dichotomizing view of the imperial world as an antagonistic struggle between self and Other," Zlotnick goes on to argue that one also needs to attend to an "alternate colonial trope . . . that depends not on an absolute, dichotomized split between self and Other but on the assimilation of Other into self." "Domesticating Imperialism," pp. 55–56.

16. The British "unification" of India under colonial rule was historically just one of the various imperial regimes that variously "unified" large portions of the subcontinent. British India "included" not only most (but not all) of the territory of contemporary India but also that of the contemporary nations of Pakistan and Bangladesh. Independent India is a result, of course, not only of British colonial rule but also of a prolonged nationalist struggle for independence.

17. Nupur Chaudhuri, "Shawls, Jewelry, Curry and Rice in Victorian Britain," in *Western Women and Imperialism: Complicity and Resistance,* Nupur Chaudhuri and Margaret Strobel, eds. (Bloomington: Indiana University Press, 1992), pp. 231–246.

18. Ibid., pp. 231–232.

19. Zlotnick, "Domesticating Imperialism," p. 65.

20. Thomas Babbington Macaulay, "Minute on Indian Education," *Selected Writings,* John Clive and Thomas Pinney, eds. (Chicago: Chicago University Press, 1972), p. 249.

21. Ibid.

22. Ibid.

23. Uma Chakravarti, "Whatever Happened to the Vedic *Dasi*? Orientalism, Nationalism and a Script for the Past," in Kumkum Sangari and Suresh Vaid, eds., *Recasting Women: Essays in Indian Colonial History* (New Brunswick, N.J.: Rutgers University Press, 1990), p. 30.

24. Ibid., p. 31.

25. F. Max Muller, *India: What It Can Teach Us,* (London: Longmans Green, 1982), p. 57.

26. Ibid.

27. F. Max Muller, *Chips from A German Workshop,* quoted in Uma Chakravarti, "Whatever Happened to the Vedic *Dasi*? p. 40.

28. I am grateful to Kristie Foell for pointing out that in the eighteenth century, Germans looked to Hebrew as the "original" precursor of German. This only reinforces my argument that the search for "Aryan" linguistic roots in Sanskrit was connected to a desire to "disown" Semitic contributions to European history and culture.

29. Susan Zlotnick, "Domesticating Imperialism," p. 56.

30. Arjun Appadurai makes the point that "at least as rapidly as forces from var-

ious metropolises are brought into new societies, they tend to be indigenized in one or other way: this is true of music and housing styles as much as it is true of science and terrorism, spectacles and constitutions." See his "Disjuncture and Difference in the Global Cultural Economy," *Theory, Culture and Society* 7 (1990), p. 295.

31. Madhu Kishwar argues, "Hindus harbor deep-seated fears of Muslims because they believe them to be innately cruel and violent. Their regular meat-eating versus the vegetarianism of upper-caste Hindus and the fact that many of the butcher community people are Muslims, feeds into the stereotype of Muslims as *kasais* (killers.)" See her "Safety is Indivisible: The Warning From the Bombay Riots," *COSAW Bulletin* 8, 3–4, (1995), p. 25.

32. For discussions of recent communal violence in India, see Sucheta Mazumdar, "For Rama and Hindutva: Women and Right Wing Mobilization"; Vibhuti Patel, "Communalism, Racism and Identity Politics"; and Paola Bachetta, "Muslim Women in the RSS Discourse," all in *COSAW Bulletin* 8, 3–4 (1995).

33. Two wonderful novels that address the theme of Partition are Salman Rushdie's *Midnight's Children* (Dover, Del.: The Consortium Inc., 1992); and Bapsi Sidhwa's *Cracking India* (Minneapolis: Milkweed Editions, 1991).

34. In my own case, the Catholic school education included schools in both India and in Uganda, which are, despite their significant differences, both former British colonies.

35. Though I focus on beef, my grandmother's caste-linked attitudes had a wider range, applying with almost equal force to the eating of nonvegetarian food in general. For an account of such sensibilities and attitudes toward eating meat, see the fictional grandmother and grandchildren in Ginu Kamani, "The Smell," in *Junglee Girl* (San Francisco: Aunt Lute Books, 1995).

36. Bapsi Sidhwa, *Cracking India* (Minneapolis: Milkweed Editions, 1991).

37. The "Pakistan" that emerged at Independence in 1947 included "West Pakistan" (which is contemporary Pakistan) and the discontiguous territory of "East Pakistan," divided from West Pakistan by a thousand miles of Indian territory, that became the present country of Bangladesh after a war in 1971. Such "crackings" and "rejoinings" of nations have thus not ended after the historical period of colonial rule, the recent history of Germa..y being another case in point.

38. These restaurants are known as "Udipi restaurants" presumably because many of those who run these restaurants originate from that part of South India.

39. In a context where "Indianness" is more taken for granted, it would be more common to specify an interest in eating *regional* cuisines, and to talk of eating "Punjabi" or "Goan" or "Gujerati" food. For an amusing account of the interest in "placing" other Indians in terms of their regional and linguistic background, see Ginu Kamani, "Ciphers," in *Junglee Girl* (San Francisco: Aunt Lute Books, 1995).

40. Zlotnick borrows this phrase from Maggie Kilgour, *From Communion to Cannibalism: An Anatomy of Metaphors of Incorporation* (Princeton, N.J.: Princeton University Press, 1990), p. 5.

41. The American equivalent of "Paki-Bashing" seems to be "dot-busting." A Jersey City hate-group called the Dotbusters, in reference to the mark many Indian women wear on their foreheads, has attacked several Indians. See Arjun Appadurai, "The Heart of Whiteness," *Callaloo* 16, 4 (1993), p. 802.

42. A recent survey showed that one-third of white Englishmen surveyed considered immigrants to be "bleeding our country dry" and were in favor of forcible

deportation of ethnic immigrants from England. Reported in "Go Back Where You Came From," *60 Minutes*, May 22, 1994. The program also cited a recent CBS survey that found that one in five Americans said they were in favor of sending immigrants home, but most of them would restrict this deportation to immigrants who entered in the last five years.

43. Kureishi's protagonist Karim says of himself and his cousin Jamila, "The thing was, we were supposed to be English, but to the English we were always wogs and nigs and Pakis and the rest of it." Hanif Kureishi, *The Buddha of Suburbia* (London: Penguin, 1990) p. 53. Karim also says that he is sick of being called "Curryface," a comment that reveals the strong connection between Indians and curry in the minds of contemporary English folk, as well as suggesting that they perceive a similarity between the color of curry and the color of Indian complexions.

44. This often comes as a surprise to many Americans who live in a context where the term "black" does not apply to people of Indian origin.

45. Salman Rushdie, *The Satanic Verses* (Dover, Del.: The Consortium Inc., 1992), p. 58.

46. Hanif Kureishi, *The Buddha of Suburbia*, p. 3. Shadwell, the theater owner says later in the novel: "What a breed of people two hundred years of imperialism has given birth to. If the Pioneers from the East India Company could see you now. What puzzlement there'd be. Everyone looks at you I'm sure, and thinks: an Indian boy, how exotic, how interesting, what stories of aunties and elephants we'll hear now from him. And you're from Orpington" (p. 141).

47. Edward W. Said, *Culture and Imperialism* (New York: Alfred A. Knopf, 1993), p. 22.

48. Susan Zlotnick, "Domesticating Imperialism," p. 56.

49. Hanif Kureishi, *The Buddha of Suburbia*, p. 51.

50. Ibid., pp. 58–61.

51. Ibid., p. 60.

52. William Makepeace Thackeray, *Vanity Fair* [1848], J. Sutherland, ed. (Oxford: Oxford University Press, 1983), p. 62.

53. Hanif Kureishi, *The Buddha of Suburbia*, p. 60.

54. Ibid., p. 64.

55. Partha Chatterjee, "The Nationalist Resolution of the Women's Question," in *Recasting Women: Essays in Indian Colonial History*, Kumkum Sangari and Suresh Vaid, eds. (New Brunswick, N.J.: Rutgers University Press, 1990), p. 238.

56. Ibid., p. 239, 243. Chatterjee's account of the gendered construction of Indian nationalism, and its symbolic distinction between the home and the external world, might help explain the odd disjunction between the roles of Indian immigrant women in family-owned grocery stores and their roles in family-owned restaurants. While immigrant Indian women are frequently seen attending to business behind the counters of Indian grocery stores, they are virtually never seen waiting tables in Indian restaurants. Anwar and Jeeta are shown to live above their grocery store, a store that Jeeta routinely helps to run. Perhaps the proximity of these grocery stores to the space of home permits women's work in these stores to be seen as more akin to their domestic tasks, while waiting tables involves work in a more "public" space. Perhaps too, women serving Indian food is too redolent of the intimacies of Indian family life to be comfortably commodified as impersonal service in a restaurant.

57. Attempts by Indian feminists to call attention to issues such as dowry-murders and domestic violence were often condemned by middle-class Indians as impositions of irrelevant "Western" agendas; see Mary Fainsod Katzenstein, "Getting Women's Issues onto the Public Agenda: Body Politics in India," *Samya Shakti* 6 (1991–92), p. 7. Such denial is also prevalent in many expatriate Indian communities, where issues of violence against women are often met with the response that "our families" do not suffer from problems seen as endemic to "Western" marriages.

58. Lata Mani, "Gender, Class and Cultural Conflict: Indu Krishnan's Knowing Her Place," in *Our Feet Walk the Sky: Women of the South Asian Diaspora,* The Women of South Asian Descent Collective, eds. (San Francisco: Aunt Lute Books, 1993), p. 35.

59. For explorations of gay and lesbian issues in immigrant Indian communities, see Pratibha Parmar's film *Khush* (1991), and Dharini Rasiah, "*Mississippi Masala* and *Khush*: Redefining Community," in *Our Feet Walk the Sky*.

60. Lata Mani, "Gender, Class and Cultural Conflict: Indu Krishnan's Knowing Her Place," in *Our Feet Walk the Sky*, pp. 34–35.

61. Jacqueline Bhabha, Francesca Klug, and Sue Shutter, *Worlds Apart: Women and Immigration and Nationality Law* (London: Pluto Press, 1985).

62. Lata Mani, "Multiple Mediations: Feminist Scholarship in the Age of Multinational Reception," *Feminist Review* 35 (Summer 1990), p. 28.

63. Ibid., p. 28.

64. Lisa Heldke, "Lets Eat Chinese: Cultural Food Colonialism," paper presented at the Midwestern Conference of the Society for Women in Philosophy, Spring 1993.

65. Ibid., pp. 4–10.

66. Ibid., pp. 19–24.

67. Anne Goldman, "I Yam What I Yam: Cooking, Culture and Colonialism," in *De/Colonizing the Subject: The Politics of Gender in Women's Autobiography*, Sidonie Smith and Julia Watson, eds. (Minneapolis: University of Minnesota Press, 1992), p. 170.

68. Lisa Heldke, "Lets Eat Chinese," p. 15.

69. I want to insist that most of us are not only ignorant about the historical and cultural contexts of the food of Others but also equally ignorant about *our own*. How many mainstream Westerners have the awareness, as they stir sugar into their morning cups of coffee, that sugar was historically a luxury item available only to the wealthy, and that the cheap and popular item now consumed as sugar has its antecedents in the colonization of the West Indies and the institution of slavery? See Sidney Mintz, *Sweetness and Power* (New York: Viking, 1985).

70. See Talal Asad, *Anthropology and the Colonial Encounter* (Ithaca: Ithaca Press, 1973); and Gerrit Huizer and Bruce Mannheim, *The Politics of Anthropology: From Colonialism and Sexism Toward a View from Below* (The Hague, Paris: Mouton, 1979).

71. For an interesting study of women's place in the fast-food industry, see Evelyn Reiter, *Making Fast Food* (Montreal: McGill-Queen's, 1991).

72. See Cynthia Enloe, *Bananas, Beaches and Bases: Making Feminist Sense of International Politics* (Berkeley, Cal.: University of California Press, 1990). Chapter 6 is entitled "Carmen Miranda on My Mind: International Politics of the Banana."

73. For an interesting discussion of the politics of global consumption, see Arjun Appadurai, "Consumption, Duration and History," *Stanford Literature Review* 10, pp. 11–33.

74. Amy Ling, "I'm Here: An Asian American Woman's Response," in *Feminisms: An Anthology of Literary Theory and Criticism*, Robyn Warhol and Diane P. Herndl, eds. (New Brunswick, N.J.: Rutgers University Press, 1991), p. 745.

75. Mitsuye Yamada, final poem in *Camp Notes* (San Lorenzo, Cal.: n.p.), quoted in A. Ling, "I'm Here: An Asian American Woman's Response," in *Feminisms: An Anthology of Literary Theory and Criticism*, Robyn Warhol and Diane P. Herndl, eds. (New Brunswick, N.J.: Rutgers University Press, 1991), p. 745.

76. I have in mind incidents such as the recent clashes between Orthodox Jews and African Americans in Crown Heights, New York; and the tensions between Asian American shopowners and their Hispanic and African American neighbors in Los Angeles in the wake of police violence against Rodney King.

77. I am grateful to David Theo Goldberg for the reminder that there are also instances where the *ethnicity* of whites plays a crucial role in particular conflicts, for instance in tensions between Italians and blacks in parts of New York City.

78. Sneja Gunew, "Feminism and the Politics of Irreducible Differences: Multiculturalism/Ethnicity/Race," in *Feminism and the Politics of Difference*, Sneja Gunew and Anna Yeatman, eds. (Boulder, Colo.: Westview Press, 1993), p. 13. To be fair to Gunew, her remark is made in the context of a deservedly critical reading of the ideological implications of a film, *No Strangers Here*, produced by the Australian Department of Immigration in the 1950s.

79. Sneja Gunew, "Feminism and the Politics of Irreducible Differences: Multiculturalism/Ethnicity/Race," in *Feminism and the Politics of Difference*, Sneja Gunew and Anna Yeatman, eds. (Boulder, Colo.: Westview Press, 1993), p. 16.

80. Louise DeSalvo, "Anorexia," *The Women's Review of Books*, 13, 10–11, July 1996. Among the complicated issues DeSalvo writes about by means of writing about food are her repugnance at what she ate at home as a child, and her coming to recognize that they ate the foods they did because they were poor and that her mother's "bad cooking" was connected to her being clinically depressed.

81. Gordon Lewis, *Slavery, Imperialism and Freedom: Studies in English Radical Thought* (New York: Monthly Review Press, 1978), p. 304.

82. Ibid.

83. Salman Rushdie, "The Empire Writes Back with a Vengeance," *The Times*, July 3, 1982. Quoted by Timothy Brennan, "The National Longing for Form" in *Nation and Narration*, Homi K. Bhabha, ed. (New York: Routledge, 1990), p. 48.

84. Sneja Gunew, "Feminism and the Politics of Irreducible Differences: Multiculturalism/Ethnicity/Race," in *Feminism and the Politics of Difference* (Boulder, Colo.: Westview Press, 1973), p. 4.

85. See Rey Chow, *Writing Diaspora: Tactics of Intervention in Contemporary Cultural Studies* (Bloomington: Indiana University Press, 1993).

86. Arjun Appadurai, "The Heart of Whiteness," *Callaloo* 16, 4 (1993), p. 799.

87. Ibid.

88. Arjun Appadurai, "Disjuncture and Difference in the Global Cultural Economy," *Theory, Culture and Society* 7 (1990), p. 297.

89. Arjun Appadurai, "The Heart of Whiteness," in *Callaloo* (1993), p. 803.

Index /